AN EVALUATION OF WORLD BANK SUPPORT, 2002–08

Gender and Development

2010
The World Bank
Washington, D.C.

Photo credits: School children in Fada, northern Chad. Photo courtesy of Kimberley Fletcher, FletcherGallery@Mac.com.

ISBN: 978-0-8213-8325-4
e-ISBN: 978-0-8213-8326-1
DOI: 10.1596/978-0-8213-8325-4

Library of Congress Cataloging-in-Publication data have been applied for.

World Bank InfoShop
E-mail: pic@worldbank.org
Telephone: 202-458-5454
Facsimile: 202-522-1500

Independent Evaluation Group
Communications, Learning, and Strategy
E-mail: ieg@worldbank.org
Telephone: 202-458-4497
Facsimile: 202-522-3125

 Printed on Recycled Paper

Table of Contents

Figures

Tables

The following are available upon request:
- Approach Paper for the Evaluation (November 24, 2008)
- Summary Findings of Staff Survey
- Summary of Consultation with Client and Other Stakeholders (with list of people met)
- List of Country Gender Assessments, Country Assistance Strategies/Country Partnership Strategies, economic and sector work, and lending activities reviewed

Abbreviations

ADB	Asian Development Bank
ARD	Agriculture and Rural Development
BP	Bank Procedure
CAS	Country Assistance Strategy
CASCR	Country Assistance Strategy Completion Report
CDC	Community Development Council
CDD	Community-driven development
CGA	Country Gender Assessment
CIDA	Canadian International Development Agency
CPIA	Country Policy and Institutional Assessment
CPS	Country Partnership Strategy
DPO	Development Policy Operation
ESW	Economic and sector work
GAP	Gender Action Plan
GDI	Gender-Related Development Index
HDI	Human Development Index
IADB	Inter-American Development Bank
ICR	Implementation Completion Report
IDA	International Development Association
IEG	Independent Evaluation Group
M&E	Monitoring and evaluation
MDG	Millennium Development Goal
OD	Operational Directive
OMS	Operational Manual Statement
OP	Operational Policy
OPCS	Operations Policy and Country Services
PAD	Project appraisal document
PREM	Poverty Reduction and Economic Management Network
PSIA	Poverty and Social Impact Analysis
RGC	Regional gender coordinator

Acknowledgments

The Country Evaluation and Regional Relations team of the Independent Evaluation Group (IEGCR) that prepared the report consisted of Gita Gopal (Task Manager), Anwesha Prabhu, Min Joo Kang, Kristen Cordell, Rajesh Vasudevan, Vikki Taaka, Gemi Thomas, and Saubhik Deb. Others who contributed included Snigdha Ali, Victoria Monchuk, Manisha J. Modi, Victor H. Orozco, Liliana Ruiz Ortega, Lily Tsang, and Robin Wyatt. C. Mark Blackden contributed to preparing chapter 3. Valuable comments from J. Michael Bamberger, C. Mark Blackden, and John Keith Rennie throughout the preparation of the report are gratefully acknowledged. Arup Banerji participated in a mission to Ghana, and the team is grateful for support and guidance received from him in undertaking the evaluation. The evaluation was prepared under the overall guidance and supervision of Ali M. Khadr (Senior Manager, IEGCR).

J. Michael Bamberger led the fieldwork in Peru and John Keith Rennie in Zambia. Others involved in the field assessments and preparation of background papers include Husnia M. Al-Kadri, Elizabeth Asiedua Asante, Molina Cerpa, Kristen Cordell, Gayatri Datar, Saubhik Deb, Cristina Elena, Shailaja Fennell, Toneema M. Haq, Monica Penuela Jaramillo, Ayaba Gilberte Kedote, Claudia Maria Cuzzi Martinez, Monica Linda Munachonga, Mukaddas Pulatova, Patrick Sakala, and Daniela Maguina Ugarte.

Peer reviewers (Ximena Vanessa Del Carpio and Kenichi Ohashi) provided guidance and comments on the approach paper and the draft report.

External panel reviewers were Ravi Kanbur and Jan Piercy.

The report was edited by Heather Dittbrenner and William B. Hurlbut. Vikki Taaka and Juicy Zareen Qureishi-Huq provided administrative guidance.

IEG acknowledges the significant cooperation, input, and financial contribution of the Swiss Agency for Development and Cooperation. That organization's support helped to deepen the evaluation and undertake the field visits.

IEG is grateful to the country directors and country teams and to the Gender Board led by Mayra Buvinic, as well as to the Regional and Country Gender Coordinators in the countries where field visits were conducted. The country teams facilitated the visits and organized stakeholder consultation meetings. The IEG team also acknowledges the contribution of several World Bank client country stakeholders who provided feedback for the evaluation.

Director-General, Evaluation: *Vinod Thomas*
Director, Independent Evaluation Group–World Bank: *Cheryl W. Gray*
Senior Manager, IEGCR: *Ali M. Khadr*
Task Manager, IEGCR: *Gita Gopal*

Foreword

The third report from the Independent Evaluation Group (IEG) on the World Bank's support for gender and development, this evaluation considers progress over the period fiscal 2002–08, following the Bank's 2001 Gender Strategy. When compared with Bank support during fiscal 1990–99, which was assessed in IEG's previous gender evaluation (IEG 2005), gender integration improved in scope and quantity during 2002–08. Although gender-related benchmarks are difficult to establish, when compared with self-assessments of other multilateral agencies, the Bank's gender integration at the project level is comparable or better, although certain bilaterals do better.

delivered good results for gender equality outcomes, yet less than a quarter did so when this was not so. The 2007 Gender Action Plan, which encourages gender integration into selected sectors, fills this lacuna to some extent, but there is the need to broaden and formalize the plan's approach to ensure sustained gender integration and institutional accountability.

Second, implementation of the Bank's gender policy, initially strong, weakened between fiscal 2006 and 2008. Country Gender Assessments, the principal tool underlying the 2001 Gender Strategy, were not being updated or undertaken, and implementation of the country-level ap-

Some 42 percent of the 138 projects reviewed in 12 countries on which the evaluation focused contributed to outcomes in gender equality in three domains—investment in human capital, access to economic assets and opportunities, and voice in development. At the country level, Bank support contributed substantially to changes in 4 of the 12 focus countries, modestly in another 6, and weakly in 2.

Two important evaluation findings suggest that action is needed to strengthen and sustain progress. First, the Bank's policy requires Country Assistance Strategies to specify operational sectors where the Bank is to integrate gender concerns into its support based on gender assessments. This approach narrows the coverage of the policy that was applicable in the 1990s, when consideration of gender was more generally required during project appraisal without being restricted to specified sectors. This evaluation finds that such a country-level approach can result in missed opportunities and reduced development effectiveness. Among 138 projects reviewed in the 12 focus countries, 63 percent of those that integrated gender considerations

proach weakened markedly. Gender integration at the project level, as seen by four complementary criteria used by IEG, declined between 2006 and 2008, but it rose (recovering to near the 2003 peak) when measured by one of these four criteria that management employs (IEG's criteria were adapted from these). Insufficient action to implement the accountability framework and to establish a tracking and monitoring system, both of which had been envisaged in the 2001 strategy, were likely contributing factors.

The evaluation recommends several actions to regain and sustain the momentum of gender integration achieved earlier in the evaluation period and to improve the development effectiveness of Bank support. In addition to strengthening management commitment to gender integration, actions include redoubling efforts to institutionalize the accountability framework and develop the monitoring system envisioned in the 2001 Gender Strategy, establishing a results framework, and broadening the requirement for gender integration at the project level.

Vinod Thomas

Executive Summary

Gender is a matter of development effectiveness. (World Bank Gender Strategy)

The World Bank's current gender policy draws on the 2001 Gender Strategy (World Bank 2002b) endorsed by the Board. Subsequently, instructions to staff were reflected in a revised Operational Policy (OP) and Bank Procedure (BP) 4.20. Together, they aim to help client countries reduce poverty and enhance human well-being by addressing gender disparities that are barriers to development.

The policy embodies a country-level approach that requires the Bank to prepare Country Gender Assessments (CGAs) for all active borrowers and to reflect the CGA findings in Country Assistance Strategies (CASs). In sector and thematic areas where the CAS has identified the need for priority gender-responsive actions, managers and staff are instructed to ensure that Bank-supported activities are gender responsive.

This evaluation, which covers the period fiscal 2002–08, finds that the Bank made progress in gender integration, compared with an earlier evaluation by the Independent Evaluation Group (IEG) on gender covering the period fiscal 1990–99. Gender integration into Bank support increased both in quantity and in scope, and more than half of relevant projects integrated gender concerns.

With regard to outcomes, detailed reviews were undertaken in 12 focus countries. The evaluation finds that Bank support likely contributed to improving gender equality-related outcomes in three domains—investment in human capital, access to economic assets and opportunities, and voice in development—substantially in 4 of the 12 countries, modestly in another 6, and weakly in 2. At the project level, 42 percent of relevant projects in the 12 focus countries generated substantial outcomes that contributed to progress in one or more of these domains.

Two sets of issues qualify these generally encouraging signs of progress. First, the evaluation finds that the implementation of the Bank's gender policy, initially strong, weakened in the latter half of this evaluation period. Insufficient steps to implement an accountability framework and to set up a monitoring system—both of which had been envisaged in the 2001 Gender Strategy—were likely contributing factors. Second, two key gaps in the Bank's current gender policy diminish its relevance: the absence of a results framework in the 2001 Gender Strategy and the replacement of what was previously a more generalized gender mainstreaming approach at the operational level with the more selective country-level one. The 2007 Gender Action Plan (GAP) broadened the focus somewhat to include certain key sectors that are typically the focus of Bank support. However, IEG is of the view that the absence of strong linkages between the GAP and the 2001 Strategy blurred the Bank's overall policy.

This evaluation recommends several actions to regain and sustain the momentum of gender integration that was evident in the first half of the evaluation period. These include redoubling efforts to institutionalize the accountability framework and develop the monitoring system envisioned in the 2001 Gender Strategy, establishing a results framework, and restoring a broader requirement for gender integration at the project level.

The Bank and Gender

In 1977 the World Bank was the first multilateral institution to appoint a Women in Development Adviser. In 1984 the Bank issued Operational Manual Statement (OMS) 2.20, which called for Bank staff to consider women's issues as part of the social analysis undertaken during the appraisal of an investment project and to assess and address through project design any disadvantageous effects on women (see figure ES.1).

A decade later, in 1994, the Bank issued OP 4.20 on Gender and Development (World Bank 1994) based on a strategy paper. Taken together, the strategy and the OP gave gender a central place in the Bank's country-level development model. Through this gender policy, the Bank aimed to address the policy and institutional underpinnings of gender disparities that constrained development effectiveness within a client country. The policy rightly underscored the importance of country ownership and commitment for Bank support to be effective in helping to reduce gender disparities. Two points of entry—one through the CAS and the other through project appraisal—provided the means to integrate gender considerations into Bank support for the next several years.

In April 2001 the Bank strengthened the country-level approach through a gender strategy paper discussed at the

Board (*Integrating Gender into the World Bank's Work: A Strategy for Action*; World Bank 2002b). The 2001 Strategy reiterated the Bank's aim to help countries reduce poverty, enhance human well-being, and increase development effectiveness by addressing gender disparities that are barriers to development. It introduced the use of a new diagnostic tool—the CGA. The Strategy promised that a CGA for every active borrower would be completed by fiscal 2005. CGAs were expected to inform CASs, which were to include, as relevant, gender-responsive interventions. In sectors and themes that the CAS identified as priorities for gender, sector managers and task teams were to ensure that gender considerations received appropriate treatment in operations.

Regarding interpretation of the Bank's gender policy, management considers that the 2001 Strategy and the subsequent OP/BP 4.20 replaced the provisions of OMS 2.20, Project Appraisal, by absorbing them into the OP/BP process. Under OP/BP 4.20, the entry point for addressing gender issues during project appraisal thus applied only to projects in sectors and themes that CASs identified as a priority for gender.

In addition to the above, four specific policies (OP 4.10 on Involuntary Resettlement, OP 4.12 on Indigenous Peoples, BP 4.30 on Forests, and OP 2.30 on Development Cooperation and Conflict) also require consideration of issues related to women, namely as part of vulnerable groups. These policies continue to maintain a project-level entry point.

Although the updated OP 8.60 on Development Policy Operations (DPOs), approved in August 2004, does not explicitly require that DPOs address gender dimensions of development, it does require that all DPOs examine the poverty and social impacts of the reform programs supported by the operation. A Good Practice Note encourages the integration of gender into such impact analysis. In 2006 the Bank launched a four-year GAP, "Gender Equality as Smart Economics" (World Bank 2006b), which it implemented beginning in January 2007. The evaluation finds that the GAP returned to the sector-specific and project-level approach of the earlier OMS 2.20, emphasizing integration of gender into operations and activities in predetermined economic sectors of importance for women's economic empowerment.

Scope of the Evaluation

This evaluation seeks to assess the effectiveness of the Bank's gender policy between fiscal years 2002 and 2008. To gauge the extent to which the Bank actually implemented its policy while keeping country coverage manageable, the evaluation selected all client countries that had a population of more than 1 million and that had implemented at least two Bank-supported investment projects during the period. This yielded a sample of 93 countries. In these

countries IEG conducted an exhaustive desk review, looking at investment projects worth $88 billion (1,183 projects, constituting 90 percent of all investment loans made during the period). Separately, the evaluation reviewed gender integration in 307 DPOs approved during the period. In addition, the evaluation reviewed all 48 identified CGAs, 74 Poverty Assessments, and 140 CASs.

To assess the outcomes of Bank support, the evaluation used in-depth country case studies. The evaluation examined Bank support in 12 countries randomly selected from a stratified weighted sample of the 93 countries. In these 12 countries, the evaluation reviewed the results of all lending activities that closed after fiscal 2003. Additionally, at the request of World Bank Board members, the evaluation team undertook a review of Bank support for gender in Afghanistan. With respect to the GAP, the evaluation was limited to assessing its objective and design, as it is too soon to assess results even on a preliminary basis. Finally, the evaluation did not focus on International Finance Corporation activities, given IEG's proposed evaluation of IFC support for gender in the near future.

Appropriateness of the Gender Policy

The objectives of the Bank's gender policy are directly relevant to the Bank's mandate of poverty reduction and economic development. The policy is sufficiently flexible that the Bank was able to respond to country-specific settings, issues, and priorities. For instance, to mitigate local sensitivities, the Bank was able to adapt and "package" its support for gender in the Republic of Yemen using a social inclusion approach; at the same time it retained a direct gender equality approach in the Philippines. However, the absence of an explicit results framework translating Bank support for gender into specific gender-related outcomes diminished the policy's relevance.

The evaluation found another factor that also tended to diminish the relevance of the Bank's gender policy: the narrowing of the entry point for gender integration at project appraisal to specific priority sectors indicated in CASs. To illustrate, if only the health and education sectors were identified in CASs as being of strategic importance for gender in a given client country (for instance, Pakistan 2006 and Bolivia 2004), under OP 4.20, Bank staff responsibilities to address gender considerations would be limited to activities in these sectors. An agricultural or a municipal services project in either country that did not integrate gender considerations, even if it were highly beneficial to do so in these specific cases, would nevertheless be fully consistent with OP 4.20 (World Bank 2003c).

In addressing strategic country-level issues, the evaluation found that the relevance of the OP/BP 4.20 was (and remains) high. Where the Bank had addressed institutional and policy reform (for example, Bangladesh, Benin, and Ghana), the evaluation found that client demand was critical for successful implementation. However, an important distinction arises between support for such policy and institutional reform and support that aims to directly increase the access of the poor to human, social, and economic services and resources. With the latter form of support, because of the different gender-related roles and responsibilities, the evaluation found that men and women often did not have equal or fair access to project benefits unless project design expressly took steps to mitigate the impact of local gender practices that inhibited such access in the first place.

Such an obligation (that is, to ensure gender-responsive project design) cannot be made contingent on client demand or only in sectors and themes identified in CASs—it is a matter of relevance, efficiency, and efficacy, and thus a matter of development effectiveness (box ES.1). This was the spirit underlying the provisions of OMS 2.20. Further-

more, given the evaluation's finding that CASs did not systematically identify priority sectors for gender integration and that the links between CASs and operations are difficult to monitor, the distinction between country-level or "strategic" policy and institutional reform and project-level design features becomes critical. The failure to make this distinction and the resulting identical treatment of the two types of Bank interventions under OP/BP 4.20 diminished the relevance of the gender policy.

Starting with its establishment in 2007, in recognition of shortfalls in gender integration at the operational level in selected sectors, the GAP encouraged gender mainstreaming by providing staff with incentives to integrate gender into predetermined sectors and activities. These steps augmented relevance (and in that respect made the GAP a positive force for change), but the introduction of the GAP without appropriate policy foundations—including the requisite backward links to CGAs and CASs as required in OP 4.20—had the effect of blurring the Bank's overall gender policy.

FIGURE ES.1   **Evolution of the Bank's Approach to Gender, 1997–2009**

1977–89

1977: Women in Development Adviser appointed.

1984: OMS 2.20, Project Appraisal, requires consideration of women's issues as appropriate, and ensures that activities enhance women's participation in development and that project design mitigates disadvantageous effects on women.

1990–2000

1994: Country-level approach requires the Bank, in consultation with the client, to address strategic issues through analysis in ongoing economic and sector work, integration of gender considerations into CASs, and subsequent integration into Bank operations.

OMS 2.20 continues to be effective.

2001–09

2001: Country-level approach strengthened in four ways:
- Country director oversees preparation of gender assessment for any active borrower.
- Country director ensures that the results of the assessment are incorporated in the CAS and reflected in the country dialogue.
- In sectors and thematic areas where the CAS has identified the need for priority gender-responsive actions, the relevant sector managers ensure that Bank-financed projects and other activities are gender responsive.
- Regional vice presidents report annually to the managing director concerned.

OMS 2.20 is replaced and its provisions absorbed into OP 4.20, which now applies only to projects in sectors and themes identified by the CAS.

2006: GAP focuses on gender integration into sectors considered important for women's empowerment.

Source: IEG.

Note: CAS = Country Assistance Strategy; GAP = Gender Action Plan; OMS = Operational Manual Statement; OP = Operational Policy.

Implementation of the Bank's Gender Policy

The quality, scope, and extent of gender integration into Bank support improved significantly in the evaluation period, compared with an earlier IEG evaluation covering 1990–99. Whereas the previous evaluation found weak integration into sectors other than those related to human

Photo courtesy of Kimberley Fletcher, FletcherGallery@Mac.com

development, this evaluation found significant expansion in integrating gender into thematic areas such as microfinance, land management and administration, and justice reform.

Overall, higher levels of gender integration occurred in Regions with lower levels of gender equality and/or greater gender-related constraints to poverty reduction. The South Asia Region posted the highest levels of gender integration and the Europe and Central Asia Region the lowest. The prevalence of gender mainstreaming in fragile states and in International Development Association countries was also higher than in International Bank for Reconstruction and Development countries—a priori a desirable pattern.

The Bank implemented its gender policy well during the first few years of the evaluation period. Many CGAs were undertaken, and subsequent CASs were more likely than previously to discuss gender issues, propose a program of action, and include at least one gender-relevant monitoring indicator. Gender integration into relevant projects increased, peaking at 64 percent in fiscal 2003.

Despite this promising start, implementation subsequently weakened. Between fiscal 2006 and 2008, only nine additional CGAs were undertaken or updated, even though the 2001 Gender Strategy had called for completion of CGAs (either as self-standing documents or otherwise) in all active borrowers by fiscal 2005. Although CASs increasingly discussed gender issues, particularly in relation to Poverty Reduction Strategy Papers and the Millennium Develop-

ment Goals, the evaluation found a decline in the frequency of meaningful gender integration into CASs.

One key weakness was that CASs often did not specify priority sectors or themes for the integration of gender concerns, which weakened the link between CASs and operations. The lack of effective monitoring of the country-level approach further weakened the implementation of OP 4.20. Gender integration at the project level declined between 2006 and 2008, after improving early in the evaluation period and peaking in 2003, when measured by four criteria that IEG used; it did rise (recovering to approximately the 2003 level) if measured by one of the four of these criteria that the Bank management uses, that is, presence of gender analysis or discussion.

Despite the lack of explicit coverage of gender issues in OP 8.60, the evaluation found increased discussion of gender issues in DPO program documents, compared with fiscal 1990–99, the period covered by the previous IEG evaluation. It also found at least one gender-related measure or action in 53 (about 17 percent) of the 307 DPOs approved for the 93 countries during the evaluation period. Most gender-related analysis, actions, and monitoring efforts remained focused on health, education, and safety nets. Gender integration outside these areas remained limited. Nevertheless, this trend represents progress that needs to be recognized, tracked, and built upon.

Finally, the evaluation finds that the introduction of the GAP in 2007—issues of fit with the Bank's gender policy as currently configured notwithstanding—laid the groundwork for revitalizing the gender integration agenda by providing fiscal incentives to address gender in Bank-supported operations and analytical work.

Institutional Arrangements and Incentives

A review of policy coherence and institutional arrangements relating to the Bank's gender policy points to several factors that may underlie the drop in implementing OP 4.20. In particular, the Bank did not establish important corporate-level institutional arrangements identified by the 2001 Strategy as necessary to underpin the shift to the country-level approach. Targeted funding to pursue gender concerns was fully available only in fiscal 2002 and not again until fiscal 2007 and 2008, after the Bank had put the GAP in place.

The 2001 Strategy promised that "an effective system of monitoring and evaluation" would be in place by fiscal 2002 to monitor the implementation of the country-level approach. This evaluation finds that the Bank did not fully implement such a system. In addition, the Bank had planned annual monitoring reports, but it presented only three such reports to the Board before fiscal 2006 (World Bank 2006c, 2004d, 2003b). Subsequently, the Bank subsumed monitoring of support for gender under the Sector

Strategy Implementation Updates, although the Poverty Reduction and Economic Management Network Gender Group has continued to prepare annual progress reports—focusing among other things on implementation of the GAP—for presentation to the Board. In addition, in fiscal 2008 the Bank's President required country directors to report on what they were (and could be) doing to enhance women's economic empowerment.

Results of Bank Support in 12 Focus Countries

IEG reviewed a portfolio of 164 Bank-supported projects and DPOs in 12 focus countries. All of these projects and DPOs closed after fiscal 2003 and before fiscal 2009, and all had an Implementation Completion Report available. IEG reviewed these projects and programs, focusing notably on how Bank support contributed to reducing gender disparities in three domains: investment in human capital, access to economic assets and opportunities, and voice in development planning and implementation. For each domain, the evaluation identified goals and objectives (from the CAS or other relevant documents). Where there was little evidence in Implementation Completion Reports, CAS Completion Reports, or other relevant documents, and where the evaluation team had not conducted a field assessment, the evaluation rated the results as modest. It used a common set of indicators identified in chapter 6.

An initial review indicated that 138 of the 164 projects and programs could plausibly have influenced outcomes related to gender equality or women's empowerment in at least one of the three domains. Many of the 138 relevant initiatives were innovative and successful in addressing gender issues—42 percent of the projects generated substantial relevant results in terms of gender outcomes.

Of the 12 countries, substantial results were achieved in four countries in at least two domains, and Bank support was judged sufficient to have plausibly contributed to systemic changes in gender outcomes. In another six countries, the Bank's contribution was modest, with results confined to one domain (or even to one sector) and unable to improve the environment for gender equality or women's empowerment significantly. The results were insufficient to address gender power relations, gender-based division of labor, local decision-making processes, or the management of resources. In the other two countries, results were weak and limited to a single domain. For these reasons, the Bank's contribution to progress in gender equality was judged to be low.

Findings and Recommendations

The evaluation finds that the objectives of the Bank's gender policy were relevant and that the Bank's support for gender over the evaluation period as a whole was stronger than in the 1990s, the period covered by IEG's previous gender evaluation. There is also some evidence that the Bank shifted its focus toward countries with higher levels of gender disparity. Outcomes were significant—42 percent of relevant projects in 12 countries achieved substantial results. Bank support was more successful in countries where demand for gender work by the client was greater, such as in Ghana and Bangladesh.

BOX ES.1

ADDRESSING GENDER ISSUES IS A MATTER OF DEVELOPMENT EFFECTIVENESS

Through conditional cash transfers and student bursaries, Bank support contributed to increased enrollment of girls in schools. Supporting microfinance institutions to provide credit to women in a culturally appropriate manner improved their decision-making powers within households. Focused attention on ensuring that women benefited from temporary work generated by Bank-supported construction created new opportunities for women and reportedly ensured equal wages for equal work. Support for enhancing women's voices at the community level helped give women legitimacy in participating in public activities in several countries. Supporting the engagement of women as decision makers in designing activities for a rural road project resulted in the construction of footpaths, which women prefer because they are the easiest and safest way to take their animals to pasture and to collect firewood and water.

In contrast to this progress with women, Bank support has not been equally effective in fostering retention of boys in schools in countries where this is an emerging issue. Similarly, providing training of trainers for extension services predominantly to men—in a context where women overwhelmingly ran family farms and were limited by local norms from attending meetings—diminished project efficacy and reduced development effectiveness. Weak support for gender-aware reform of the agricultural sector could have exacerbated inequities for women, who constitute a significant group of the informal labor in many countries. Failure to integrate gender into Bank support for local governments reduced development effectiveness and resulted in missed opportunities to ensure gender-aware development at the local level, where the risks of elite male capture are typically high. Finally, individual women's needs differ, depending on their responsibilities and roles. Consulting only wives of community leaders resulted in the provision of insufficient water at inconvenient times to women from poorer households.

Source: IEG.

However, the evaluation found that although the implementation of the country-level approach envisaged in the 2001 Gender Strategy and reflected in OP/BP 4.20 began well, it weakened markedly after fiscal 2005, both at the country and project levels. This decline in gender integration shows that the momentum evident in the first half of the evaluation period was lost. The 2007 GAP helped reinvigorate the agenda, but any such initiative needs to be sustainably institutionalized and set within a policy framework covering the project level, with a clear overall results framework.

The evaluation found that to be effective, gender integration needs to address strategic issues (institutional and policy reform) that would help facilitate and sustain gender and development outcomes in the field. By their nature, strategic issues need to be addressed selectively and opportunistically, for such support can be effective only with client commitment and ownership. At the operational level, ensuring a gender responsive project design, when appropriate, is necessary for development effectiveness. Because of the different roles and responsibilities of men and women, the evaluation found that in roughly 75 percent of Bank operations, women (and, in some untypical cases, men) will participate less and benefit relatively less from project activities if the design does not mitigate such impact. The GAP attempts to compensate for this, and its policy base should be strengthened and formalized, either through revision of OP 4.20 or through restoration of broader gender-related provisions along the lines of OMS 2.20.

To strengthen accountability, it is important to formulate a results framework to underpin the gender policy. This would help target a coherent and mutually reinforcing set of outcomes to support the gender and development goals of Bank clients. Additionally, a well-functioning monitoring system to assess implementation of gender-related policies and the results at the operational and country level, as envisaged in the 2001 Gender Strategy, is essential. In addition, accountability for policy implementation needs strengthening through provision of resources and training for all Bank managers.

Finally, the Bank needs to use the significant flexibility provided by its gender policy in tailoring its support to different contexts. In countries with higher levels of gender parity (such as Colombia or the Philippines), it may be sufficient to focus on gender issues in a single sector. However, in countries with higher levels of gender inequality, there is a need to mainstream gender issues within and across different sectors in a mutually reinforcing manner if desired outcomes are to be achieved. In these countries, it is also critical to strengthen Bank support for gender-aware institutional reform, particularly at the subnational and local government levels, and to reinforce the demand for reduced gender disparities through appropriate incentives.

To ensure a better understanding of the gender policy and to ensure its effective implementation in a manner that will contribute to reducing gender disparities and empowering women in the Bank's client countries, the evaluation recommends several measures:

- Foster greater clarity and better implementation of the Bank's Gender Policy by—

  - Establishing a results framework to facilitate consistent adoption of an outcome approach to gender integration in the Bank's work.

  - Establishing and implementing a realistic action plan for completing or updating country-level diagnostics, giving primacy to countries with higher levels of gender inequality.

  - Extending implementation of the 2007 GAP while formalizing and strengthening its policy basis. An alternative would be to reinstate and strengthen provisions along the lines of OMS 2.20 to restore a sector- and/or project-level entry point for gender.

- Establish clear management accountability for the development and implementation of a system to monitor the extent to which Bank work adequately addresses gender-related concerns, including effective reporting mechanisms. The pivotal role of country directors needs to feature centrally in the accountability framework.

- Strengthen the incentives for effective gender-related actions in client countries by continuing to provide incentive funding through the GAP to strengthen the collection, analysis, and dissemination of gender-disaggregated, gender-relevant data and statistics.

Management Response

I. Introduction

Management regards the Independent Evaluation Group (IEG) evaluation of the World Bank's support for gender and development as a serious effort to assess the implementation of the Bank's gender and development work. The evaluation findings reflect work conducted through a mix of desk reviews, a few field reviews, and a project portfolio review in 93 countries, with a special focus on results in a sample of 12 countries.

Emphasis on strengthening the Bank's gender support. The emphasis of the report in strengthening the Bank's gender and development work is especially welcome. We note the evaluation's finding that the Bank made progress in integrating gender issues during the 2002–08 period as compared to the 1990–99 period, but, in agreement with IEG, Bank management recognizes that gender issues are not yet adequately mainstreamed across sectors and Regions, and that new measures need to be adopted to speed up progress. This recognition led to the launch in 2007 of a four-year World Bank Group Gender Action Plan (GAP), which IEG notes has revitalized the gender agenda in the Bank and helped increase gender coverage in economic sectors such as agriculture, rural development, finance, economic policy and infrastructure.

Policy relevance and recommendations for new measures. Bank management agrees with the report's finding that the current policy framework for gender and development is adequate and with IEG's recommendations to strengthen monitoring, the results framework, and management accountability. Management also agrees with the importance of ensuring sufficient budget resources to implement the Gender Strategy and with the recommendation to continue the use of incentive funding to strengthen gender and development work. Although progress has been made on some of these crucial elements, IEG's observations will assist future actions. In addition, drawing on the lessons from the GAP, which uses innovative mechanisms to increase gender coverage in operations in key sectors that are not easily mainstreamed, we propose both to tackle gender capacity building using nontraditional training vehicles and to continue making the "business-case" forcefully for gender equality as smart economics, to help increase client country interest.

Analysis of IEG data. Management is grateful to IEG for granting access to its data, which allowed further unpacking of IEG's ratings and results. This enabled two new and useful findings. First, it revealed encouraging performance in the economic sectors during the last two years of the review period, which saw gender coverage increase in these traditionally less-receptive sectors, for instance, from 58 to 71 percent of projects in agriculture, and from 15 to 18 percent in infrastructure. This finding corroborates the Bank's Annual Monitoring Reports, which show that the overall fall in gender coverage in Bank operations leveled out in fiscal 2006 and has since trended upward—an improvement coinciding with the GAP, which targets these sectors. This trend is encouraging, and although levels are still too low, it may indicate that innovative mechanisms, such as the ones put in place by the GAP, can bring about change in sectors that traditionally have been less receptive to gender mainstreaming.

Second, it showed that criteria to measure gender integration need to be adjusted, given the growing complexity of the Bank's portfolio. The aggregate decline found by IEG since fiscal 2006 is largely explained by IEG rating sector-wide institutional reform loans in education low, mainly because they lack individual-level indicators and therefore do not monitor gender-disaggregated impact. Yet these "second-generation" projects, which address sector-wide issues such as curriculum development, teacher training, and education sector salary scales, make up an increasing share of the Bank's education portfolio and target what in many countries may be the largest constraint for girls' education today: schooling quality. Going forward, the analysis of trends in gender mainstreaming needs to take into account both project objectives and portfolio composition.

II. General Comments

Management has comments on the overall policy framework, the results focus of Bank work, and the role of the GAP.

Overall policy framework

Relevance of Operational Policy. Management agrees with IEG on the relevance of the Bank's Operational Policy (OP/BP4.20) on gender to address strategic, country-level gender issues. The policy calls for gender assessment to be discussed in Country Assistance Strategies (CASs). In sectors and thematic areas where the CAS has identified the need for gender-responsive interventions, the Bank's assistance incorporates measures to address this need. Management notes that the policy is flexible on how the gender assessment is to be done. Management agrees with IEG that it is not the case that a specific piece of economic and sector work (ESW) called a Country Gender Assessment (CGA) is required. The gender assessment may be a stand-alone assessment or it may be carried out as part of other Bank ESW, such as poverty assessments, country economic memoranda, public expenditure reviews, development policy reviews, poverty and social impact assessments, or institutional analyses. Alternatively, it may be an assessment that has been carried out by the country or an organization other than the Bank. Going forward, it is important to ensure that CASs are more consistently informed by gender assessment.

The policy's selective and flexible approach. Management and IEG have discussed and agreed on the appropriateness of the policy's selective approach and the flexible means for undertaking country-level gender diagnostics. This approach goes hand in hand with the movement by all development partners from a fragmented project focus to a more effective and efficient country focus—the aid effectiveness agenda. The Bank's business model calls for a comprehensive assessment of a country's poverty reduction and growth agenda but a selective, prioritized set of activities to support the achievement of the goals of CASs. The gender policy follows that model—calling for periodic analytical work assessing gender issues at the country level that feeds into CASs and selective country programs. It takes into account a long history of IEG findings on the importance of country ownership and working together with other donors based on comparative advantage.

Results focus of Bank's work

Projects and gender—A focus on results. IEG suggests that the gender policy restricts the entry point for gender integration only to sectors mentioned in the CAS. Management notes that the Bank's gender policy framework is wider. Under the current policy framework, project-level entry points are triggered by several factors, which are determined separately for Development Policy Operations, and investment lending operations, notably projects involving safeguards where women's special needs are relevant. This policy framework is consistent with the current strategy.[1] However, and more importantly, the Bank follows a results focus in all operations. Projects outside sectors highlighted in the CAS often mainstream gender concerns when it is a matter of development effectiveness; Bank policy does not require that a gender-informed operation be in a sector highlighted as priority in a CAS.

Gender diagnostics and policy dialogue. IEG's assessment of weak implementation is based on trends in gender integration in investment lending and decreased gender inte-

gration into CASs, which it in turn largely attributes to a significant decline in the number of CGAs undertaken. Management concurs with IEG on the need for country-level gender diagnostics and the importance of integrating gender issues into CASs. We recognize that the treatment of gender in CASs is an area that needs improvement and is a focus of management attention (see World Bank 2009c). We consider stand-alone CGAs as just one of many ways to undertake the required country-level gender diagnosis. As noted above, other options, specified in the gender policy, include integrating gender analysis into key ESW or using analysis produced by the country or an organization other than the Bank. Management's self-evaluation shows that the number of ESW with highly satisfactory or satisfactory integration of gender issues has more than doubled in the latter part of the evaluation period, starting in fiscal 2005 (see World Bank 2009d). Seventy-two of 108 active countries had satisfactory or better gender diagnostics in the 2002–08 period, when counting ESW that according to the policy qualify as full country-level gender diagnostics. Management strongly favors embedding gender assessment in key country diagnostic work and will work with staff to ensure that all gender-informed ESW is properly recognized.

Implementation of the Gender Policy: Analysis of gender integration in investment lending. Management welcomes IEG's efforts to evaluate the progress in policy implementation and acknowledges that measuring progress in gender mainstreaming, by its very definition, is a complex exercise. Management is encouraged by IEG's finding that, as compared to the previous evaluation period (1990–99), there is a significant improvement in the quality, scope, and extent of gender integration in the lending portfolio. We also agree with IEG's assessment based on the current evaluation period (fiscal 2002–08) that there is much room for improving gender integration in the Bank's investment lending portfolio.

Specific actions proposed by management

Strengthen the results framework and monitoring system. Management welcomes this recommendation and notes that the Bank has a gender monitoring framework and reports regularly to senior management on progress in the gender strategy. In addition, the GAP has a results framework and reports regularly to the Board. Nevertheless, the monitoring system can and should be strengthened. As part of the GAP transition plan, management will present to the Board during the second quarter of 2010 a strengthened results framework with quantitative targets and accompanying indicators for key sectors and Regions. These targets will be set in a process involving relevant sector boards and Region departments, based on an exercise carried out in 2008 to quantify senior management's commitment to increase gender mainstreaming in the Agriculture and Rural Development portfolio.[2]

Work under way on strengthening the existing monitoring system for the Gender Policy. Information on the number of project beneficiaries, disaggregated by gender, is now required for all International Development Association–supported investment projects that have an approval date of July 1, 2009, or later. We plan, through the GAP transition plan, to assist Bank task teams in fulfilling this new requirement. In addition, management is reviewing current and proposed Core Sector Indicators to see which ones could be meaningfully disaggregated by gender.

Management agreement on the need to establish clearer accountability for implementing the Gender Policy, particularly at the level of country director and above. Management proposes to strengthen accountability at the senior level through Managing Director–chaired reviews of the Bank's annual monitoring reports on implementing the gender policy by the operational vice presidents. In contrast with past practice, this reporting will include progress in implementing the quantitative targets defined above, giving the exercise teeth. As part of the GAP transition plan, it is likely that funding incentives will play a role, notably with regard to country gender diagnostics in key ESW in targeted countries.

Role of the GAP: "Gender equality as smart economics"

The GAP's fit with the Bank's policy framework. Management is encouraged by the evaluation's finding that the GAP, launched in 2007, has revitalized the gender and development agenda at the Bank. Both IEG and management agree that the GAP is an attempt to address weaknesses in gender mainstreaming that have been identified in the Bank's annual monitoring of the Gender Strategy. Management notes that the GAP focuses on those sectors identified in the 2001 IEG review as being poor performers in gender mainstreaming, precisely in order to improve their performance. Thus, the GAP was a response to reinvigorate gender mainstreaming and does not represent a return to the project-level approach or diminished links to gender assessment and CASs. As noted in the IEG evaluation, the extent of gender analysis in project appraisal documents improved between fiscal 2006 and 2008. Given the additional insights from the analysis of IEG data, management

would like to add that this increase in gender integration in the last two years (fiscal 2006–08) has occurred in a portfolio in which infrastructure and other economic sector operations traditionally characterized by low gender integration make up an increasing share.[3] The GAP is an instrument to improve performance of the Bank's country-led approach, based on the CAS and delivered through tools that include ESW and operations. A total of $4.2 million in GAP funds has supported 56 pieces of analytical work, many directly linked to key country policy dialogue; country-specific programs in Afghanistan, Ghana, Kenya, Lao PDR, Liberia, and Sudan, among others; and policy research to build the business case for gender equality. Sharing this research and analysis with partner countries increases country demand for gender support.

Furthering the GAP. The GAP is a time-bound effort launched to address weak implementation of the gender mainstreaming strategy in a subset of lagging sectors. As such, a transitional mechanism is needed that, though firmly anchored in the Bank's existing gender policy, builds on the momentum and lessons of the GAP to strengthen gender coverage in mainstream Bank operations. To this end, as requested by the Board, management is developing a GAP transition plan, to be presented to the Bank's Board of Directors in the spring of 2010. It will be informed by the independent midterm review of the GAP completed in June 2009.

III. Recommendations

Management's responses to IEG recommendations are included in the attached Management Action Record matrix. However, management would go further and note other actions we see as potentially equally or more important in preserving the positive momentum in gender mainstreaming generated by GAP beyond its closing date. These steps include the consideration of a World Development Report on gender equality to demonstrate the importance of gender in poverty reduction and growth and provide concrete assessments of what works and why, to increase client demand for gender equality work. Management will identify additional options in the transition plan scheduled for presentation at the Board in 2010.

Management Action Record

IEG Recommendation	Management Response
Foster greater clarity and better implementation of the Bank's gender policy, notably by—	Management agrees that the implementation of the Bank's gender policy needs improvement and will detail steps to be taken in the GAP transition plan to be presented to the Board in the fourth quarter of fiscal 2010. Management will also prepare and issue a guidance note to staff on the Bank's gender policy framework.
• Establishing a results framework to facilitate consistent adoption of an outcome approach to gender integration in the Bank's work.	Management notes that the Bank has a gender monitoring framework and reports regularly to senior management. Of course, it can be improved and made more results focused. The GAP transition plan will set out how the framework will be strengthened.
• Establishing and implementing a realistic action plan for completing or updating country-level diagnostics, giving primacy to countries with higher levels of gender inequality.	Management sees the CAS as the link between diagnostics and implementation and as the right place to determine gender priorities in Bank support to all countries in which the Bank has an active program. As noted in the CAS Retrospective (World Bank 2009c), management will work to improve the treatment of gender in CASs and will further monitor that the gender assessment adequately informs the CAS, as required in the policy. Management will report on results in regular gender monitoring reports.
• Extending implementation of the 2007 GAP while formalizing and strengthening its policy basis. An alternative would be to reinstate and strengthen provisions along the lines of OMS 2.20 to restore a sector- and/or project-level entry point for gender.	Management and IEG agree that the GAP is filling an implementation gap in the Bank's gender policy framework. At the Board's request, management is preparing a transition plan that will extend the gains of the GAP once it ends. The policy basis for the GAP and future action plans is fully adequate. The Bank's relevant policies already determine project entry points for gender.
Establish clear management accountability for the development and implementation of a system to monitor the extent to which Bank work adequately addresses gender-related concerns, including effective reporting mechanisms. The pivotal role of country directors needs to feature centrally in the accountability framework.	Management agrees with the recommendation to strengthen accountability for implementation of the Bank's gender policy, including country directors and operational vice presidents. Management notes that it has monitoring systems in place, but agrees that further work is needed to improve their impact. Starting with the current fiscal year, management commits to an annual Managing Director–level discussion of the comprehensive annual progress report, drawing on inputs from operational vice presidencies.
Strengthen the incentives for effective gender-related actions in client countries by continuing to provide incentive funding through the GAP to strengthen the collection, analysis, and dissemination of gender-disaggregated, gender-relevant data and statistics.	Management agrees that incentive funding continues to be needed for gender disaggregated data and statistics, but adds that transitional incentive funding for analytical and operational work has proven to be effective, as demonstrated by GAP results.

Summary of Discussions of Executive Directors and of the Board Committee on Development Effectiveness

On December 17, 2009, the Executive Directors (EDs) discussed the document entitled *Gender and Development: An Evaluation of World Bank Support, 2002–08,* prepared by the Independent Evaluation Group (IEG), and the revised draft Management Response. For this discussion, additional data and analysis were shared by IEG and management. Previously, the Board Committee on Development Effectiveness (CODE) considered the IEG evaluation report and draft Management Response on October 28, 2009. A statement by the External Advisory Panel was also made available for the Committee meeting. Based on its review of the IEG report and draft Management Response, the Committee had recommended a subsequent Board consideration.

At the Board meeting held on December 17, there was concurrence with IEG's evaluation that gender was an essential and core development function, and with its findings that the Bank was improving in integrating gender in scope and quality. The EDs and management also agreed with IEG that the Bank can do better on gender mainstreaming. IEG's findings resonated with the Board on the areas identified as key to strengthening gender mainstreaming, including (i) the results framework, (ii) managerial accountability, (iii) Bank budget resources, and (iv) country-level diagnostics. Noting management's intention to address these areas, EDs urged management to quickly take action. In strengthening the integration of gender in the Bank's operations, they emphasized that gender analysis be reflected in Country Assistance Strategies (CAS). It was noted that the IEG evaluation report and final Management Response would be disclosed.

At the earlier CODE discussion, Committee members welcomed the timely report, noting that the Bank's gender work had been a topic at the IDA15 mid-term review and that the report would have broader relevance for the process leading up to IDA16. They found it encouraging that integration of gender overall improved during the period covered by the IEG evaluation when compared to the 1990s and took note of IEG's finding that the implementation of the Bank's gender policy weakened in the latter half of the evaluation period. Committee members suggested subsequent

discussions and exchanges between IEG and management to help develop an understanding on the implementation of the Gender Policy Operational Policy/Bank Procedure (OP/BP 4.20) in areas where there were disagreements, for example, the definition and effectiveness of country gender diagnostics and the analysis of gender mainstreaming trends. In addition, Committee members emphasized the need to strengthen Senior Management accountability, the importance of having sufficient resources to implement the Gender Strategy, and the continued use of incentive funding. In view of the differences expressed by IEG and management, Committee members underlined the importance of an appropriate communication plan for disseminating the IEG's findings and management's response, which was confirmed at the Board meeting.

Main Issues Discussed

Differences between IEG and Management. At the Board meeting, IEG and management commented on their fruitful exchanges on the issues in the evaluation. When the IEG evaluation report and draft Management Response had been considered by CODE, many members had expressed difficulty in reaching a conclusion given the differences, including on methodology and data issues. However, both during the Board and Committee discussions, some speakers viewed IEG and management's differences in a positive light. IEG had noted that there had been significant consultations with management in the preparation of the evaluation report, including on the data used, and additional exchanges to reduce differences and clarify where differences remained.

During the Board discussion, management emphasized that the data and ratings shared by IEG following the CODE meeting generated new and useful findings that clarified the differences between IEG's and management's reporting of trends and led to a fruitful discussion with IEG. The Director-General, Evaluation (DGE) concurred that the additional exchange of data with management following the CODE meeting helped to develop an understanding of the three issues on which differences remain, that is, integration of gender considerations into economic and sector work; statistical association between the preparation of a gender assessment and integration of gender in the CAS; and trends in gender mainstreaming at the project level. The DGE also noted that, in addition to the usual communications that are coordinated with management, IEG is working with management to support regional workshops to engage operational staff and client stakeholders. Furthermore, IEG has initiated its own program to raise its evaluators' awareness of the need to address gender-related issues.

Country-Level Gender Diagnostics. At the Board discussion, EDs re-emphasized the importance of country gender assessment, possibly using other diagnostic tools, to meet the requirement under OP/BP 4.20. Moreover, they underlined the need to ensure the integration of gender diagnostics in CASs. Management agreed that country gender diagnostics are important, while avoiding across-the-board prescriptions, to inform a country-specific approach to gender that is reflected in CASs. In this connection, the importance of country ownership and addressing gender issues to take into account the country context including cultural sensitivities was stressed.

At the Committee meeting, some speakers supported a return to preparing Country Gender Assessments (CGAs). Several others favored a flexible approach; a few of them noted that gender diagnostics could be integrated in other analytical work; some others encouraged the Bank to draw on gender assessments prepared by others or to prepare them with other development partners. One speaker cautioned against mandating CGAs. A few specific comments were made related to the need to assess the diagnostic value of CGAs, and interpreting IEG's recommendation as a call for a realistic implementation plan for country-level gender diagnostic work, without being prescriptive. Management elaborated on economic and sector work that in its view met the requirement for gender assessments ranging from core gender analyses to Poverty Assessments, Country Economic Memoranda, Poverty and Social Impact Analyses, and Public Expenditure Reviews.

2001 Gender Strategy and OP/BP 4.20. There was general agreement at the Board and Committee on the continued relevance of the 2001 Gender Strategy and OP/BP 4.20, and the need for management to focus on practical initiatives to improve implementation and results focus. During the Committee discussions, some speakers wondered whether there had been a shift away from the Bank's Gender Strategy, as suggested by the IEG; management stressed that there has been no shift—that both the Gender Strategy and OP/BP 4.20 call appropriately for a country-led approach. In supporting a greater focus on managerial accountability, many speakers echoed the external panel in highlighting the importance of training and linking gender work with managers' performance evaluations; this was reiterated at the Board meeting.

At both the Board and Committee meetings, speakers emphasized the importance of improving the development effectiveness of gender support; of allocating budgetary resources from the Bank instead of relying on external funding; of improving the results framework for monitoring and evaluation; of pursuing a demand-driven and country owned approach; and of keeping in mind that gender issues involve both men and women. Stressing the importance of gender for development, the topic was proposed as the theme for the 2012 World Development Report.

Gender Action Plan (GAP). Responding to comments made at the Board and CODE meetings on the role and limited focus of GAP on economic sectors, management noted that the GAP both covered more than 50 percent of the current lending portfolio and, through innovative mechanisms such as incentives-based funding, had yielded results particularly in sectors that historically have had lower gender coverage. Building on its experience with innovative mechanisms, management remarked that the GAP Transition Plan would support sectors not targeted by the GAP such as Education and Health. Management declared its intention to use the Transition Plan to help address the specific issues identified by both management and IEG, for instance by developing new targets and time-bound action plans for specific quantifiable indicators for sectors and Regions.

Advisory Panel Statement

Ravi Kanbur and Jan Piercy

We welcome this comprehensive evaluation of Bank support for gender and development during 2002–08. The period follows the introduction of the Gender Strategy in 2001 and includes the introduction of the Gender Action Plan (GAP) in 2007. We note also management's responses to key elements of the findings and the interchanges with the Independent Evaluation Group (IEG), as recorded in the end notes of the chapters.

The report finds that the Bank's performance was better during 2002–08 than during 1990–99, the period covered in an earlier evaluation. However, it also finds that performance weakened in the latter part of the period, compared with the first part of the period under evaluation. We recognize that there are significant issues in measuring "performance." For example, of four measures, one improved and three deteriorated. Management in its analysis focused on the measure that improved. (See the exchange between management and IEG in endnote 14 in chapter 4). However, overall and taking into account the caveats, we endorse the report's findings and now briefly discuss their implications. We would be happy to expand on or explain the basis for our conclusions, but are being succinct in accord with guidelines for this response.

A central contention of the report is that Country Gender Assessments (CGAs), introduced after the 2001 Strategy to provide diagnostics to facilitate the integration of gender considerations into country strategies and projects, were not being undertaken or were not being updated, in the latter part of the 2002–08 period. This may have led to dissipation of focus and may thus account in significant measure for the weakening in performance. Management appears to reject this argument (endnote 1 of chapter 2), asserting that consideration of gender is incorporated into a wide range of reports: "A CGA does not need to be labeled as such to provide an actionable gender diagnostic."

Respecting this point, it is our view, however, that although individual pieces of work such as Country Economic Memoranda, Poverty and Social Impact Analyses (PSIAs), employment studies, and so forth can and should integrate attention to gender, this does not substitute for the CGA, with gender as focal point leading the analysis and providing the policy focus. The CGA can help provide accountability

for gender, highlighting actions needed across sectors and should itself thereby be an important source document for economic and sector work such as the PSIA. This is not to say that the Bank has to do a CGA on its own; indeed, collaborating with other development partners is ideal, creating broader engagement cost effectively and enabling country participants to be involved in one process rather than repetitively with multiple donors/lenders. In some cases, where work of other donors covers what a CGA would undertake, the Bank should utilize this analysis, although it should be imported into a document which management endorses, to maintain focus and accountability on gender and development. We were pleased to see budgets cited for CGAs, as assessing the value of any analysis appropriately should take costs into account.

The failure to follow through on the commitment to produce CGAs for all active borrowing countries without announcing this change in strategy is troubling on governance grounds as well. The GAPs that management appears to regard in some measure as alternatives to the CGA are financed by external funding and will cease when this outside support ends. The Bank's commitment to gender analysis and action is, however, an ongoing responsibility, all the more so given the established link between progress in addressing gender barriers and achievement of the Millennium Development Goals.

> We therefore support the report's recommendation for "establishing and implementing a realistic action plan for completing or updating country-level diagnostics, giving primacy to countries with higher levels of gender inequality."

The report highlights the importance of integrating gender into the broad country strategy, as well as into specific operations. Country Assistance Strategy (CAS) inclusion of gender improved significantly in the period under review compared with the earlier period, although performance weakened toward the end of the period (the peak seems to have come in 2003). The report also highlights a tendency to better integrate gender into projects in sectors identified in the CAS as being particularly relevant for gender issues. This contrasts with a gender perspective permeating project design and appraisal for all projects. There is a debate on this between management and IEG (see endnote 19 in chapter 4), but in our view a gender strategy has to walk on both legs—integration into the overall country strategy and integration to the extent appropriate operation by operation.

We therefore support the recommendation for "extending implementation of the 2007 GAP while formalizing and strengthening its policy basis. An alternative would be to reinstate and strengthen provisions along the lines of [Operational Manual Statement] 2.20 in order to restore a sector- and/or project-level entry point for gender."

The report also has recommendations on enhancing management's accountability and incentive funding for gender integration. Although endorsing these points in general terms, we have the following observations:

1. We would have liked to see consideration of what characteristics in managers may be associated with more effective gender integration. In particular, it would have been interesting to include such variables as gender and training of managers in the econometric analysis. We would also have liked to know extent to which management performance reviews take into account gender performance.

2. The findings on training are symptomatic and, quite frankly, shocking:

   A second prong of the Gender Strategy was to broaden and strengthen gender expertise in the Bank through training and capacity enhancement, thus minimizing the need for gender specialists. The effect of training and capacity building within the Bank appears mixed. RGCs observe that among higher-level staff—those responsible for integrating gender into operations—training sessions on gender are not popular. Thus, these sessions are instead largely attended by gender specialists and consultants. Further, at an institutional level, a gender module was integrated into the Bank's orientation course for all new staff. Between fiscal 2003 and 2006, the PREM Gender Group prepared and presented this module, but it has since been discontinued..... An examination of data available from the Bank's Learning Management System appears to confirm the observations that higher-level staff do not typically attend gender training (see chapter 5).

   We believe that these findings deserve a direct and targeted response from management.

3. We note that the evaluation does not cover the International Finance Corporation because a separate evaluation is due for those operations. However, the findings of this report, and the debates surrounding them, should be fully taken into account in the design of that evaluation.

We conclude by recognizing the report's finding that the Bank's performance has indeed improved over the previous decade. This is welcome. However, the weakening in performance in the latter part of this decade highlighted by the report gives cause for concern. Focus on how to maintain and improve the Bank's performance on integrating gender considerations into its work is required. No doubt the detail of the recommendations will be debated, but their broad thrust is sound, and management needs to take them on board purposively.

Chapter 1

EVALUATION HIGHLIGHTS

- The Bank's approach to gender has evolved through a variety of approaches.

- The current state of gender policy in the Bank is a country-level one, but with a sector- and project-based focus reemerging in recent years.

- Operational Policy (OP) 4.20 abrogated the provisions of Operational Manual Statement 2.20 (which called for the consideration of gender issues during project appraisal) except as required by the OP in sectors and thematic areas identified as priority for gender in the Country Assistance Strategy.

Evolution of the World Bank's Gender Policy

The World Bank was the first multilateral development institution to make women's issues an explicit item of attention. This occurred in 1977, during the United Nations Decade for Women, when the Bank began requiring consideration of women's issues as part of a project's social analysis. Over the next three decades, Bank approaches kept pace with international development in this area, shifting from a focus on women to a focus on gender equality.

The vehicle for identifying and addressing these issues shifted from the project's social analysis to the Country Assistance Strategy (CAS), with the issues diagnosed by a Country Gender Assessment (CGA) and addressed as part of the overall support for economic growth and poverty reduction in a country. This chapter describes the evolution of the Bank's gender policy and presents the objectives and scope of the Bank's current policy.

1977–2001: Enhancing Women's Participation in Development

In 1997, against the backdrop of the United Nations Decade for Women (1976–85),[1] the Bank appointed a Women in Development Adviser. In 1984, the approval of Operational Manual Statement (OMS) 2.20 on Project Appraisal (World Bank 1984) called for Bank staff to consider issues related to women as part of the social analysis undertaken during appraisal of investment projects where "women are sometimes a particularly important group of project participants and beneficiaries." Clearly, this did not apply to every project, but it has been suggested that a preliminary analysis is required in most cases to identify the project beneficiaries (IEG 2001b, appendix 1). OMS 2.20 called for Bank staff to mitigate disadvantageous effects on women and to encourage women's participation in development. Bank staff were asked to examine whether the implications for women were included in the provisions for monitoring the impact of the project.[2,3]

> As early as 1977, the Bank initiated a focus on women and development issues.

In 1991, after the 1990 World Development Report on poverty (World Bank 1990), the approach to gender shifted to consideration of women's issues as part of the Bank's overall poverty reduction mandate. This was first reflected in the 1990 Operational Directive (OD) on poverty reduction.

Four years later, the strategy paper "Enhancing Women's Participation in Economic Development" (World Bank 1994) set out the goal of reducing gender disparity in human development and enhancing the economic participation of women as part of the Bank's overall support for poverty reduction in a client country. This required sound analysis of gender issues (as part of regular economic and sector work [ESW]) and the integration of relevant gender issues into the design of CASs and subsequent country programs.

These principles were incorporated in Operational Policy (OP) 4.20, Gender and Development, issued in 1994, which took a country-level approach and proposed to address strategic country-level issues[4] by requiring integration of gender considerations into CASs and country programs. Because of the importance of country ownership in addressing strategic gender issues, the OP required that such activities be country led and integrated into Bank support in close collaboration with the client.

At the same time, OMS 2.20 continued to apply to the appraisal of investment lending; in this case, Bank staff were obliged to implement its provisions as appropriate, and it was not a matter of client demand or of Bank staff's choice. The two

> In 1994, the Bank added a country-level approach that required it to consider and address gender issues as part of its support for poverty reduction in each client country.

approaches were complementary and together constituted a "gender mainstreaming" approach. However, until 2001, it was unclear whether OP 4.20 applied to policy-based lending (now categorized as Development Policy Operations [DPOs]).

2001–09: Strengthened Country-Level Approach

In 2000, 189 signatory governments accepted gender equality as an explicit objective in the Millennium

Development Goals (MDGs). Against this background, the Bank introduced a gender strategy the following year that emphasized "gender equality" and focused on disparities between the sexes without concentrating exclusively on cases where females are disadvantaged, relative to males.

By 2001, the Bank had shifted to a focus on gender equality as a means to help reduce poverty.

This 2001 Gender Strategy (*Integrating Gender into the World Bank's Work: A Strategy for Action*; World Bank 2002b)—referred to as the 2001 Gender Strategy—endorsed by the Board, set out a four-step approach (see figure 1.1) and provided an instrument for country-level diagnosis, namely the CGA.

For investment lending, the 2001 Strategy recognized OMS 2.20 as an important element of the Bank's policy framework for gender. However, it noted that the treatment of gender issues in the appraisal of investment lending would be considered as part of the process of converting OMSs to OP/Bank Procedure (BP) statements (World Bank 2002b, p. 55). It recommended integrating a gender dimension "into the social impact analysis associated with DPOs in high-priority sectors (as identified in the CGA)" (World Bank 2002b, p. 26), and noted that the treatment of gender considerations would be taken up in other relevant operational statements related to DPOs (World Bank 2002b, p. 57).

In 2003, a revised OP 4.20 was issued, with a new parallel BP (4.20) to set out the associated procedures. The OP/BP contained substantive and detailed guidance to country directors, sector managers, and task teams on gender integration in Bank support—significantly more than previously. For investment lending, OP 4.20 replaced the provisions of OMS 2.20 related to consideration of gender issues at project appraisal. It updated the language and absorbed these provisions into the four-step process.[5,6]

With respect to DPOs, the updated OP 8.60, approved in August 2004, does not explicitly require these instruments to address gender dimensions of development. This said, OP 8.60 requires that all DPOs examine the poverty and social impacts of the reform programs supported by the operation. The Good Practice Note on using Poverty and Social Impact Analysis to support development policy operations

(World Bank 2004c) provides guidance on how gender issues can be integrated into such analysis. However, OP 8.60 makes no reference to the CGA or to the identification of policy issues described in BP 4.20.

In addition to the above, four specific policies (OP 4.10 on Involuntary Resettlement, OP 4.12 on Indigenous Peoples, BP 4.30 on Forests, and OP 2.30 on Development Cooperation and Conflict) also require consideration of issues related to women as part of vulnerable groups. These policies continue to maintain a project-level entry point.

In 2007, the Bank introduced a Gender Action Plan (GAP) that focused on four key markets—land, labor, agriculture, and finance—as well as on infrastructure related to access to these markets. The GAP aimed to advance women's economic empowerment in Bank client countries by making these four markets work for women and by empowering women to compete in these markets. As one of its four action points, it provided resources to Bank staff to integrate gender considerations into analytical work and operations

Figure 1.1 Strategic Mainstreaming— A Four-Step Approach (OP 4.20)

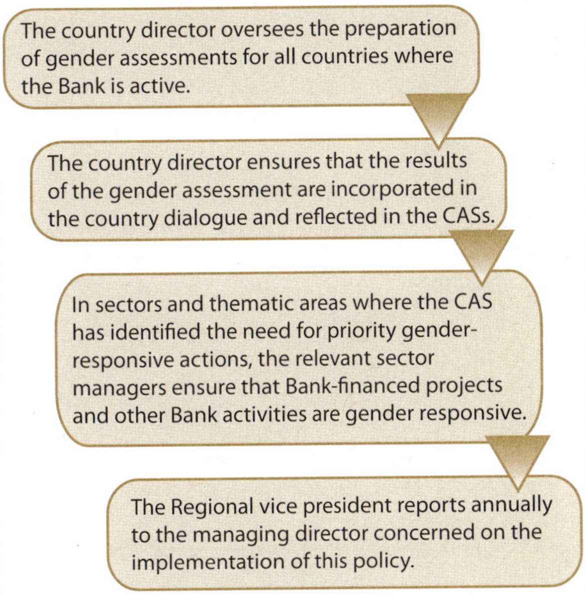

The country director oversees the preparation of gender assessments for all countries where the Bank is active.

The country director ensures that the results of the gender assessment are incorporated in the country dialogue and reflected in the CASs.

In sectors and thematic areas where the CAS has identified the need for priority gender-responsive actions, the relevant sector managers ensure that Bank-financed projects and other Bank activities are gender responsive.

The Regional vice president reports annually to the managing director concerned on the implementation of this policy.

Source: IEG.

Note: CAS = Country Assistance Strategy; OP = Operational Policy.

in predetermined economic sectors that influence these four markets.

The Independent Evaluation Group (IEG) is of the view that by encouraging gender integration into operations without explicit reference to the CAS or CGA, the GAP thus adopted an approach more reminiscent of the project-level approach of OMS 2.20 than of the country-level approach of the Bank's current policy, OP/BP 4.20.[7, 8]

To conclude, for the purposes of this evaluation, the Bank's policy on gender is interpreted consistently with OP/BP 4.20 as requiring the four-step process (figure 1.1) in each country where the Bank is active. The OP/BP 4.20, read along with the 2001 Gender Strategy, is the guiding document for policy implementation. Thus, except in cases identified in other specific policies, there is no requirement that gender considerations be integrated into activities in sectors not noted in CASs.

Chapter 2

EVALUATION HIGHLIGHTS

- The Bank's gender policy requires a country-level diagnostic in all countries in which the Bank has an active assistance program, identification of key gender and development constraints, and integration into CASs and programs.

- Such "strategic mainstreaming" is to be undertaken in close consultation with the client.

- This evaluation reviews how the Bank implemented its gender policy and to what extent it has supported the reduction of gender disparity and enhanced women's empowerment.

Design of the Evaluation

IEG has previously conducted three evaluations of Bank support for gender. The first, in 1994 (IEG 1994), traced the concept of women in development and how gender came to be reflected in Bank policies and lending. In 1997, a second evaluation (IEG 1997b) reviewed lending and nonlending work for evidence of progress in implementing the Bank's 1994 policy. The third evaluation—conducted in two phases (IEG 2001a, 2001b) and published together as *Evaluating a Decade of World Bank Gender Policy, 1990–1999* (IEG 2005)—assessed gender mainstreaming in Bank support between 1990 and 1999.

One of the key findings of the 2001 IEG evaluations was that although gender was integrated into the majority of the human development sectors, integration was weaker in sectors that influenced the participation of women in economic activities. (Subsequently, this finding was validated independently by the Gender Group; World Bank 2006b.) At the institutional level, the evaluation found no consensus on the scope of the Bank's strategy (IEG 2001a).

> This evaluation builds on previous IEG assessments in 1994, 1997, and 2001.

The evaluations concluded that the Bank had not established processes to institutionalize or operationalize its policy and that monitoring of gender-related inputs, outputs, and outcomes was weak. IEG recommended that the Bank clarify its gender policy, require the integration of gender considerations into CASs based on comprehensive diagnoses, strengthen client institutions to support the implementation of national gender policies, and establish monitoring and evaluation (M&E) systems to measure progress toward policy objectives.

Given the evolution in how the Bank has approached gender since the 2001 evaluation (including the revised Gender Strategy in 2001, OP/BP 4.20 in 2003, and the GAP in 2007), it is an opportune time to undertake another evaluation of Bank support for gender and development. The purpose of this evaluation is primarily to foster learning and motivate appropriate course corrections based on the assessment of Bank experience, with the aim of enhancing the development effectiveness of future Bank interventions. The evaluation did not focus on International Finance Corporation activities, given IEG's proposed fiscal 2012 evaluation of gender integration into support by the Corporation.

Evaluation Approach and Methodology

The main evaluation questions are as follows:

- **Relevance and appropriateness of the Bank's gender policy:** To what extent is the World Bank's policy resulting in the "right" gender issues (that is, issues relevant for poverty reduction and economic growth, as noted in OP/BP 4.20) being adequately addressed at the country level?

- **Integration of gender into Bank support:** To what extent did the Bank implement its 2001 Strategy and OP/BP 4.20?

- **Results of the policy:** To what extent has the Bank contributed to documented results in reducing gender disparities and enhancing women's empowerment in selected countries? To what extent has the Bank supported the development of gender-disaggregated data in client countries in these areas? What has worked well? What needs to be strengthened?

To answer the first two questions on relevance and policy implementation, IEG selected all countries with a population of more than 1 million to ensure a manageable evaluation sample. Because OP 4.20 applies only to investment projects, the evaluation included all countries that had received at least two investment projects during the evaluation period and that had prepared a CAS or an equivalent document between fiscal 2002 and 2008 (appendix A lists the 93 countries).

> IEG assessed the relevance and implementation of the Bank's 2001 Gender Strategy by looking at programs in 93 countries.

To assess relevance, IEG reviewed whether the objectives of the gender policy were relevant for the Bank's mandate of poverty reduction and economic growth and for client countries. IEG undertook a literature review to understand better the links among gender equality, economic growth, and poverty reduction. It also reviewed the appropriateness by focusing on whether the policy approach allowed tailoring of Bank support to country-specific contexts, whether it reflected a clear accountability framework, and whether the approach was consistent with international conventions on gender equality and women's empowerment.

To assess policy implementation in these 93 countries, IEG reviewed objectives, gender discussion, and the matrices of 140 CASs and other strategy documents including CAS progress reports prepared during the evaluation period. It assessed the extent of gender integration in 48 CGAs and 74 Poverty Assessments prepared in the 93 evaluation countries.[1] It also reviewed project appraisal documents (PADs) of 1,183 projects approved during the evaluation period, excluding Emergency Rehabilitation Loans and supplementary financing, to understand how gender was integrated in the various sectors.

In all, the evaluation covered 90 percent of the investment lending commitments. Figure 2.1 details the criteria used for each of these assessments (detailed rating scales are provided in the relevant chapters). IEG also undertook a rapid examination of 307 DPOs, approved during the evaluation period to better understand how gender issues were addressed in these operations. It also looked at the extent and nature of gender discussion in the program documents, inclusion of gender-related actions or triggers, and the extent to which the gender dimensions were being measured and monitored.

To answer the third question on the results of Bank support, IEG selected 12 countries, using a weighted stratified sampling procedure of the 93 countries (see appendix A). In 10 of those countries, CASs had been prepared between fiscal 2002 and 2004. IEG tried to understand how the Bank achieved its strategic objectives during the period. In two countries, CASs were prepared late in the evaluation period; for these, the evaluation relied on project-level objectives in one and a 2001 CAS in the other. In the 12 countries, IEG examined 164 operations (both DPOs and investment projects) that closed after fiscal 2003 and before fiscal 2009 and for which an implementation completion report (ICR) was available.[2] At the

request of members of the Bank's Board, IEG reviewed Bank support to Afghanistan as a separate study and examined the design and results of DPOs.

The evaluation assessed results in 12 of the 93 countries.

Answering the question on outcomes of Bank support was challenging. The 2001 Strategy did not include an explicit results framework, so the evaluation team constructed one based on the Bank's strategy. It focused on how Bank support contributed to achieving outcomes in three domains that the 2001 Gender Strategy indicates are important for achieving gender equality: enhanced human capital, equal access to economic assets and opportunities, and enhanced voice of men and women in development planning and implementation.[3]

IEG assessed the efficacy of Bank support and its results based on goals and objectives stated in the CAS or other relevant documents. Where there was little evidence in Bank ICRs, CAS Completion Reports (CASCRs), or other relevant documents, and where field assessments were not conducted, IEG rated the results as modest. It used a common set of indicators and subindicators, as identified in chapter 6.

In answering the relevance and integration questions, IEG employed a before-and-after comparison, using the results of the previous evaluation for the "before" phase. In answering the third evaluation question in the 12 countries, it proved difficult within the constraints of this evaluation to use a with-and-without design. Appendix A describes the methodology in two countries where field assessments were undertaken (Peru and Zambia). In three other countries (Ghana, Tajikistan, and the Republic of Yemen), IEG conducted focus group discussions or surveys with both male and female beneficiaries and nonbeneficiaries to get a better idea of the results for project beneficiaries.

In conducting the evaluation, IEG used multiple methods to validate and supplement its findings, including semi-structured interviews of Bank staff and donor representatives and consultations with client stakeholders. It also held three consultative sessions with the Bank's Gender Board, the first before preparation of the Approach Paper (IEG

FIGURE 2.1 Criteria for Rating Gender Integration in CGAs, CASs, and Projects

A CGA with high gender integration (48 CGAs reviewed)

Fully meets the following criteria (from OP/BP 4.20 and the Gender Group's 2004 guidance for CGAs):
- Is user friendly and published
- Analyzes gender issues using a cross-sectoral approach with good data covering socio-economic roles, productive resources, human development, and participation in development decision making
- Includes consultation with client stakeholders during the preparatory process or once the recommendations are drafted
- Identifies a limited set of policy and operational interventions that the analysis and consultations suggest are key to removing gender-related barriers to development

A CAS with high gender integration (140 CASs reviewed)

Fully meets the following criteria (adapted from the Gender Group's criteria for assessing CASs and OP/BP 4.20):
- Includes gender diagnosis (around the three domains)
- Integrates gender into the relevant sectors in the CAS matrix (or explains why this was not necessary)
- Includes at least one monitoring indicator in the overall results framework other than on reproductive health and primary education

A project with high gender integration (1,183 projects reviewed)

Fully meets the following criteria (adapted from the Gender Group's criteria for assessing gender integration at the project level):
- Includes gender diagnosis within country and sector context, backed by some quantitative or qualitative data, and identifies issues to be addressed
- Includes consultation with both men and women, either during project design or implementation (as noted in the PAD or other related design documents), and some discussion of the implications
- Includes measures to address key identified issues or notes that diagnosis indicates that no actions are needed
- Includes at least one gender-disaggregated or gender-related indicator

Source: IEG.

Note: CAS = Country Assistance Strategy; CGA = Country Gender Assessment; OP/BP = Operational/Bank Policy; PAD = project appraisal document.

2008b), the second midway through the evaluation, and the final one to discuss emerging findings. Additionally, it consulted with external stakeholders both in client countries and in Washington, DC. The literature review also helped the evaluators to understand new thinking in this area since the last evaluation.

To deepen understanding of the results, IEG undertook field assessments and relied on other independent assessments, as well as impact assessments commissioned by the Bank. Where feasible, IEG attempted to isolate the results

> In conducting the evaluation, IEG triangulated the desk review findings through a variety of methods.

of Bank support at the project and sector levels and then assess how the specific results could have contributed posi-

tively or negatively to the three desired outcomes. Some research was also undertaken in the 12 countries to identify other extraneous factors that could have influenced or contributed to the results.

Organization of the Report

The next chapter examines the relevance and appropriateness of the Bank's gender policy, chapter 4 examines how the Bank implemented its policy, and chapter 5 reviews the institutionalization of the policy. Chapter 6 then seeks to understand the results of Bank support and examines what worked best and what did not work as well, and why. Chapter 7 provides the evaluation's conclusions, overall lessons, and suggestions for moving ahead. Appendixes provide further information on the evaluation methodology and other relevant information.

Chapter 3

EVALUATION HIGHLIGHTS

- The Bank's gender policy is closely linked to the overall mandate of poverty reduction.

- It is appropriately flexible and allows tailoring of Bank support to suit country-specific needs and priorities.

- The lack of a results framework reduces the policy's relevance, leaving unclear precisely how the Bank aims to translate the goal into results.

- Provision in the policy for selective (rather than generalized, as in the past) gender integration at the project level further weakens the appropriateness of the policy.

Relevance and Appropriateness of the World Bank's Gender Policy

To assess relevance, in conducting the evaluation, IEG focused on whether the objectives of the gender policy are consistent with the Bank's mandate of poverty reduction and economic growth, as well as appropriate for meeting client country priorities and needs. To assess the appropriateness of the design, IEG examined whether the policy (which directs how the Gender Strategy should be implemented) facilitated tailoring of Bank support to suit country contexts, whether it included a clear accountability framework, and whether the overall approach was consistent with international conventions in this area.

IEG concludes that the objectives of the Bank's gender policy are highly relevant to its poverty reduction mandate as well as to the clients' development needs and priorities. The policy is also flexible enough to facilitate country-specific responses and includes an accountability framework. Weak elements lie in the lack of a results framework, as well as the narrowing of the requirement that gender issues be considered at project appraisal only in projects in sectors and themes identified in CASs.

Relevance of Policy Objectives to the Bank's Mandate

The Bank's gender policy aims to "assist member countries to reduce poverty and enhance economic growth, human well-being, and development effectiveness by addressing the gender disparities and inequalities that are barriers to development, and by assisting member countries in formulating and implementing their gender and development goals" (World Bank 2002b, p. xii). For the Bank, gender equality is an instrument to help achieve the institutional mandates of poverty reduction and economic growth.

A literature review undertaken for this evaluation confirms the linkages between gender equality and poverty reduction (appendix B). The literature suggests that improving gender outcomes in education and health; expanding women's participation in the labor force, entrepreneurship, and access to productive assets; and strengthening women's voice and rights can lead to better development outcomes across a range of sectors.

Gender-based inequalities in education decrease availability of human capital for a country.

Many studies find that gender-based inequalities in education reduce economic growth, because when either girls or boys of school age are unable to attend school, the overall availability of human capital within the country is decreased. Several studies have documented the positive externalities of educating women—and the important intergenerational effects of female education. Educated women contribute to the welfare of the next generation by reducing infant mortality, lowering fertility, and improving the nutritional status of children (Klasen 1999; Smith and Haddad 1999; World Bank 2001a, 2005b; Lagerlöf 2003).

Country studies confirm the significant effect of educating women on health and educational outcomes. In India, children of literate mothers spend two hours more per day studying than children of illiterate mothers (Behrman and others 1999). In Guatemala and Nigeria, educated mothers are more likely to adopt health-seeking behaviors such as immunization (Pebley, Goldman, and Rodriguez 1996; Gage and others 1997). In Brazil, income received by mothers has four times the impact on children's growth than the same amount received by fathers (Thomas 1990). Within the household, educated women have a stronger bargaining position, which in turn contributes to better intrahousehold resource allocation. The long-term impact on adolescent girls is striking (box 3.1).

Since the 1994 International Conference on Population and Development in Cairo, the basic importance of women's health for countries' economic and social development—as well as family well-being in general—has been increasingly recognized by the international community and its public health agenda (Germain and Kyte 1995; UNDP 1995; Dixon-Mueller and Germain

2007). Within the health arena, reproductive health matters have received by far the most attention. Although the MDGs appear to concentrate more specifically on improving the slightly narrower category of maternal health (to which one of the eight goals—number five—is devoted exclusively), consensus has emerged that ensuring universal access to reproductive health care—covering family planning and sexual health more generally—is vital for the realization of all of the MDGs (Sachs 2001; WHO 2002; Singh and others 2003; United Nations Millennium Project 2005).

> Development literature recognizes the importance of women's health for family well-being and for a country's economic and social development.

However, on this particular MDG, progress worldwide has been poor, compared with progress on the poverty and the gender parity goals (Bourguignon and others 2008). More than 500,000 women still die each year during pregnancy and childbirth (UNICEF 2006; Ban 2009). In terms of development indicators, maternal mortality rates show the widest gender gap. UNICEF data from 2005 show that the maternal mortality rate across the industrialized world was 8 per 100,000 live births, but in developing countries it was 450 per 100,000, and in the least developed countries it was 870 (UNICEF 2008, p. 45).

Empirical evidence shows that women have less ownership of economic resources and assets than men do, and several studies suggest that enhanced access to such assets and resources leads to their increased productivity (Blackden and Bhanu 1999; Bamberger and others 2002; World Bank 2001a, 2002e). This in turn improves household welfare through better bargaining power (Doss 1996; World Bank 2006b). There is also growing empirical evidence that, although there are forms of structural discrimination against women in relation to access to credit networks (Mayoux 2001), female borrowers have a lower risk of default because women's group have a lower prevalence of corruption and bribes, and women borrowers have higher repayment rates (Khandker 1998; Swamy and others 2001; Khandker and others 2008). Such findings have strengthened demands for gender-based policies to ensure that women are given improved access to economic opportunities.

Increasing women's control over land can have a strong and immediate effect on the welfare of the following generation, as well as on the pace at which physical and human capital are accumulated (World Bank 2003c). For example, in Ghana, women's land rights are more precarious than men's, which has been found to have direct implications for productivity and yields

> Empirical evidence shows that women can be empowered by being encouraged to participate in community activities.

(Goldstein and Udry 2008). Analysis of data from Honduras and Nicaragua suggests a positive correlation between women's land rights and their overall role in the household economy: women gain greater control over agricultural income, gain higher shares of business and labor market earnings, and more frequently receive credit (Katz and Chamorro 2003).

Power and authority differentials between women and men are not restricted to the private sphere; they also play out in

---

BOX 3.1

LONG-TERM EFFECTS OF FEMALE EDUCATION

The education of girls provides a strong test of a government's commitment to equality of opportunity. Many formidable obstacles stop girls from completing their schooling: family financial pressure, lack of safety, even things as basic as inadequate toilet facilities. But if these obstacles can be overcome, the payoff is very high. Educated women have fewer, healthier children, and they have them when they are older. The result is children who are more successful in school, largely because they benefit from their mothers' education. Educating girls and integrating them into the labor force is one way to break an intergenerational cycle of poverty.

Source: Commission on Growth and Development (2008).

the public sphere, affecting prevailing forms of local governance. There is evidence that encouraging the participation of women in community activities can lead to their empowerment and increased presence in community affairs and activities. Goetz (2004), for example, discusses the establishment of rules to secure institutionalized spaces for women's participation in planning, monitoring, auditing, and reviewing expenditures, ring-fencing portions of budgets for women-only deliberations, and conducting gender-sensitive revenue and spending analyses. Deininger, Galab, and Olsen (2005) find that in India, women's involvement in community-driven development (CDD) has led to improvements in their participation that appear to transcend the realm of the family and extend to the community.

The literature review, however, indicates that the evidence on the extent to which gender inequality is linked to growth outcomes is tentative at best. The reliance on cross-country regressions in some of the analyses during the late 1990s is problematic for many reasons.[1] Recent reviews highlight the conceptual, methodological, and data challenges faced in seeking to establish empirical— let alone causal—relationships among gender inequality, poverty, and growth (Stotsky 2006; World Bank 2007e). The conclusions of a review of the available evidence are summarized in box 3.2, and there appears to be a need for stronger evidence to explain the observed correlations among gender equality or women's empowerment, poverty reduction, and economic growth.

The link between gender equality and economic growth needs to be strengthened.

Overall, despite the methodological challenges, the literature suggests that gender-based differences in health, education, access to economic assets, and voice affect overall economic choices and opportunities for both men and women. They affect the labor productivity of men and women, the performance and potential of their businesses, and the incentives they face as economic agents. These differences also have longer-term, intergenerational effects, influencing the education, welfare, and future economic potential of children.

All these factors can affect the nature, pace, sustainability, and impact of economic growth and poverty reduction— and thereby the effectiveness of development interventions in achieving their goals. As a recent International Monetary Fund survey concluded, "Societies that increase women's access to education, health care, employment, and credit, and that narrow differences between women and men in economic opportunities, increase the pace of economic development and reduce poverty" (Stotsky 2006).

Gender differentials in access to health, education, economic assets, and decision making affect the pace and nature of poverty reduction.

Consequently, this evaluation concludes that the objective of the Bank's gender policy is very relevant to the Bank's central poverty reduction mandate. Addressing the gender disparities that are barriers to development is one of the important ways the Bank can contribute to sustainable and equitable growth and poverty reduction.

Relevance of Objectives for Bank Client Countries

IEG assessed the relevance of objectives for client countries by reviewing the country's status on international conventions in this area, as well as through a review of domestic policies in the 12 focus countries.

All 93 countries included in this evaluation are signatories to the Convention on the Elimination of All Forms of Discrimination against Women. All are also signatories of the Beijing Declaration (1995), which endorsed gender mainstreaming as the optimal approach to achieve gender equality, and the Millennium Declaration (UN 2000) and its associated MDGs, which specifically include "gender equality and empowerment of women" as one of the eight goals (MDG 3).

BOX 3.2

GENDER, POVERTY, AND GROWTH: SOME KEY CONCLUSIONS

"Poverty incidence tends to be lower in countries with greater gender equality.... Economic growth also appears to be positively correlated with gender equality.... Simple correlations across countries—while suggestive—do not imply a causal relationship between gender equality and poverty reduction or economic growth: gender equality could 'cause' faster growth and accelerated poverty reduction, but faster development could also spur improvements in gender equality. Alternatively, the causal arrows may point in both directions, or a third factor may be responsible for both faster development and greater improvements in gender equality—perhaps better governance."

Source: World Bank (2007e).

CLIENT COUNTRY DEMAND FOR ADDRESSING GENDER-RELATED OBJECTIVES

Despite the formal acceptance of gender equality or women's empowerment by client countries, 87 percent of 167 Bank staff respondents to an IEG survey identified the lack of demand in client countries as the most important constraint in addressing gender issues in their work. The fact that fewer than 10 percent of projects (of 1,183) have explicit gender objectives for at least one component underscores the point that gender issues are not of high priority for most countries. However, several client stakeholders pointed out that this demand depends on whom Bank staff consult in countries. They stressed the need to ensure wider participation (outside the Ministry of Finance and other line ministries) in this dialogue.

Sources: IEG survey, client consultation, and project-level review.

In this respect, country ownership of the gender equality agenda is evident, even as country-specific objectives and approaches range from women's advancement and empowerment to promoting gender equality. Consequently, development assistance in support of gender equality, women's advancement, and empowerment as an instrument to enhance economic development and poverty reduction is consistent with the stated policy objectives in these countries (box 3.3).

Additionally, each of the 12 focus countries has a country-level policy or strategy for gender equality or women's advancement. Spurred by the commitments made at Beijing and follow-up conferences, each of these countries has invested significant resources to establish institutional mechanisms, albeit with varying responsibilities and resources, to implement their policies and strategies (table 3.1).

Appropriateness of Policy Design

IEG assessed the design of the current gender policy (based on the 2001 Gender Strategy) against three subquestions (issues of resources and staffing are discussed in chapter 5):

- To what extent did the gender policy provide the ability to tailor Bank support to country-specific needs and priorities?

- To what extent did the gender policy reflect a clear accountability and reporting framework to support implementation of the strategy?

- To what extent was the gender policy consistent with international conventions on gender equality?

In formulating the 2001 Gender Strategy, the Bank relied on its own analysis and self-assessments. Just before the

TABLE 3.1	Commitments to Gender Equality in Focus Countries			
Country	Date of CEDAW ratification	Constitution prohibits discrimination on grounds of sex	Government statement on gender or women	Institutional machinery to implement policy
Bangladesh	1984[a]	Y	1995	Y
Benin	1990	Y	2001	Y
Colombia	1982	Y	1994[b]	Y
Ghana	1986	Y	2004	Y
Lebanon	1997[a]	Y	2005[c]	Y
Nigeria	1985	Y	2006	Y
Peru	1982	Y	2006	Y
Philippines	1981	Y	1989	Y
Tajikistan	1993[a]	Y	1998	Y
Turkey	1985[a]	Y	2008	Y
Yemen, Rep. of	1984[a]	N[d]	2003	Y
Zambia	1996	Y	2000	Y

Source: World Bank.
Note: CEDAW = Convention on the Elimination of All Forms of Discrimination Against Women.
a. Includes some reservations.
b. For rural women.
c. Part of a ministerial statement.
d. "Women are the sisters of men. They have rights and duties, which are guaranteed and assigned by Shari'ah and stipulated by law" (from the Constitution of Yemen).

evaluation period, a Bank policy research report made a strong case for why gender equality matters for development (World Bank 2001a). Furthermore, as noted in chapter 2, IEG also undertook an evaluation of Bank support for gender and development in 1999 (IEG 2005), which fed into the formulation of the 2001 Gender Strategy, as reflected in the Management Action Record included in the Bank's 2001 Gender Strategy.

Ability to tailor country-specific support

The gender policy stresses that the Bank is to be supportive but proactive in (i) helping client countries address gender disparities and inequalities that are barriers to poverty reduction and enhanced economic growth and (ii) formulating and implementing countries' own gender and development goals. The gender policy's four-step process is sufficiently flexible to accommodate this kind of tailoring.

The four-step process provides flexibility for country-specific tailoring of Bank support.

The first step requires a country-specific assessment (CGA) to support the client in identifying critical gender constraints to development. The second step requires integration of an appropriate gender response into the CAS, based on the CGA findings. The third step requires gender integration into projects and activities in sectors and thematic areas that the CAS identifies as strategic priorities from a gender perspective. Finally, the 2001 Gender Strategy anticipated that a "new monitoring and evaluation system for tracking and evaluating gender mainstreaming in the World Bank's work" would be delivered in fiscal 2002.[2]

Accountability framework for policy implementation

A key element for determining the commitment of an institution to implement a policy lies in the accountability framework for implementation. Such a framework requires an articulation of the objectives and of the desired results (a results orientation), clear assignment of responsibilities, and an M&E system to allow for understanding of results. The Bank's Gender Strategy and the subsequent OP/BP 4.20 reflected two of these three elements.

OP/BP 4.20 clearly stated responsibilities for policy implementation. The country director would "oversee" preparation of the CGA in each country where the Bank is active and ensure that the results were reflected in the subsequent CAS.[3] The sector manager would ensure that projects and activities in the relevant sectors identified in the CAS were gender responsive. In terms of M&E, as discussed in the previous section, Regional vice presidencies were to report on policy implementation annually to

the managing director, and the Gender and Development Board was to consolidate the reports into a Bank-wide summary. Thus, two elements of the accountability framework were well laid out in the Bank's 2001 Gender Strategy.

The lack of a clear results framework reduces the relevance of the gender policy.

The results framework was weak, however, even though the 2001 Gender Strategy included significant illustrations of integrating gender into a variety of sectors and thematic areas. Although the 2001 Strategy noted the framework in the 2000/2001 World Development Report *Attacking Poverty* (World Bank 2000a)—security, opportunity, and empowerment—as well as that in the 2001 engendering development report (World Bank 2001a)—equal rights, equal access to resources, and equal voice and participation—it stopped short of specifying the framework for achieving the Bank's objectives.[4] This has resulted in the arbitrary and inconsistent treatment of gender issues. For example, gender issues considered important in a first CAS were sometimes not seen as important by the time of the second CAS (or the other way around), with insufficient justification provided for the switch in approach. This weakened the accountability framework.

Consistency of approach with international gender-related conventions

Several international conventions stress the importance of gender mainstreaming. The 1995 Beijing Convention endorsed gender mainstreaming as the most effective approach to address gender inequalities (box 3.4). As recently as 2005, the Paris Declaration reiterated the importance of strengthening donor harmonization in addressing gender equality.

The 2007 GAP also states that gender mainstreaming is the "sound and viable appropriate strategy to address gender inequalities" (World Bank 2006b) Recognizing the weak integration of gender considerations into specific sectors, the GAP defines a four-year plan to give gender issues more traction at the operational level. The GAP is, therefore, highly relevant.

The GAP was a reaction to low institutionalization of the Bank's Gender Strategy.

IEG considers that the lack of a wider project-level entry point reduces the overall development effectiveness of Bank support. To illustrate, in Tajikistan, the Farm Privatization Support Project provided training of trainers for extension services predominantly to men and by men. However, IEG's Project Performance Assessment Report

DEFINITION OF GENDER MAINSTREAMING

"The process of assessing the implications for women and men of any planned action, including legislation, policies or programmes, in all areas and at all levels. It is a strategy for making women's as well as men's concerns and experiences an integral dimension of the design, implementation, monitoring and evaluation of policies and programmes in all political, economic and societal spheres so that women and men benefit equally and inequality is not perpetuated. The ultimate goal is to achieve gender equality."

Source: ECOSOC (1997).

(IEG 2008b) found that family farms in Tajikistan are overwhelmingly run by women (because many men have migrated), and local cultural norms constrain women from attending official meetings.[5] Male extension trainers missed an important target population, reducing the possibility of introducing change and supporting gender equality. Before fiscal 2003, a project of this sort that did not include gender considerations would have been inconsistent with OMS 2.20 (to the extent that it was being implemented). But the lack of gender integration in such projects would not have been inconsistent with OP 4.20, because the project was not in a sector identified in the CAS as important for gender.

To conclude, the objectives of the gender policy are highly relevant for the Bank's mandate of poverty reduction and for development plans of client countries. The implementation approach is appropriately flexible and responsive to ensure relevance for the client and to address country-specific priorities. The gender policy specifies an accountability framework for the Bank and proposes a strong monitoring system.

However, the absence of an explicit results framework and the lack of clarity on appropriate outcomes has weakened implementation of the policy. Further, the abrogation of the provisions of OMS 2.20 to generally consider gender issues during project appraisal has also weakened the design of the Bank's overall gender policy framework as it existed prior to the 2001 Gender Strategy. This is of particular concern, given the evaluation finding that CASs are typically not strong in articulating clear gender responses (chapter 4), thereby significantly weakening the link between CASs and gender integration into projects. On balance, therefore, the relevance of the Bank's gender policy could be further strengthened to meet the Bank's mandate and address client needs.

Chapter 4

EVALUATION HIGHLIGHTS

- Implementation of OP/BP 4.20 was high during the first few years of the evaluation period, but it declined after 2003.

- The 2007 GAP appears to have been the focus of attention in the final years of the evaluation period.

- Whether the focus is on the country-level approach (required by the Bank's OP 4.20) or the project-level approach (not required by the OP), implementation of the gender policy appears to have weakened during the latter part of the evaluation period.

Implementation of the Bank's Gender Policy

IEG assessed the Bank's implementation of its gender policy from two angles. First, it reviewed the extent to which the Bank implemented the requirements of OP/BP 4.20 (the four-step process of country-level diagnosis, integration of findings into CASs, and selective intervention in priority sectors and thematic areas).

Second, it examined the extent to which projects were designed consistent with sector strategies that recommend gender integration. In order to do this, the evaluation team undertook an extensive review of Bank documents, including 48 CGAs, 74 Poverty Assessments, and 140 CASs, as well as 1,183 PADs approved or prepared in the countries during the evaluation period. Table 4.1 categorizes the CASs and projects reviewed by the relevant country's score on the gender equity criterion of the Country Policy and Institutional Assessment (CPIA).

To better understand the nature of gender integration into Bank support, the 2002 CPIA rating for the gender equality criterion (CPIA 7) was used as a proxy for the level of gender equality in a country (box 4.1). Given that the mean CPIA 7 rating was 3.5 and the largest number of countries had a rating of 3.5, a rating below that was considered to signify the presence of critical gender constraints to development or the presence of lower levels of gender equality. A country with a CPIA 7 rating of 4 or above was considered to have fewer critical gender constraints or higher levels of gender equality. This analysis indicates that International Bank for Reconstruction and Development (IBRD) countries have significantly higher levels of gender equality than International Development Association (IDA) countries.

Overall, IEG found that the gender policy was well implemented during the first few years of the evaluation period, when many CGAs were undertaken and a larger number of subsequent CASs integrated gender considerations as required. Gender integration at the project level increased significantly compared with the previous evaluation period (fiscal 1990–99) and expanded to sectors beyond health and education, although it is difficult to confirm the links with CASs. However, in the latter half of the evaluation period (fiscal 2006–08), the number of CGAs being undertaken or updated declined[1] and the percentage of CASs with good gender integration decreased.

There has also been a significant decline in gender integration at the project level, from a high in fiscal 2003 to a low in fiscal 2008. As a result, the evaluation concludes that the implementation of the gender policy appears to have weakened in the latter half of the evaluation period. Appendix C presents the econometric analysis undertaken to test the statistical significance of the findings presented in this chapter.

TABLE 4.1	Categorization of CASs and Projects Reviewed by Gender Equality Criterion of CPIA					
CPIA 7 rating (2002)	IBRD CASs	IDA/Blend CASs	Total	IBRD projects	IDA/Blend projects	Total
2.5	2	7	9	13	53	66
3	4	20	24	53	165	218
3.5	12	32	44	108	263	371
4	18	19	37	197	162	359
4.5	12	3	15	81	28	109
5	9	—	9	47	—	47
6	2	—	2	13	—	13
Total	59	81	140	512	671	1,183

Source: World Bank.

Note: CAS = Country Assistance Strategy; CPIA = Country Policy and Institutional Assessment, IBRD = International Bank for Reconstruction and Development; IDA = International Development Association.

Diagnosing Country Context through CGAs[2]

Issued in 1993, OP 4.20 stated that country-level gender assessments may be conducted as part of other ESW. The 2001 Gender Strategy, however, went a step further by introducing the CGA as the "principal means" for a country analysis. The Strategy stated that preparing such a CGA would be the responsibility of the country director, that CGAs would be completed by fiscal 2005 for all countries where the Bank had an active program, and that updates to CGAs would be undertaken approximately once every five years.[3] The 2001 Strategy also noted that for purposes of monitoring and quality assurance, it would be important that CASs discuss the CGA and identify the rationale for particular gender-responsive actions (or their absence). However, the Strategy provided significant flexibility regarding its format and methods.[4]

The evaluation team took several steps to ensure that it captured all CGAs undertaken in these 93 countries without restricting the count to self-standing reports. First, it assessed 140 CASs in the 93 countries to see whether a CGA in any form was indicated as having been undertaken. The evaluation team accepted draft CGAs, gender notes, strategic gender briefs, and chapters in other ESW (provided it was mentioned in the CAS or otherwise noted as being a gender assessment). In addition, it confirmed that the evaluation's list covered all CGAs noted on the Bank's gender Web site. Finally, it contacted Regional gender coordinators and staff in the Gender Group of the Poverty Reduction and Economic Management Network (PREM) to help confirm that the evaluation had a comprehensive list.

Using these methods, IEG found that by 2008, CGAs had been prepared in about half of the 93 countries (49). Country-specific CGAs had been completed in 32 countries and brief gender notes in another seven. Two Regional CGAs had been conducted in the Latin America and the Caribbean Region, covering nine countries.[5] Two poverty/labor assessments (for Albania and Mozambique) were identified as CGAs by the country CAS.

Consistent with the gender policy, CGAs were undertaken in countries displaying a wide range of gender equality levels. If the countries were divided into two groups according to whether critical gender constraints to development were present, then CGAs were undertaken in both groups (table 4.2). The pattern was similar when the CGAs were disaggregated according to whether the country was IBRD, IDA, or blend (table 4.3).

> Consistent with the gender policy, the preparation of CGAs was concentrated in countries with both high and low levels of gender inequality.

The Europe and Central Asia Region prepared the lowest percentage of CGAs. However, the Region also had the highest average CPIA 7 rating of 4.2, and 11 of the 15 countries for which CGAs were not prepared had high levels of gender equality, reflected in a CPIA 7 rating of 4 or above. The need

---

BOX 4.1

CPIA 7 RATING FOR GENDER EQUALITY

The CPIA is an annual assessment of the quality of a country's policy and institutional framework. Gender equality is one of 16 criteria used for the assessment. The gender equality rating assesses the extent to which the country has enacted laws and put in place enforcing institutions and programs that promote equal access for men and women to human capital development opportunities; promote equal access to productive and economic resources; and give both genders equal status and protection under the law. A number of other gender indices were considered for this analysis, such as the United Nations Gender Development Index and the Global Gender Gap index, but CPIA 7 was the only gender-related rating available for all years between fiscal 2002 and 2007. A recently completed evaluation of the CPIA suggests that CPIA 7 correlates well with similar gender rating indices. For the 93 countries, the ratings were as shown in the table.

Rating	Frequency of countries
2.5	7
3	18
3.5	29
4	21
4.5	11
5	5
6	2
Total	93

Source: World Bank.

TABLE 4.2	CGAs by CPIA 7 Rating for Gender Equality		
CPIA rating 2002	Evaluation countries	CGAs prepared	% completed
2.5–3.5	54	30	56
4–6	39	19	49

Source: World Bank.
Note: CGA = Country Gender Assessment; CPIA = Country Policy and Institutional Assessment.

TABLE 4.3	CGAs by IBRD, IDA, and Blend Countries		
IBRD/ IDA	Number of countries	CGAs prepared	% completed
IDA/Blend	56	31	55
IBRD	37	18	49

Source: World Bank.
Note: CGA = Country Gender Assessment; IBRD = International Bank for Reconstruction and Development; IDA = International Development Association.

for CGAs was arguably lower in these 11 countries, because gender was not a critical development constraint, although CASs did not explicitly make this argument, as required by the policy. A similar assertion cannot be made for Middle East and North Africa and Africa, where several of the countries in which CGAs had not been undertaken had lower CPIA 7 ratings (3 of 4 in the Middle East and North Africa, and 13 of 17 in Sub-Saharan Africa with a CPIA 7 rating of 3.5 or lower).

In all Regions except Sub-Saharan Africa, CGAs were prepared in countries with higher levels of gender inequalities.

There is a high level of variability in the quality and scope of CGAs, ranging from short policy notes to extensive analysis and in-depth consultation (figure 4.1 and box 4.2). A quarter of the CGAs were prepared quickly as policy notes to feed into CASs, rather than coming from a more lengthy process that would generate client commitment or ownership. In such cases—for example, Benin and Ghana—the draft CGAs fed into gender-aware CASs but did little to strengthen greater commitment to gender (in Ghana) or to the Poverty Reduction Strategy Paper (in Benin). In the Russian Federation, Honduras, and Zambia, CGAs influenced CASs, but this influence appears to have been lost by the time of the subsequent CAS.

FIGURE 4.1   Criteria to Assess Quality of CGAs

CGAs rated high
- Is user friendly and published
- Analyzes gender issues using a cross-sectoral approach with good data covering socio-economic roles, productive resources, human development, and participation in development decision making
- Includes consultation with client stakeholders either during preparation or once the recommendations are drafted
- Identifies a limited set of policy and operational interventions that the analysis and consultations suggest are key to removing gender-related barriers to development

CGAs rated substantial
- Is published but not user friendly
- Includes a cross-sectoral analysis of required elements but with little data or explanation for any absence thereof
- Includes consultation with client stakeholders either during preparation or once priority recommendations are drafted
- Identifies a set of recommendations, not necessarily prioritized
- **OR** meets all four criteria substantially

CGAs rated modest
- Is not published, but is user friendly
- Includes partial analysis of the required elements with limited data
- Includes weak consultation with client stakeholders either during preparation or once the priority recommendations are drafted
- Identifies an unprioritized set of recommendations

CGAs rated low
- Is neither published nor user friendly
- Includes weak and partial analysis of required elements and no data
- Includes no consultation with clients or other development partners
- Includes no recommendations or actions

Source: World Bank (1999a).
Note: CGA = Country Gender Assessment.

QUALITY OF CGAS

IEG found that only half of the CGAs were of good quality. Good-quality CGAs generally had the following properties: they were prepared collaboratively (with governments and/or other development partners), included rigorous analysis of country-specific issues and political economy factors surrounding gender equality, reflected a realistic assessment of country institutional arrangements and capacity, and recommended a feasible set of actions that kept capacity and other constraints in mind. Such CGAs were more expensive because of the need to interact with clients at different levels, but they generally had more impact on client country policies and programs.

- The Egypt CGA ($154,000) was done jointly with the National Council for Women. It was anchored in relevant gender-disaggregated data, and its recommendations were mindful of the country-level context. This internal report became an effective tool to raise gender awareness in Egypt and reportedly influenced country-level policies in several areas.

- The Chile CGA ($153,000) (World Bank 2007d) was a good-practice "focused" CGA that analyzed gender and labor market issues. It was prepared in close collaboration with the government, which requested the analysis, and with the Inter-American Development Bank (IADB). Using cross-country evidence and micro data simulations, the study concluded that an increase in female labor force participation from the present low level of 37 percent to around 50 percent—the regional average—could increase growth significantly and have a sizable effect on poverty reduction. The CGA influenced client policies and helped to integrate gender into the CAS.

- The Nepal CGA ($1 million) (World Bank and DFID 2006)—Unequal Citizens, Gender, Caste, and Ethnic Exclusion in Nepal—was prepared in a highly participatory manner, and it strengthened the gender content of the country's Poverty Reduction Strategy Paper. Data are disaggregated by gender, caste, and region and are cross-sectoral in nature, including in-depth integration in the hard sectors. Several client stakeholders in Nepal consider this a seminal piece of work that draws attention not only to gender issues but also to linkages with caste and ethnicity.

Several CGAs of lower quality did not reflect a good understanding of the specific country context. Less expensive assessments for other countries (costing an average of $25,000) were essentially draft notes prepared for internal Bank consumption. Client stakeholders were generally unaware of these pieces of work and were not involved in their preparation. The CGAs did not focus on the extent to which the capacity and institutional arrangements in client countries could support the design and implementation of gender-aware development activities or include an analysis of political economy constraints. Consequently, the analyses were quite general, less moored to the country context, and led to only general recommendations.

Source: IEG desk review of CGAs.

CGA costs were also highly variable but averaged about $59,000 each. The average excludes three reports undertaken in South Asia, each costing more than $500,000. CGAs in the Sub-Saharan Africa Region were the least costly, averaging $47,000 (table 4.4). This low average cost likely reflects the predominance of quick policy notes among the CGAs and perhaps also explains why about half of them were of middling quality. About half of the CGAs did not clearly prioritize policy and operational interventions to address gender-related barriers to poverty reduction and economic growth. Most suggested a multitude of actions, making it difficult for a reader to understand how and where to prioritize.

TABLE 4.4	CGAs by Region				
Region	CPIA average (2002)	Evaluation countries	CGAs prepared	% completed	Average cost
East Asia and Pacific	3.5	8	6	75	$84,000
Latin America and the Caribbean	3.7	20	14	70	$51,603
South Asia	2.8	5	3	60	$526,000[a]
Middle East and North Africa	2.8	7	3	57	$143,650
Sub-Saharan Africa	3.5	31	15	48	$47,000
Europe and Central Asia	4.2	22	8	36	$113,000

Source: World Bank.

a. Excludes Nepal, which cost about $1.0 million.

Interviews with Bank staff confirmed that one of the main benefits of the CGA was the preparation process and the discussion and awareness it generated within the country team. To a great extent, staff said, the quality of the CGA did not play a role in this process. At the same time, CGAs that have influenced country-level policies—such as those in Chile and Nepal—were of high quality and were more expensive (box 4.2).

The use of the CGA as a diagnostic tool steadily declined through the evaluation period to the point that none were updated or undertaken in fiscal 2008 (figure 4.2).[6] Several CASs from fiscal 2005 and 2006 suggested that CGAs would be undertaken, although ultimately they were not done. The 2006 Gender Monitoring Report also noted that the pace of completion of CGAs had slowed and added, "CGAs continued to have no significant impact on CASs," although the basis for this conclusion is not clear, given the evaluation findings reflected below (World Bank 2006c).

Undertaking or updating CGAs is no longer common.

In summary, CGAs were completed in more than half of the countries where the Bank was active.[7] However, their preparation and update has declined significantly, and no CGAs were identified in fiscal 2008. Given that CGAs were billed in the Bank's 2001 Gender Strategy as the principal means for formulating responses, this evaluation considers that the failure to undertake and periodically update them, particularly in countries with lower levels of gender equality, has been a weak link in the implementation of OP 4.20.

Integration of Gender Issues into CASs

The evaluation assessed 140 CASs prepared between fiscal 2002 and 2008 in the 93 countries to understand how they addressed gender issues and whether the presence of a CGA affected the manner in which a CAS addressed gender issues. Each CAS was assessed on the extent to which it incorporated a strategic gender approach based on a set of indicators (figure 4.3).[8]

Overall, discussions of gender issues in CASs have increased significantly since the previous gender evaluation—almost 89 percent of the 140 CASs examined have some reference to gender issues (compared with 64 percent in the previous evaluation). The higher levels of discussion of gender issues in this decade may in part be a result of the discussion of MDG 3 on gender equality, because more than three-quarters of the CASs discussed the achievement of MDGs. Despite increased discussion of gender issues, the shift to a strategic mainstreaming approach to gender issues at the country level is found in only 44 percent of the 140 CASs.[9] In 56 percent of CASs, despite the discussion, the quality was considered to be inadequate. These CASs included limited or weak diagnosis, reflected no results framework, provided no explanation for the inclusion of a few isolated activities (often related to human development), did not identify or suggest important sectors for integration at the project level, and typically did not integrate relevant monitoring indicators.

Gender discussion in CASs has increased significantly since IEG's previous evaluation (2005), but a strategic mainstreaming approach is found in only 44 percent of CASs.

On average, CASs did better at integrating gender considerations in countries with lower CPIA 7 ratings (figure 4.4). CASs in IDA countries also integrated gender somewhat better than those in IBRD countries (an IEG rating of 2.3 for IBRD compared with 2.6 for IDA). At the same time, CASs have demonstrated that they can address gender issues even in countries with higher levels of gender equality, consistent with the gender policy. Good gender integration was undertaken in 46 percent of IBRD countries and in 42 percent of IBRD and IDA countries with CPIA ratings of 4 and higher.[10]

Gender integration in the CAS is strongly correlated with the preparation of a CGA prior to the CAS. In countries where CGAs were prepared, 65 percent of the CASs included a better discussion of gender issues and proposed actions and integrated gender into the overall results framework. In countries where CGAs were not prepared, only about 33 percent of the CASs dealt with gender issues in a similar manner. An econometric analysis indicates that even after control-

FIGURE 4.2 Number of CGAs Undertaken by Fiscal Year

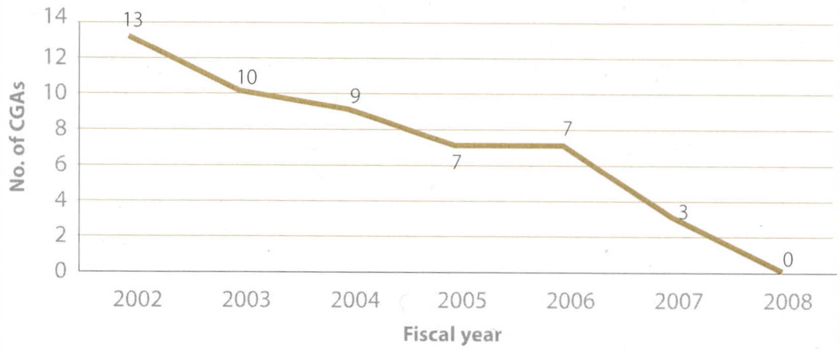

Source: IEG.

Note: CGA = Country Gender Assessment.

FIGURE 4.3 Criteria to Assess CAS Quality

CASs rated high	CASs rated substantial	CASs rated modest	CASs rated low
• Includes diagnosis of gender issues (focused on or integrated into any discussion on the three domains) • Formulates a strategic response that integrates gender into the relevant sectors in the CAS matrix (or explains why this was not necessary) • Includes at least one monitoring indicator in the overall results framework other than on reproductive health or access to primary education	• Includes a gender analysis that summarizes issues in the country but does not focus on all three domains • Identifies a few actions in two of the three domains (in the CAS matrix) • Includes at least one monitoring indicator in the overall results framework other than on reproductive health and education • **OR** Explains that gender is not an issue for development and hence proposes no actions	• Includes some discussions on gender or women, limited to a sector or subsector • Identifies issues but mentions no action or only includes actions for reproductive health and education without any explanation of why other issues are not addressed • Includes indicators on reproductive health or access to education as part of the discussion on MDGs	• Includes some references to women or gender • Includes no action, or an action for reproductive health or primary education • Includes no indicators

Source: Adapted from PREM Gender Group's criteria for assessing CAS quality.
Note: CAS = Country Assistance Strategy; MDG = Millennium Development Goal.

ling for CPIA, income level, and gender outcome variables, countries with prior CGAs are significantly more likely to have integrated gender better into CASs.

To conclude, CASs have increased discussion of gender issues, and about 44 percent of the CASs examined included a strategic response (box 4.3) in that they integrated an appropriate diagnosis of gender issues, focused on relevant outcomes that would support gender equality or women's empowerment, and integrated gender considerations into the overall CAS results framework. However, such integration of gender issues occurred more frequently during the initial years of the evaluation period. By fiscal 2006, the occurrence of high or substantial gender integration had declined (figure 4.5). A shift in approach to gender in CASs may be one reason (box 4.4). The shift to more Country Partnership Strategies (CPSs) could be another, because only 20 percent of all CPSs had satisfactory gender integration, although two-thirds of the CPSs were for IBRD countries.

The above findings are broadly consistent with those of the gender monitoring report prepared by the PREM Anchor Gender Group (World Bank 2006c). It notes that attention to gender issues in CASs decreased in fiscal 2006 after a peak in fiscal 2003, when 83 percent of CASs included an analysis of gender issues and proposed actions in one or more sectors (IEG found 71 percent).[11]

FIGURE 4.4 CAS and CGA Quality across CPIA 7 Rating

Source: IEG.
Note: Two CASs in countries with a CPIA 7 rating of 6 were excluded. CAS = Country Assistance Strategy; CGA = Country Gender Assessment; CPIA = Country Policy and Institutional Assessment; IBRD = International Bank for Reconstruction and Development; IDA = International Development Association.

Gender Integration by Sector Board

In its evaluation, IEG excluded about 25 percent of the 1,183 projects for which gender was considered to be of "low" relevance. That was the case if a project was likely to benefit both men and women (based on a review of its objectives, components, and social analysis) and did not include involuntary resettlement or affect indigenous peoples. The following sections present the findings on gender integration into the remaining 890 projects using the criteria shown in figure 4.6.

Forty percent of Bank commitments during the evaluation period were assigned to the health, education, social protection, social development, and agriculture and rural development sectors (figure 4.7); CASs have identified these as high-impact sectors. Together, the energy, transport, urban development, and water sectors account for nearly half of total support (48 percent). Although gender issues in these sectors have not typically been emphasized in CASs, Bank sector strategies and related programs emphasize the importance of integrating gender into these sectors to reduce the burden of unproductive domestic chores, increase women's access to markets, and improve opportunities for productive purposes.

Another set of projects, mainly in public sector governance and financial and private sector development, do not have strategies that showcase any particular benefits of integrating gender issues, although the development literature, by both the Bank and others, indicates that these are often associated with severe gender constraints. Together, they constitute 11 percent of the commitments.

Projects designed by the health, nutrition, and population and agriculture and rural development (ARD) sectors show strong levels of integration (figure 4.8). Although causality is virtually impossible to impute rigorously, the improvement in the energy and mining and urban development sectors between fiscal 2006 and 2008 may well be linked to the gender efforts of the Energy Sector Management Assistance Program and to the injection of funds in these sectors by the 2007 GAP.

The high incidence of quality integration in ARD (maintained throughout the evaluation period) may be linked to knowledge management and dissemination efforts, as well as to the provision of significant resources and tools spearheaded by the gender and agriculture thematic group. A similar effect is not evident in transport and water, where integration has declined over the years despite the highly gender-aware transport strategy of 2008 and the additional GAP funding.

There has also been a decline in the education sector, particularly in countries where gender parity has been achieved; projects addressing reform in teacher training or vocational training reflect weak levels of gender integration. The shift to programmatic lending may be one reason for the observed decline in these sectors. Further, integration has been significantly less common in the financial as well as in private sector development sectors, although some increase was observable in the last two years.

> ARD and health, nutrition, and population are the two best-performing sectors in terms of high or substantial gender integration in operations.

BOX 4.3

SATISFACTORY TREATMENT OF GENDER ISSUES IN CASs

The **2003 Vietnam CAS** (World Bank 2002f) includes a good discussion on gender equality, supports the government's gender strategy through several measures that address institutional constraints, proposes to mainstream gender into high-impact projects in the Bank's portfolio, and includes gender-aware monitoring indicators. A follow-up CGA is proposed to coincide with Vietnam's preparation of its next five-year plan for the advancement of women.

The **2008 Nicaragua CAS** (World Bank 2007f) includes a diagnosis that identifies priority issues, proposes to address strategic policy and institutional reform, and includes some specific monitoring indicators. It is also notable in that the gender strategy was prepared through a series of gender-focused studies prepared in coordination with the IADB. The UK's Department for International Development funding also helped provide a gender specialist to participate in the CAS process, and specific workshops were held to review the results of gender mainstreaming efforts in Bank operations, as well as to inform government stakeholders, donors, and other groups about the focus on women's economic empowerment in the Bank's GAP. The challenge, based on the evaluation findings, will be to ensure follow-through.

The **Pakistan CAS (2002)** (World Bank 2002c) diagnoses the gender status in the country, aims to improve equity through support for pro-poor and pro-gender equity policies, presents a strategic set of actions to empower women and to generate gender-aware data, and includes indicators to measure the progress of Bank support and government interventions. The CAS also reflects country-level donor collaboration in addressing gender issues.

Source: IEG assessment of CASs issued during evaluation period.

IEG also finds in the evaluation that gender integration has broadened beyond the traditional human and social development sectors. For example, more than 67 percent of 68 relevant projects that aimed to address land administration and management, 44 of which were managed by the ARD sector board, addressed gender issues in a substantial manner. Similarly, among 14 projects classified with a theme for access to justice—the majority managed by the Public Sector Governance Board—two-thirds integrated gender based on the recognition that there are differences in the "justice needs" of men and women. In contrast, gender integration in the design of projects with a climate change dimension remains weak.[12]

FIGURE 4.5 Quality of High or Substantial Gender Integration into CASs

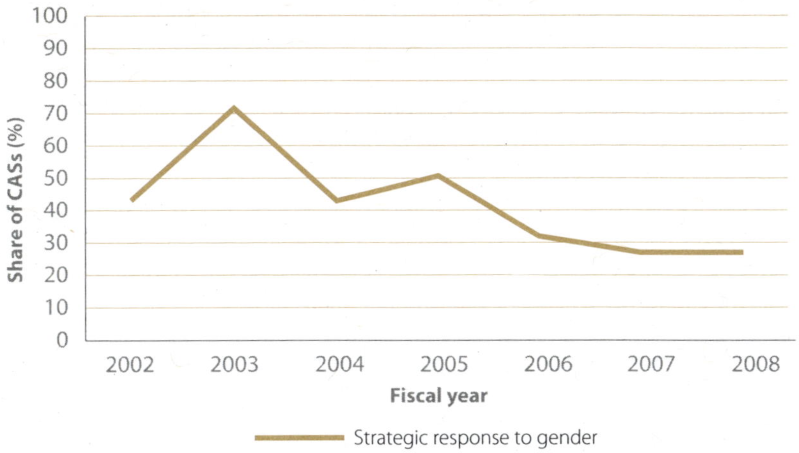

Source: IEG.
Note: CAS = Country Assistance Strategy.

Gender Integration in Project Design

IEG reviewed the link between priority gender-related sectors identified in CASs and gender integration at the project level. Overall, this link was difficult to establish, given changing priorities and in some cases the lack of clear identification of priority sectors in CASs, and changes in sectoral priorities between two CASs. Additionally, in some cases where a link was present, the evaluation found no significant change in integration at the project level in specified sectors either before or after the CAS.

About 25 percent of the CASs proposed gender mainstreaming into operations. However, an analysis indicated that the difference between gender integration in operations in countries where CASs indicated that gender would be mainstreamed into operations and those that did not

Gender integration has broadened beyond the health and education sectors.

was only about 4 percentage points. Thus, the link between the CAS and subsequent operations is not evident, and the

---

BOX 4.4

CHANGING APPROACH TO GENDER IN CAS RETROSPECTIVES

Following the patterns established by the 1998 and 2000 CAS retrospectives, the report "Country Assistance Strategies: Retrospective and Future Directions" (World Bank 2009c) made the case for gender as a cross-cutting issue essential to addressing poverty reduction through CASs. It placed the retrospective in the context of past gender work. The retrospective concluded that CASs must "explicitly address whether gender is a priority for the Bank in the country, and where that is not the case, the CAS should explain why."

By 2005, *Results Focus in Country Assistance Strategies: A Stocktaking of Results-Based Country Assistance Strategies* (World Bank 2005g) relegated gender issues to a footnote about the ever-expanding range of issues that a CAS is expected to cover: "In more or less order of arrival, these now include: governance, gender, the MDGs, donor harmonization, capacity building, extractive industries, country financing parameters, and many others." A second reference appeared in a case study of the Cameroon CAS, which used a gender-relevant indicator. Similarly, a draft concept note for the Operations Policy and Country Services (OPCS) CAS retrospective circulated for discussion did not mention gender at all. The subsequent draft report examines the treatment of gender issues as part of poverty diagnosis in CASs and illustrates how this was done well in the Ghana CAS (a good practice also identified by the evaluation) but does not go any further. The final CAS retrospective, however, discusses the integration of gender into CASs, noting that on average 71 percent of CASs adequately addressed gender issues between fiscal 2002 and 2008, although it adds that the percentage has fallen to 60 percent in fiscal 2007 and 2008. It concludes that Bank programs outlined in CASs reflect the actual country demand for Bank services, including on ways to address gender disparities.

Source: IEG.

FIGURE 4.6 Assessing Gender Integration into Project Operations

Projects rated high	Projects rated substantial	Projects rated modest	Projects rated low
• Includes gender diagnosis within country and sector context backed by quantitative or qualitative data; identifies issues that need to be addressed • Includes measures for consultation in project design with both men and women during social assessment or during project design or implementation, and some discussion of the implications • Includes measures to address key identified issues or notes that diagnosis indicates that no actions are needed • Includes at least one gender-disaggregated or -related indicator	• Includes gender analysis that summarizes and identifies issues • Includes consultation but no discussion of any implications • Includes some measure to address at least one of the identified issues • Includes at least one gender-disaggregated or -related indicator • **OR** Explains that gender is not an issue for development and hence proposes no actions	• Includes little discussion on relevant gender issues or focuses on women • Includes consultation with stakeholders but does not suggest that both male and female opinions were sought • Typically mentions that women will benefit but without any clearly identified follow-up action • Includes no gender-disaggregated or -related indicators	• Includes little consultation • Includes no actions • Includes no indicators

Source: Adapted from PREM Gender Group's criteria for assessing gender integration at the project level.

FIGURE 4.7 Distribution of Investment Projects by Sector

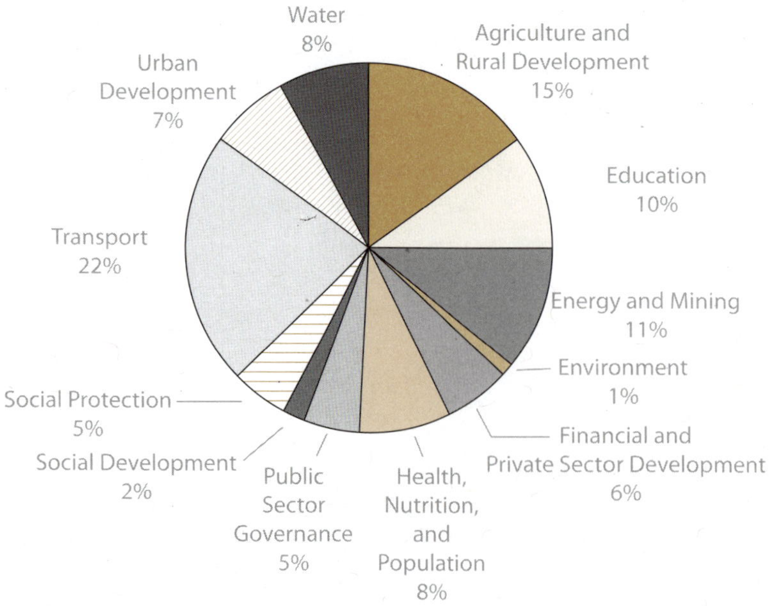

Water 8%
Agriculture and Rural Development 15%
Urban Development 7%
Education 10%
Transport 22%
Energy and Mining 11%
Environment 1%
Social Protection 5%
Financial and Private Sector Development 6%
Social Development 2%
Public Sector Governance 5%
Health, Nutrition, and Population 8%

Source: World Bank internal database (commitments worth about 1 percent in 3 sectors were excluded).

country-level approach in OP 4.20 does not come through as guiding implementation and integration at the project level.

Despite the above, there are several reasons to look more closely at gender integration at the project level. First, most development agencies assess the extent of gender mainstreaming in their portfolios at the activity or project level, which provides a comparator that can be useful in benchmarking the Bank's integration of gender issues against that of other development partners (box 4.5). Second, responses to the staff survey[13] suggest that the project is still perceived as the primary entry point for gender integration. Finally, such analysis provides a way to compare gender integration across Regions within the Bank.

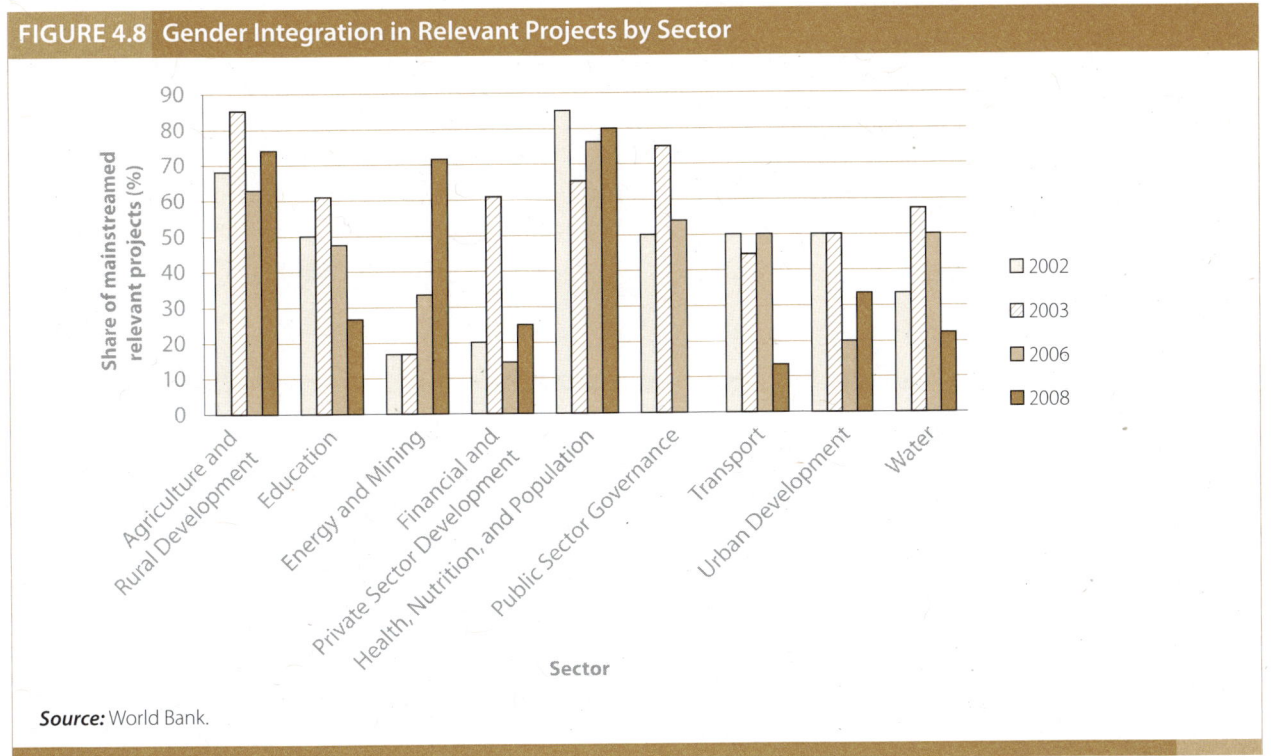

FIGURE 4.8 Gender Integration in Relevant Projects by Sector

Source: World Bank.

Except for benchmarking with other development partners, this section discusses gender integration into 890 of the 1,183 projects where gender was considered relevant. Finally, this section presents the findings of a review of how IEG integrated gender into its review of project ICRs.

Overall, 56 percent of the 890 relevant projects integrated gender into project design. At a Regional level, integration was consistent with the average CPIA 7 rating—South Asia had the highest levels of gender integration and Europe and Central Asia the lowest (table 4.5). The percentage of gender mainstreaming in low-income countries under stress (CPIA 7 rating of 3) and IDA countries (CPIA 7 rating of 3.5) is higher than in IBRD countries (CPIA 7 rating of 3.9); that is consistent with the levels of gender equality. When disaggregated by CPIA 7 rating, gender integration is higher in countries with a lower CPIA 7 rating (figure 4.9). Thus, higher levels of gender integration are occurring in Regions with higher levels of gender inequality and/or more binding gender-related constraints to poverty reduction.

Overall, gender is being integrated better in Regions with lower CPIA 7 ratings.

The above findings regarding gender integration in projects are consistent with the findings of a similar project-level review by the PREM Gender Group of lending operations in two years, fiscal 2006 and 2008. Both IEG and the Gender Group found that the extent of gender analysis in project ap-

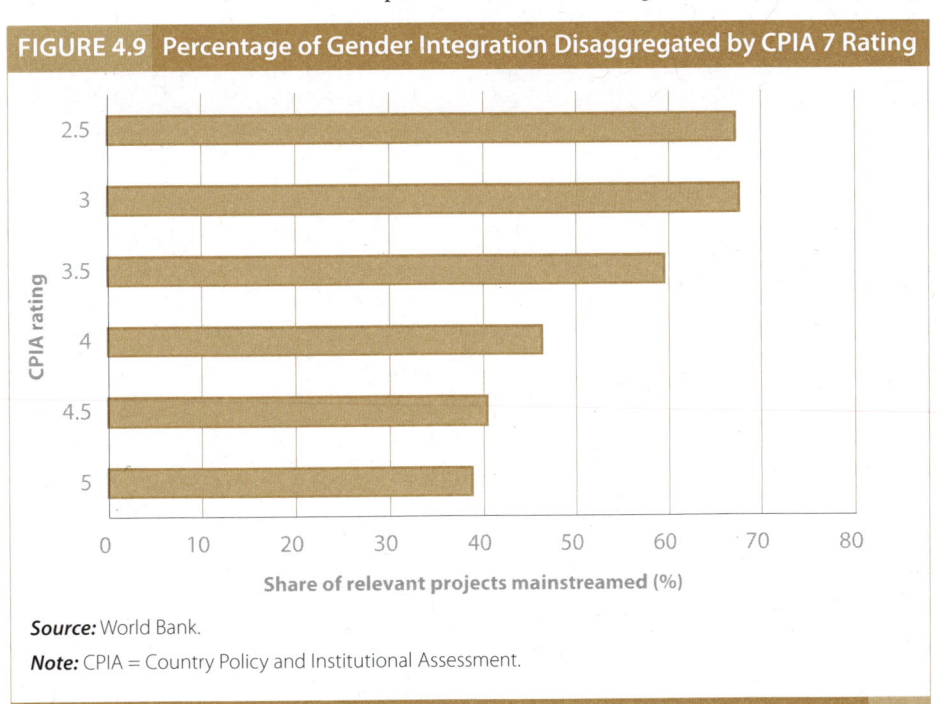

FIGURE 4.9 Percentage of Gender Integration Disaggregated by CPIA 7 Rating

Source: World Bank.

Note: CPIA = Country Policy and Institutional Assessment.

TABLE 4.5

Region	Number of countries	Average CPIA 7 rating (2002)	Share of relevant projects with high or substantial integration
South Asia	5	3.2	72
East Asia and Pacific	8	3.6	64
Sub-Saharan Africa	31	3.4	61
Middle East and North Africa	7	3.5	56
Latin America and the Caribbean	20	3.9	54
Europe and Central Asia	22	4.2	33

TABLE 4.5 Percentage of Gender Integration in Projects across Regions

Source: World Bank.

praisal documents improved between fiscal 2006 and 2008 (figure 4.11). Using all four criteria (which IEG considers more rigorous), however, the evaluation found that there was a significant decline in gender integration in projects, similar to that at the country level (figure 4.10; see also box 4.6).[14]

Econometric analysis indicated that even after controlling for CPIA 7 rating, Region, Sector Board, country income level, and loan size, gender integration in projects approved in fiscal 2008 was more likely to be lower than in previous years. The highest levels of integration were around fiscal 2003 (64 percent), and the lowest were in fiscal 2008 (46 percent). The funds injected by the GAP may reverse this trend, as has perhaps occurred in the energy and mining and financial and private sector development sectors; however, this finding confirms that a project-level integration approach is not yet institutionalized, despite the policies of the 1990s.

> The project-level findings appear broadly consistent with that of the Gender Group for two of the eight years where there was information.

This decline may be due to one or more of several factors. It may have been a result of the shift as reflected in OP/BP 4.20 that required the integration of gender considerations at the project level only in sectors and themes identified as priorities by the CAS. The availability of incentive funding in fiscal 2001–02 may have led to the higher levels of integration identified between 2002 and 2003. Such incentive funding resumed only in mid-2007 with the GAP, the impact of which is not yet fully evident.

The decline may also have been related to the shift to programmatic lending. Finally, it may be attributable to a lack of requisite skills or awareness among Bank staff of newer or second-generation gender issues, such as improving quality of education (as opposed to reducing gender disparity in access) or integrating gender into support with a climate change dimension.[15]

Gender Integration in DPOs

The 307 DPOs approved for the 93 countries constituted about 33 percent of total Bank lending during the evaluation

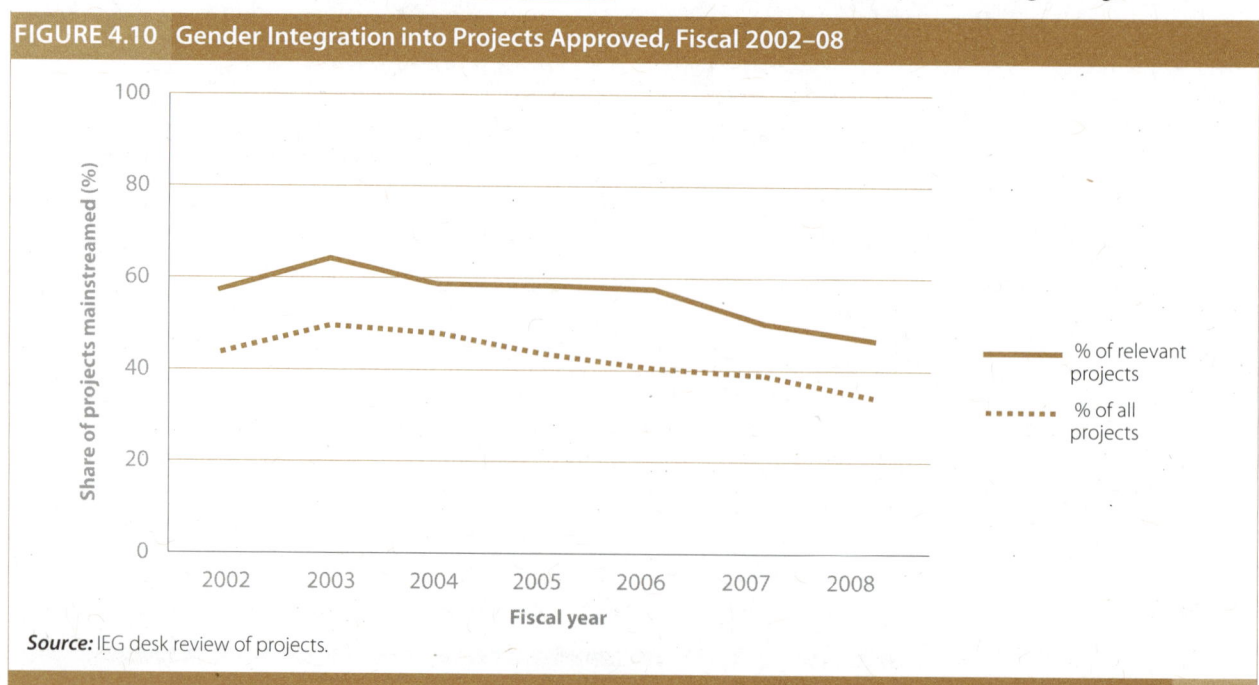

FIGURE 4.10 Gender Integration into Projects Approved, Fiscal 2002–08

Source: IEG desk review of projects.

BOX 4.5

SELF-ASSESSMENTS OF GENDER INTEGRATION

The level of gender integration in the 1,183 investment projects in the 93 countries averages 43 percent across the evaluation period. This level of gender integration in investment projects is considerably higher than that seen during the previous evaluation period (fiscal 1990–99). Using fairly similar criteria, the previous evaluation found only 25 percent satisfactory integration in its review of 112 investment projects in four sectors (health, nutrition, and population; education; ARD; and transport). The equivalent number in these four sectors for the current evaluation would be 60 percent.

With the caveat that criteria used by other agencies to assess gender integration are only broadly similar, the Bank's average compares well with self-assessments of other multilateral organizations (Asian Development Bank [ADB], European Commission, and IADB), but does not compare equally well with those of several bilateral donors.

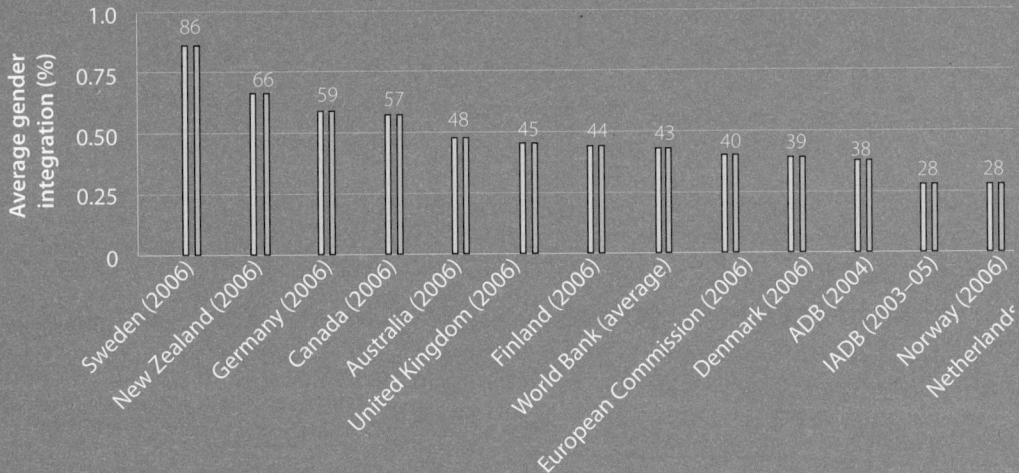

Sources: IDB (2003); ADB (2006); Organisation for Economic Co-operation and Development–Development Assistance Committee creditor rating system statistics as of July 2008.

---

period. The highest level was in 2002 (50 percent of the total commitments) and the lowest in 2008 (26 percent). Many of these credits are different in nature from the previous generation of structural adjustment credits. They aim to bring about specific poverty-related outcomes and include measurable indicators for monitoring progress during implementation and the evaluation of outcomes on completion. IEG assessed the extent of gender analysis in these program documents, the extent of gender-related measures or actions, and the extent to which gender-related results were targeted and monitored.

Attention to gender issues increased in programmatic lending over the previous evaluation period (fiscal 1990–99).

An increased number of DPOs, particularly in the health and education sectors, have integrated gender considerations.

The change is particularly notable in the health and education sectors, the same sectors in which integration of gender issues into projects typically starts. More than half of the documents (56 percent) contain focused discussion on gender issues (particularly in the health and education sectors); however, fewer than one-third of the documents considered the gender-differentiated implications of programs, and then it was mostly in the human development sectors (box 4.7). There were exceptions, such as consideration of the gender implications of land reform in Uganda and Yemen. As with investment lending, the weakness is in monitoring the gender-differentiated impact of the program outside the human development sectors.

Fifty-three (17 percent) of the 307 DPOs approved in the 93 countries between fiscal 2002 and 2008 included at least one women-in-development or gender-related measure. These constituted less than 1 percent of the total measures in these 307 programs, and about 70 percent of them were in countries with a CPIA 7 rating of 3.5 or lower. This is a clear increase over the previous evaluation period.[16]

About 70 percent of these measures related to reproductive health and girls' education. Pakistan had ten DPOs (related to girls' education and women's health), and there were five in Ghana (education and reproductive health), three in Argentina (maternal health and social protection), and three in Bolivia (reproductive health). Some, mainly under the

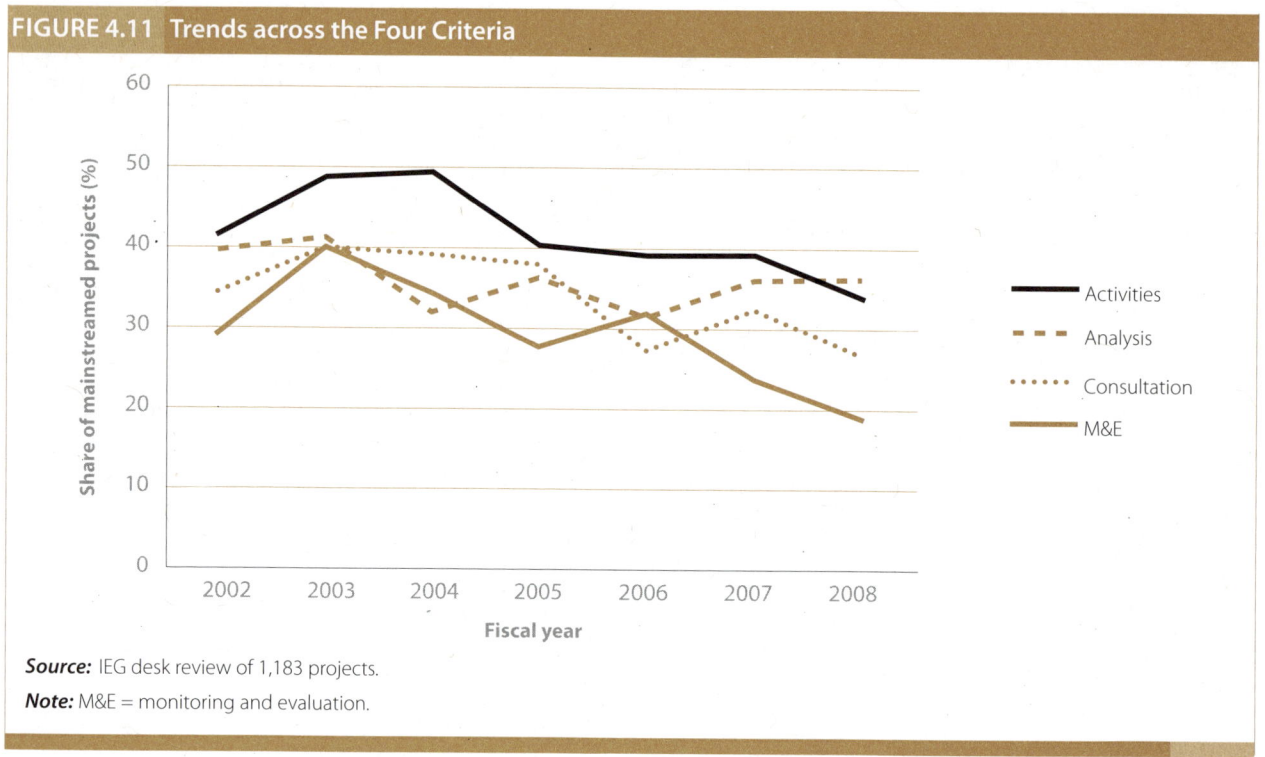

FIGURE 4.11 Trends across the Four Criteria

Source: IEG desk review of 1,183 projects.

Note: M&E = monitoring and evaluation.

Economic Policy Sector Board, tried to address other strategic gender-related issues:

- **Uganda:** Three measures in three different DPOs related to gender and land issues, including a draft proposal of specific actions to strengthen the land rights of women.

- **Pakistan:** Twenty-four of the 27 measures spread across 10 DPOs focused on some aspect of girls' education, including toilets, free textbooks, and female teachers. There was one measure related to revision of three laws to encourage female labor participation and one measure related to gender budgeting in the National Women's Development Ministry.

- **Vietnam:** Three measures in three different DPOs focused on unification of the legal framework to address

gender disparities and increase women's participation in decision making and allocation of institutional responsibilities and resources for the implementation and monitoring of gender equity.

- In **Benin, Burundi, Ethiopia**, and **Niger**, measures in a single DPO focused on the preparation of country-level GAPs.

- In **Rwanda**, a measure required gender discrimination of all forms to be abolished in all forthcoming legislation.

Conclusion

The implementation of the gender policy increased during the early part of the evaluation period, reaching a peak around 2003–04. At the country level, increasing numbers of CGAs were completed, and more CASs integrated gender issues in a strategic manner. At the project level, gender integration was highest in fiscal 2003 (49 percent of all projects and 64 percent of all relevant projects).

By 2008, however, implementation had declined significantly at both the country and project levels.[17] Although causality cannot be inferred, the decline at the project level, after the peak in 2003–04, began at around the same time that the OMS 2.20 provisions related to women were abrogated and the Bank's policy related to investment lending narrowed.[18]

Implementation of the Gender Strategy peaked in fiscal 2003–04 and then declined through fiscal 2008.

To fully implement its 2001 "strategic gender mainstreaming," the Bank needs to complete and update its CGAs and integrate their findings into CASs.[19] If the shift to CPSs makes this more challenging, staff will need guidance on how best to do it when country strategies focus on programs that may not consider gender integration an important development issue.

Additionally, although the GAP addresses a hole in the Bank's policy framework, it needs to be aligned much better with the country-level approach so that it complements the implementation of the Bank's formal policy as reflected in OP 4.20.[20] It is also important to determine how gender integration at the sector or project level will be sustained without an institutional mandate for such integration.

CGAs need to be undertaken or updated as necessary if the gender strategy is to be effectively implemented.

Better-quality gender integration is evident in sectors where technical support has been provided, such as in access to education issues, in several subsectors in ARD, in transport, and in energy. Although causality is difficult to infer, the gender and transport initiative, as well as efforts of the gender and agricultural thematic group (including the process of developing a widely publicized *Gender in Agriculture Sourcebook* [World Bank, FAO, and IFAD 2009]), are likely to have contributed to this improved quality. If so, similar efforts are needed to improve the quality of gender integration in activities related to climate change, private and financial sector development, governance, and local governments, as well as with second-generation gender issues such as those in education projects. At the same time, the drop in the levels of gender integration in such sectors as transport[21] suggests that it is necessary to institutionalize such processes if integration of gender issues is to be sustained.

Provision of sustained resources and appropriate tools leads to better gender integration.

Chapter 5

EVALUATION HIGHLIGHTS

- Institutionalization of the gender policy was weak.

- The accountability framework specified in the gender policy was not fully established.

- Incremental budget materialized for only three of the eight years covered by the evaluation.

- There is some evidence that the Bank has maintained an adequate level of staff with gender experience.

- Partnerships appear strong at the global level, but available evidence suggests this is not so at the country level.

Institutional Arrangements and Incentives

To help ensure its effective implementation, the 2001 Gender Strategy aimed to improve and align institutional arrangements and resources. These included an articulated accountability framework, adequate staffing, availability of budgetary incentives, and partnerships. The Strategy also stressed M&E, including the development of a new monitoring system and the provision of annual reports by the Regional vice presidencies.

Overall, the evaluation found that the gender policy was weakly institutionalized within the Bank.[1] The accountability framework, well laid out in the Gender Strategy, was not operationalized, and the monitoring system was not fully established.[2] On gender-related staffing, budgeting, and partnerships, there is little information.

Accountabilities for Gender Integration

The rather elaborate accountability system outlined in the Gender Strategy (see chapter 1) was not institutionalized. No standard systems or processes were put in place to assess, reward, or sanction staff and managers' work engagement or outputs. In IEG's view, the President's call in April 2008 for country directors to report on the status of gender work is indicative of—among other things—a perceived need to act more forcefully and systematically to implement the accountability framework called for in the 2001 Gender Strategy and reflected in OP 4.20 (box 5.1).

> The accountability framework specified in the gender strategy was not effectively implemented.

At the corporate level, no control systems were established for gender integration. The difference in approach is clear when the processes for implementing the gender policy are compared with those for implementing the environmental policy (table 5.1).[3] Further, some Regional processes to monitor gender integration during the previous evaluation were eliminated during this period. Thus, there are few or no control systems at any level to ensure implementation of the gender policy.

The 2001 Gender Strategy had anticipated that each Region would establish a three-year GAP with time-bound results indicators (World Bank 2002b, p. 74). All Regions had action plans, though they varied widely in structure and content. Three Regions—Middle East and North Africa, East Asia and Pacific, and Latin America and the Caribbean—maintained action plans for mainstreaming gender. In the

Middle East and North Africa, for example, gender equality is an explicit objective of the Regional strategy. A flagship gender report covering all active and inactive client countries in the Region was launched at the Annual Meetings in Dubai (2003) and disseminated widely within the Region. This report (World Bank 2004b) contributed to policy dialogue on gender issues with senior policy makers in client countries. Country-level operations, however, were not covered, because the country focal points were mapped to the External Affairs Vice Presidency.

In East Asia and Pacific and Latin America and the Caribbean, in contrast, the primary focus was more on mainstreaming gender into country operations than on Regional initiatives. Other Regions had some form of strategies reflected in their reports or as a presentation made to the Regional management teams. However, not all these action plans were fully resourced, and reporting was undertaken only during the first few years.

Finally, there are no incentives (other than the financial ones provided by the 2007 GAP) for implementing the gender policy.[4] Thus, managers and staff who integrated gender well into CASs and other documents were not rewarded, and those who did not do so were not put on notice.

Staffing and Skills

The Gender Strategy had envisaged that Regions would provide technical expertise in gender and development to assist staff in gender analysis and strategic mainstreaming, especially during the initial years of implementation. It is difficult to assess whether adequate staffing was maintained in this area.

> Evidence is inconclusive on the adequacy of staff and skills for implementation of the gender strategy.

At the corporate level, 16 staff members were formally mapped to the gender sector in the PREM anchor as of May

2009. Beyond this, data on the number of gender specialists in the Bank are difficult to obtain. Further, staff other than gender specialists also spend time on gender issues, which is very difficult to quantify. A rough estimate by the Gender Group in PREM suggests that staff at the Bank working on gender full or part time number about 64 full-time staff (about 0.59 percent of total staff as of fiscal 2006). This is broadly confirmed by an examination of recruitment figures in the Bank between fiscal 2003 and 2009—staff recruited and mapped to the Gender Network constitute 0.50 percent of all staff recruited (table 5.2).

At a Regional level, those with gender skills included regional gender coordinators (RGCs); at the country level, country focal points were the locus of those skills. Interviews with RGCs suggest that the time spent on gender work has declined over the evaluation period, with RGCs and country focal points taking on multiple responsibilities unconnected with gender, or the gender responsibility being added to the work of staff fully engaged with other responsibilities.

It is difficult to conclude whether the Bank maintained adequate gender specialists during the evaluation period. During the same period (fiscal 2003–09), the Bank hired almost four times the staff for the environment sector, and as of May 2009, there are more than 16 times the staff formally mapped to environment (267) than to gender (16).

At the same time, a comparison of gender staffing in multilateral institutions by an external agency, using a different method of calculation, confirms the small numbers but indicates that the Bank has the highest percentage of gender specialists, at 0.8 percent. The IADB and the African Development Bank have 0.70 percent (CIEL 2007).[5] Management notes that a growing number of Bank staff not recognized as "gender experts" are doing gender work and asserts that the GAP has been effective in motivating new work on gender and reaching a wider Bank audience, enlarging the pool of gender expertise at the Bank (and training Bank staff on gender issues "by doing").

A second prong of the Gender Strategy was to broaden and strengthen gender expertise in the Bank through training and capacity enhancement, thus minimizing the need for gender specialists. The effect of training and capacity building within the Bank appears mixed. RGCs observe that among higher-level staff—those responsible for integrating gender into operations—training sessions on gender are not popular. Thus, these sessions are instead largely attended by gender specialists and consultants. Further, at an institutional level, a gender module was integrated into the Bank's orientation course for all new staff. Between fiscal 2003 and 2006, the PREM Gender Group prepared and presented this module, but it has since been discontinued. An examination of data available from the Bank's Learning

---

BOX 5.1

THE PRESIDENT'S SIX NEW WORLD BANK GROUP COMMITMENTS ON GENDER EQUALITY

1. To measurably improve the integration of gender equality into our agriculture and rural development projects by the end of the implementation of the Gender Action Plan in December 2010

2. To channel, through the International Finance Corporation, at least $100 million in credit lines at commercial banks for women entrepreneurs by the end of 2012

3. To have World Bank country directors report to me, by June 1 (2008), on what we are doing and what more we should be doing to empower girls and women economically in countries that we support

4. To launch a work program on young women count for economic development, starting with an event prior to the 2008 Annual Meetings

5. To create a Private Sector Leaders' Forum and convene the first meeting on the margins of the 2008 Annual Meetings

6. To increase IDA investments for gender equality

Source: World Bank.

TABLE 5.1	Processes for Environmental and Gender Integration—A Comparison	
Dimension	**Environment**	**Gender**
Country-level approach	OP and BP 4.02 require the Bank to encourage and support the efforts of borrowing governments to prepare and implement an appropriate Environmental Action Plan. The Bank works with each government to ensure that information from the Environmental Action Plan is integrated into the CAS and informs the development of program- and project-level details in a continuing environmental planning process.	**Similar obligation**
Project-level requirements	OP and BP 4.01. The Bank requires environmental assessment (EA) of projects proposed for Bank financing to help ensure that they are environmentally sound and sustainable, and thus to improve decision making. EA is a process the breadth, depth, and type of analysis of which depend on the nature, scale, and potential environmental impact of the proposed project. *Responsibility:* EA for a proposed Bank-financed operation is the responsibility of the borrower. Bank staff assists the borrower, as appropriate. The Region coordinates Bank review of EA in consultation with its Regional environment sector unit and, as necessary, with the support of the Environment Department.	**No equivalent obligation** **Previously**. OMS 2.20 required Bank staff to appraise whether the project design adequately took into account local circumstances that impeded or encouraged the participation of women; contributions that women could make to achieve the project objectives; changes that the project would introduce that might be disadvantageous to women; and whether the implications for women were included in the provisions for monitoring the impact of the project.
Project preparation	The Bank undertakes environmental screening of each proposed project to determine the appropriate extent and type of EA. It classifies the project into one of four categories, depending on the characteristics and the nature and magnitude of its potential environmental impacts.	**No equivalent obligation** **Previously**. South Asia and East Asia and Pacific were reviewing the treatment of gender issues as part of the regionally required clearance for social development. *This does not happen anymore.*
Project implementation	The borrower reports on compliance with measures agreed with the Bank based on the findings and results of the EA, including implementation of any Environment Management Plan (EMP), as set out in the project documents; the status of litigator measures; and the findings of monitoring programs. The Bank bases supervision of the project's environmental aspects on the findings and recommendations of the EA, including measures set out in the legal agreements, any EMP, and other project documents.	**No equivalent obligation** **Previously.** The project supervision report included a check box on meeting gender objectives, if applicable. This has been removed.
Project completion	Guidelines suggest the need to consider impact on the environment.	**Improvement:** The ICR includes a section headed "Poverty Impacts, Gender Aspects, and Social Development," and guidelines encourage consideration of gender impact. **Previously.** The guidelines only encouraged consideration of gender impact.

Source: Adapted from IEG (2001a, 2001b).

Note: BP = Bank Policy; CAS = Country Assistance Strategy; EA = Environmental Assessment; EMP = Environment Management Plan; ICR = Implementation Completion and Results Report; OP = Operational Policy; PSR = public sector reform.

TABLE 5.2	Gender and Environment Staff Hired between Fiscal 2004 and 2008		
Fiscal year	Total	Number of staff mapped to gender	Number of staff mapped to environment
2004	305	2	10
2005	231	1	8
2006	245	3	4
2007	306	1	3
2008	303	0	5
Total	1,390	7 (0.50% of total staff)	30 (2.15% of total staff)

Source: World Bank.

Management System appears to confirm the observations that higher-level staff do not typically attend gender training (table 5.3).

The absence of gender as a theme made it difficult to identify gender-related training activities. IEG, therefore, sought information on all training with titles that included certain gender-related words[6] (there may have been many more activities with a gender component). These data indicate that between fiscal 2003 and 2009, 91 training sessions focused on gender, constituting 3 percent of all training provided. Seventy-two percent of the participants were female. The largest set of participants was ungraded and likely to be consultants or from external agencies. One-third of the other participants were from GF–GG levels, and only 13 percent were from GH+ levels (in 2008, GH+ staff constituted 37 percent of all staff).

The number of gender experts in the Bank is small compared with some of the other thematic areas, but the Bank appears to have maintained gender staff comparable to, and in some cases better than, other multilateral agencies. That said, given that the accountability framework envisaged in the Gender Strategy is not in place and that efforts at train-

ing appear not to have been fully successful, this area continues to need close monitoring.

Incremental Budget for Gender Integration

The 2001 Gender Strategy had estimated "incremental" costs of implementation to be about $2 million in fiscal 2001, about $3 million per year in the three subsequent years, and approximately $2.5 million per year thereafter. Establishing whether this budget was allocated for gender mainstreaming is difficult, because funding for gender is not tracked systematically at the country, sector, or project levels.

The lack of a gender code in the Bank's budget system means that budget for gender integration is not systematically tracked.

Corporate incentive funding of $0.6 million was set aside for fiscal 2001–02, and the Regions had committed more than twice this amount as matching Bank budget. Management, therefore, assured the Board that the commitment for 2001 was fully met during a Board discussion in 2002.

TABLE 5.3	Participant Profile in Gender Training since Fiscal 2003						
		Participation			Percent		
Grade group	Location	Female	Male	Total	Female	Male	Total
GA–GD	CO	6	—	6	1	0	0
	HQ	63	5	68	6	1	4
GE	CO	11	—	11	1	0	1
	HQ	67	6	73	6	1	5
GF–GG	CO	48	38	86	4	9	6
	HQ	326	156	482	30	36	32
GH+	CO	—	2	2	0	0	0
	HQ	100	94	194	9	22	13
Ungraded	CO	12	3	15	1	1	1
	HQ	456	129	585	42	30	38

Source: World Bank database.
Note: CO = country office; HQ = Washington, DC, headquarters.

This infusion of institutional funds for gender mainstreaming perhaps accounts for the higher levels of gender mainstreaming in 2002–03.[7]

However, the incentive funding was discontinued between fiscal 2003 and 2007, when the GAP provided additional funds of $36.8 million (including Bank budget of about $11.3 million, of which $3 million was from the Development Grant Fund and $1 million from the Marrakesh Action Plan) for gender activities.[8] Thus, the incremental funding for gender activities was more than met in the last two years of the evaluation period, although strictly speaking it did not contribute to implementing the country-level approach of OP 4.20.[9]

Estimating the amount of incremental funding provided for implementation of the 2001 Gender Strategy between 2003 and 2007 is more challenging. Anecdotal information obtained from RGCs suggests that during the evaluation period, each RGC was able to devote about 50 percent of his or her time to gender issues.[10] In addition, the RGCs received on average $50,000–$100,000 for the staff time of country-level gender focal points and for activities to support gender mainstreaming. These are small amounts.

In the Middle East and North Africa, for example, staff estimate that about 0.30 percent of the annual Regional administrative budget was spent on gender integration. Furthermore, although in Europe and Central Asia such funds were regularly available, in other Regions funds from the Bank budget varied from year to year, which made planning more difficult. All RGCs note that they relied mostly on Trust Funds for gender work. A rough calculation indicates that this falls short of the additional $3 million estimated for implementation of the gender strategy. Additionally, there proved to be little difference in the availability of such resources before and after the 2001 Strategy.[11]

About half of the respondents to the IEG survey identified lack of funds as one of five reasons for not addressing gender issues. RGCs confirm that once the incentive funding was terminated in fiscal 2003 and until the GAP started disbursing funds in 2007, funds for gender integration were limited. Incremental budget as envisaged in the Gender Strategy was thus available only for 2001 and then through the GAP for the last two of the eight years (fiscal 2007 and 2008).

Partnerships

IEG focused on how partnerships have led to generation of gender-disaggregated or -related data at the global level. GenderStats, a system developed during the evaluation period, provides gender-related information (box 5.2). An important focus of GAP funding is a series of data collection programs to improve the range of available gender-disaggregated data and statistics.

The Bank is engaging in partnerships—including the United Nation's Inter-Agency Expert Group on Gender and Statistics—to promote a global collaboration in producing and using data on women. In partnership with the Luxemburg Income Study, the GAP has launched an initiative on key gender employment indicators, a set of gender-disaggregated indicators on employment in 27 Organisation for Economic Co-operation and Development and middle-income countries, including data on gender earnings ratios, employment status by gender, and percentages of males and females in specific industries. Together these efforts have increased the availability of data during this evaluation period relative to the earlier evaluation period.

Partnerships at the global level supported good outputs; collaboration at the country level was more limited.

At a country level, East Asia and Pacific and Latin America and the Caribbean lead the way in collaboration. In both

---

BOX 5.2

GENDER-RELATED DATA

The GenderStats electronic database was established by the PREM Gender Group to provide a comprehensive gender reference database for Bank staff and development partners. It provides the most recent gender-disaggregated statistics and gender-relevant data on population, health, education, employment, political participation, and programs and policies for most countries in the world—information needed for all major Bank processes and instruments. It also makes baseline and diagnostic information on gender at the country level available to users all over the world.

Data sources include national statistics, United Nations databases, and World Bank-conducted or -funded surveys. This has been an important contribution in providing information to task teams within the Bank. Additionally, the 2007 GAP pushed the frontier forward and should be credited for integrating gender into some of the most "ungendered" pieces of Bank work, such as the Global Monitoring Report.

Source: World Bank PREM Gender Group.

Regions, there is an understanding between the Bank and the regional multilateral agencies on a division of labor regarding country gender assessments. For example, in the Philippines, Vietnam, Mongolia, and Lao PDR, ADB is responsible for undertaking and updating gender assessments; in other countries, the Bank leads the way. Yet there are general issues that constrain collaboration. For example, the fact that IADB and the World Bank have different fiscal years can make an ESW product less helpful for one agency than for the other.

Collaboration at the country level is less evident in the 12 focus countries. The Philippines is an example of good practice on close country-level coordination, with the Bank being an active partner in the Official Development Assistance—Gender and Development Network (box 5.3).[12] In Yemen, Ghana, and Tajikistan, IEG missions were told that country gender coordinators rarely participated in gender consultative groups organized by the development partners, as they were juggling a variety of other tasks.

Several donor representatives assessed gender collaboration at the country levels using their own instruments. Findings of such assessments[13] suggest that the evaluation findings on collaboration with development partners at the country level are valid.

Monitoring and Evaluation

An improved M&E system was scheduled for delivery in calendar year 2002, according to the 2001 Gender Strategy. The Strategy noted that this system would involve annual monitoring, partly through the submission of regional gender mainstreaming plans and year-end reporting by the Regional vice presidencies on the implementation of these plans, and partly through reporting on benchmarked statistics about regional actions and outputs.

The Regional vice presidencies were expected to submit progress reports annually to the managing directors, which the Gender and Development Board would consolidate into a Bank-wide summary to be submitted with the Regional vice presidents' reports to the Management Committee and, in turn, to the Board of Executive Directors. In addition, OPCS was responsible for monitoring the implementation of the Bank's country-level approach in collaboration with the Gender Group.[14]

The tracking and evaluation system envisaged in the gender strategy was not fully implemented.

The new system was not effectively established.[15] Consistent with the policy, the PREM Gender Group prepared annual gender mainstreaming monitoring reports that tracked integration in Bank products (country diagnosis, policy dialogue, analytical work, and lending), based on annual monitoring reports provided by the Regions during the first few years (for fiscal 2002–05). These reports were based on findings by the Quality Assurance Group on gender integration in a sample of activities each year, supplemented by some primary review undertaken by the Gender Group.

In 2006, however, gender became part of the new streamlined process for reporting on sector strategies, a process endorsed by the Bank's Board and obviating the need to produce stand-alone annual gender monitoring reports.[16] In 2007, the GAP was also initiated. The PREM Gender Group continued to prepare monitoring reports in fiscal 2008, but the focus was now primarily on progress in implementing the GAP.[17]

During the evaluation period, the Gender Group spearheaded several systems through which the Bank monitors results in countries. These include annual updating of the CPIA 7 rating on gender equality; the World Development Indicators, which include a table on gender and reports all available gender-disaggregated information; and the Global Monitoring Report, which tracks performance and progress toward achieving the MDGs.

The absence of an effective systematic monitoring system is noted by other donor assessments. For example, the other

---

BOX 5.3

THE PHILIPPINES LEADS THE WAY IN DONOR COLLABORATION ON GENDER

In 2004, with World Bank and other donor support, the government of the Philippines developed harmonized guidelines for gender integration into development interventions, providing donor organizations and proponent/implementing agencies with a common tool for ensuring the gender responsiveness of programs and projects in the various stages of the project cycle. The first edition was revised in 2007, with the help of a technical grant from the ADB.

These guidelines prescribe processes more stringent than those of the Bank and include the mandatory allocation of 5 percent of each public agency's budget to target gender-related activities. The external and independent audit agency of the Philippines has started conducting regular gender audits on the use of these resources.

Source: World Bank.

donor assessments of the Bank's Gender Equality Institutional Assessment rates the Bank 2 on a scale of 1–4, with 4 being the best. CIDA notes that institutional monitoring at the Bank did not focus on outcomes, reporting instead on "anecdotal achievements."

On the operational side, monitoring of results is weak. ICRs available for the closed gender-relevant projects in 12 countries and about 449 Implementation Status Reports indicate that consideration of gender aspects during implementation is not common. In 43 of the 93 evaluation countries that had prepared two CASs during the evaluation period, only one-third of the CASCRs discussed the achievement of objectives stated in previous CASs. Thus, important lessons and knowledge that could have been gleaned from the Bank's vast range of activities are not systematically captured or disseminated.

Key Findings

Key arrangements to implement the policy were not institutionalized within the Bank. Most notable was the lack of an accountability framework and an effective M&E system, both envisaged in the 2001 Gender Strategy. This resulted in little systematic understanding of how the strategy was being implemented and weakened accountability for implementation at an institutional level.

Additionally, although the lack of a control system to integrate gender may have been a deliberate strategy, the simultaneous lack of incentives to address gender resulted in little institutionalization. Thus, gender integration within the Bank, with some exceptions, appears more a reflection of staff commitment and advocacy efforts by the PREM Gender Group and the Regional gender coordinators than a result of effective implementation of the gender policy.

It must be noted, however, that these findings are typical of other development agencies as well. A synthesis report prepared by Norad (2005), based on evaluation reports of eight development agencies (including the Bank), found that these issues were common across agencies (see also Moser and Moser 2005; Mehra and Gupta 2006). The Norad report noted that "work on institutionalizing the empowerment of women and gender equality have had low priority, there have been insufficient resources to implement policies and strategies, the focus has shifted to other areas, and there is no systematic reporting of results in this area" (p. 5).

Chapter 6

EVALUATION HIGHLIGHTS

- The Bank did not have a results framework for supporting gender equality.

- Outcomes of Bank support were assessed around three key domains: enhanced human capital, increased access to economic assets and opportunities, and enhanced voice of men and women in development.

- In 10 of the 12 countries, support has mainly been through a discrete set of project-level activities.

- Strengthening institutions to be more gender aware and supporting the formulation of gender-aware policies was not a common feature of Bank support.

- Consequently, although these activities may have good results at the project level, they have influenced country-level results only in 4 of the 12 countries.

Results of Bank Support—What Worked Well? What Did Not?

Of the 93 countries, a stratified random sample of 12 was selected for assessing the results of Bank support: Bangladesh, Benin, Colombia, Ghana, Lebanon, Nigeria, Peru, the Philippines, Tajikistan, Turkey, Yemen, and Zambia. IEG reviewed all 164 projects and programs in these countries that closed after fiscal 2003 and before fiscal 2009 and for which an ICR was available.

An initial review indicated that only 138 of the 164 projects and programs could have potentially influenced outcomes related to gender equality or women's empowerment in the three domains. CASs, PADs, ICRs, Implementation Status and Results Reports, and other relevant documents were examined. This desk review was supplemented with rapid field assessments of a few projects each in Benin, Ghana, Peru, Tajikistan, Yemen, and Zambia.

Assessing results proved challenging because only about a third of the CASCRs and half of the ICRs reported meaningfully on gender outcomes. In addition, the CASs and projects themselves did not follow a common results framework in addressing gender issues.

Thus, IEG examined how the Bank contributed to outcomes in three domains. Table 6.1 specifies the indicators for assessing outcomes; these are further detailed in this chapter. For each country, the subindicators were defined based on Bank support, and baselines and benchmarks were gleaned from relevant CASs or PADs.[1] Thus, if the Bank provided support for land administration, then the evaluation used available data in project documents to assess the gender implications of the Bank's support. Quantitative data to help understand results were available mainly for outcomes in health, education, and labor force participation. The evaluation had to rely on qualitative data in other areas.

Given the broad sweep and data limitations, this evaluation did not rate results using conventional IEG rating scales. Where Bank support generated sustainable results in at least two of the three domains, contribution of Bank support for gender equality was considered "substantial." Where this happened in only one domain, or when support to all three domains generated modest results, Bank support was considered "modest." Where support did not lead to sustainable and substantial results in at least one domain, the contribution was considered "low" (table 6.2).

Even in the field assessments, attribution of the results to the Bank cannot be argued with certainty.[2] In countries where the evaluation found that Bank support contributed to greater progress toward gender equality or to women's empowerment, the governments had a positive attitude, there were civil society organizations working in this area, and several other development partners con-

TABLE 6.1	Indicators to Assess Support for Gender Equality
Enhanced human capital	• Reduced gender disparity in access to education (assessed along with completion rates) • Reduced maternal mortality • Increased access to clean water for both men and women
Equal access to economic assets and opportunities	• Increased equality in access to financial and economic services and assets • Increased equality in access to economic opportunities • Enhanced capacity or skills of both men and women for productive purposes
Enhanced voice of men and women in development planning	• Increased participation in development decision making at the community level • Increased accountability of local institutions for gender equality • Institutional strengthening for gender equality through making institutions more accountable for gender equality

Source: IEG.

tributed to the overall gender agenda. It therefore became impossible to state with any certainty whether progress toward gender equality may have been achieved without the Bank's contribution. At best, what could be established was whether the Bank could reasonably be said to have contributed to progress in the three domains.

Results of Bank Support in 12 Focus Countries

About 42 percent of the 138 closed and relevant projects delivered substantial gender-related benefits. Forty-seven percent of the 138 projects integrated gender considerations during project design, and about 63 percent of these projects delivered substantial or high outcomes. Of the 53 percent that did not integrate gender considerations at appraisal, 22 percent of these (in the Philippines, and some in Colombia) appear to have benefited women nonetheless.

About 42 percent of all closed and relevant projects generated substantial gender-related benefits.

In Bangladesh, Ghana, Peru, and the Philippines, Bank support contributed significantly to gender equality (or women's empowerment) by reducing gender disparities and empowering women in at least two of the three domains. In the Philippines, the results stem from highly gender-aware and effective domestic systems, processes, and incentives, which caused gender considerations to be introduced during implementation and generated positive results for both men and women.

In 4 of the 12 countries, the results of Bank support substantially influenced gender-equality outcomes.

TABLE 6.2	Criteria for Rating Results in 12 Evaluation Countries		
Rating	**Enhanced human capital**	**Improved equality of access to assets and opportunities**	**Improved voice in development**
Substantial	Significant achievement of stated objectives in the following areas where the Bank provided support: • Enhanced parity in access to education (with completion rates maintained) • Decreased maternal mortality rates • Increased access to water	Significant achievement of stated objectives in the following areas where the Bank provided support: • Increased equality in access to resources (credit, economic services, and land) • Increased equality in labor force participation • Enhanced productive skills and capacity for both men and women	Significant achievement of stated objectives in the following areas where the Bank provided support: • Increased voice of men and women in development decision making at the community or other level • Increased accountability of local institutions for gender equality • Enhanced institutional capacity to design and implement policies and rules to support gender equality or women's empowerment
Modest	Partial achievement of stated objectives in areas, as discussed above	Partial achievement of stated objectives in areas, as discussed above	Partial achievement of stated objectives in areas as discussed above
Low	Weak achievement of stated objective in the areas, as discussed above	Weak achievement of stated objective in the areas, as discussed above	Weak achievement of stated objective in the areas as discussed above

Source: IEG.

In Benin, Colombia, Tajikistan, Turkey, Yemen, and Zambia, the contribution of Bank support to gender equality was modest, although it may have been substantial in one of the three domains. Thus, there were some very positive results at the local level, but they were limited to one domain or remained at the local level and were not of a scale that would likely affect gender inequalities. In Nigeria and Lebanon, there was little gender-responsive Bank support, and ICRs were either silent or outcomes were limited, even in the health and education sector in Nigeria.[3]

The evaluation sought to understand the Bank's contribution to gender equality and women's empowerment at a country level by examining differences in CPIA 7 rating between fiscal 2002 and 2008 and the Global Gender Gap Index (table 6.3).[4] The analysis shows that gender equality has improved in Bangladesh, Peru, and Ghana. In the Philippines, although the CPIA 7 rating shows no change, the Global Gender Gap Index indicates some positive change. At the same time, Bank support appears to have contributed only modestly to improved gender equality ratings in Colombia and Tajikistan, where there were similar positive changes at a country level.

Enhanced Human Capital

The evaluation assessed the provision of services in three sectors—education, health, and water. Box 6.1 describes some good practices in social protection; a literature review, combined with evaluation findings in the 12 countries, showed this may be helpful in designing responses to the current economic crisis.

Getting more girls into school

The Bank successfully worked with clients to increase enrollment of girls in primary and secondary schools. It did not have the same success in enhancing the quality of education and has only started limited attempts to address male gender issues.

In Bangladesh, Benin, Ghana, Turkey, and Yemen, the Bank provided analytical work and lending to reduce gender disparity at different levels of education. In Turkey, conditional cash transfers targeted the poorest 6 percent of the population, and the use of basic education services has improved access for girls from economically vulnerable homes (see box 6.2).[5] In Bangladesh, gender disparity was removed, partly because of substantial attention to the issue and lending that began as a CAS-mandated priority. In Ghana, DPOs and investment loans focused on deprived regions. Although national targets were met, there is no information on enrollments in the 40 most deprived regions.[6]

In other countries, Bank support has not been similarly successful (box 6.3). In Zambia, this was because the Bank—though it set ambitious goals before the evaluation period—stopped lending for the education sector. In 2008, the Zambia CAS (World Bank 2004g) returned to addressing gender disparity in education through analytical work.[7] Another reason for less success in the Philippines and Peru was that the Bank did not set specific goals or actions for gender mainstreaming in education because, as noted in CASs, gender parity had already been achieved.[8]

In Colombia, although the CGA identified several gender issues in education (both male and female) and the CAS identified male gender issues, gender was not well integrated into the Bank's large portfolio in the sector. In secondary education, meanwhile, the gap has widened in favor of girls. In Nigeria, lack of attention to gender issues resulted in low efficacy.[9]

TABLE 6.3	Changes in CPIA Ratings over the Evaluation Period	
Country	Change in CPIA ratings between 2002 and 2008	Change in GGG between 2006 and 2008
Bangladesh	Positive	Positive (0.0261)
Benin	No change	Negative (−0.0198)
Colombia	—	Negative (−0.0105)
Ghana	Positive	Positive (0.0026)
Lebanon	—	Not available
Nigeria	No change	Positive (0.0235)
Peru	—	Positive (0.0340)
Philippines	—	Positive (0.0052)
Tajikistan	Positive	Negative (−0.0038)[a]
Turkey	—	Positive (0.0003)
Yemen, Rep. of	No change	Positive (0.0069)
Zambia	No change	Negative (−0.0155)

Source: World Bank.

Note: CPIA = Country Policy and Institutional Assessment; GGG = Global Gender Gap Index; — = IBRD countries.
a. Data available only for 2007 and 2008.

ECONOMIC CRISIS—LESSONS FROM EXPERIENCES

An economic crisis has different implications for each gender, particularly where men and women have different social and economic roles. For example, men may return home when they lose jobs or migrate in search of work, and women's participation in the labor market and in community affairs may increase as a mechanism to cope with reduced family or household incomes (Silvey 2000; Brown and Lapuyade 2001; Jokisch and Pribilsky 2002; Tanga, Mbuagbo, and Fru 2002; Fiszbein, Giovagnoli, and Thurston 2003). In the workplace, women may encounter low wages, long hours, no state benefits, considerable health hazards, harassment, and few rights. In addition, structural reforms in the wake of economic crises have tended to reduce social expenditure, introduce fees for basic public services, and remove state support, all of which also have differential implications for men and women (Elson and Cagatay 2000; Lim 2000; Young 2003).

Differential effects are specific to a locale, and a "global crisis" cannot be addressed through a "global" approach. For example, research in some developing countries shows that families protect their investments in sons at the expense of their daughters during economic crises (Özler 1999; UNRISD 2005). In other countries, girls fare no worse than boys (Correia 2002; Levine and Ames 2003). Some studies show that the changes wrought by an economic crisis can help empower women and increase their decision-making role within the household (Parrado and Zenteno 2001; Hamilton 2002; Lee 2005; Munné 2005). Others show that stresses caused by such crises have helped increase male violence (Correia 2002; Douglas and others 2003; Ćopić 2004). Thus, effects are contextual and depend on gender norms in different locales.

To be effective, therefore, interventions need to be carefully designed. An assessment of safety nets in Bangladesh, supported by the Bank and undertaken by the International Food Policy Research Institute, showed that cash-based programs had greater beneficial impact on household savings and female empowerment measures, whereas food-rationing programs had more impact on increasing household income (Ahmed and others 2007). Adding conditions on who receives transfer payments (women or men, for example, in the case of schemes oriented toward gender outcomes, such as work requirements or keeping children in school) can help further poverty reduction aims (Ravallion 2008).

An examination of closed operations in Colombia, Peru, and the Philippines suggests that support has focused on targeted programs for the poor to deal with the aftermath of such crises. Such support has included opportunities to improve skills, participation in wage labor, and cash transfers for accessing health and education services. Mostly, these efforts specifically target women (as opposed to households), although some, such as the Social Safety Project in Colombia, focus on families. They appeared to benefit both men and women, but ICRs provided little or no information on gender-related outcomes.

At the same time, Bank support typically has not gone beyond such programs to actively support gender integration into labor market reform and trade liberalization strategies or to redirect public expenditure in a manner that would help to weaken the underlying gender inequalities that cause these differentiated effects.

Source: IEG.

Gender disparity in completion rates—even as enrollments go up—proved to be a challenge in 11 of the 12 countries (Colombia being the exception), and in some countries such disparity was a result of decreasing male enrollments. This was also partly linked to quality of education, particularly critical for girls, because returns to education can otherwise be very low for them.[10]

For example, an International Food Policy Research Institute assessment found that enrollments increased the most in Bangladesh when there were additional grants to improve quality. A subsequent survey by that country's government found that dropout rates for both boys and girls had increased. Completion rates also fell below the baseline at project appraisal, at both the primary and secondary levels.[11]

A concern in several countries was the decreasing number of boys in school, an issue the Bank has yet to con-

sider fully. In Bangladesh and Yemen, although demand-side interventions have made it less costly to send girls to school, more boys are now being kept at home to help support their families. Male gender issues are also emerging in Colombia and the Philippines. The evaluation found that the Bank took some concrete actions to address this issue in Bangladesh.[12]

Reducing maternal mortality[13]

In 11 of the focus countries (all except Lebanon), CASs or projects identified maternal mortality as a key constraint.

> Bank support was not very effective in reducing maternal mortality rates.

Bank support for reducing maternal mortality, however, has not yet contributed to significant outcomes (box 6.4). This is despite considerable focus on reproductive rights of poor women in both Bank projects and DPOs.

THE DESIGN OF CONDITIONAL CASH TRANSFERS IS CRITICAL

A 2007 International Food Policy Research Institute study in Turkey (Adato and others 2007) found that although state legitimization of social change through the successful Bank-supported program of conditional cash transfers may provide opportunities for women to spend time outside their homes and to engage with institutions such as banks, in some regions, sociocultural biases against schooling for girls can be more powerful than cash incentives. In such cases, complementary approaches are needed to overcome these constraints. In Mexico, the approach of a cash transfer for beneficiaries aged 70 or older worked, as did a cash incentive for high school graduation that was conditional on its investment in higher education. Cash incentives also appear to have worked in Bangladesh.

However, educated women who received conditional cash transfers were more likely to espouse attitudes of gender equality in education for their children, and less about it among spouses. In both cases, local nongovernmental organizations catalyze the process of change at the community level in a socially accepted manner.

Source: IEG desk review of Bank support for Turkey.

Bank support contributed to a slow, steady decline in maternal mortality in Bangladesh and achieved stated targets in Peru. However, it is unclear whether the objectives were fully achieved in both countries.[14] In Ghana, the maternal mortality rate significantly improved between 2003 and 2005 through abolition of user fees for poor women, supported by the Bank. However, underfunding and the abolition of the exemption for delivery fees by a new government, as well as the health worker strike of 2007, left local health facilities stranded and unable to provide required support (Witter and others 2007).

Contributions were weaker in Colombia, the Philippines, Yemen, and Zambia. Although the Bank identified maternal mortality as a key issue in Colombia and the Philippines, it provided little by way of targeted lending during the evaluation period.[15] In Yemen and Zambia, maternal mortality was not directly addressed; rather, it was addressed through HIV/AIDs and malaria projects.[16] Additionally, social fund projects financed health subprojects that supplied infrastructure and training personnel. Although these benefited women in general, the support

did not positively influence maternal mortality rates, which increased in both countries (World Bank 2009f).

Provision of water to households

Provision of water at the household level can help reduce the time spent collecting water for domestic use—a female responsibility in most countries—and contribute to better

> Bank support was successful in getting water to households, but sustainability remains a concern.

health. The size of the support for this, however, was low in about half the 12 countries, compared with overall lending. Sustainability was also of concern in some projects.

In Benin, Poverty Reduction Support Credits supported access to safe water for the rural population. The ICRs for the Benin Poverty Reduction Support Credits noted that the percentage of rural poor with access to safe water increased from 35 percent in 2002 to 44 percent in 2006, but the CAS target of 64.5 percent by 2006 was not met.

SUSTAINED LENDING, DEMAND-SIDE INCENTIVES, AND CIVIL SOCIETY PARTICIPATION HELPED INCREASE GENDER PARITY IN EDUCATION

Bank support in Bangladesh and Ghana was more successful in contributing to results in the education sector because, unlike in Zambia, gender-aware lending was sustained. Furthermore, in Bangladesh and Ghana, although Bank support focused on the supply side (classrooms, female teachers, and textbooks), it also created sufficient demand for the services through support for various incentives designed to remove constraints.

In both countries, government ownership and commitment were important, but Bank support encouraged the involvement civil society at the local level, which helped to enhance and strengthen awareness of the importance of ensuring that girls are encouraged to go to school. In countries such as the Philippines and Colombia, there is a need to recognize that gender parit in enrollments is not necessarily the achievement of gender equality and that there is a need to address gender issues relatec to quality (such as in curriculum, teaching methods, and access to labor markets).

Source: IEG review.

ADDRESSING MATERNAL MORTALITY REQUIRES CROSS-SECTORAL SUPPORT AND CONTEXT-SPECIFIC STRATEGIES

Tackling gender issues such as maternal mortality requires a considered multidimensional and cross-sectoral approach tailored to local contexts.

- Narrowly focusing Bank support on interventions in the health sector has in many cases limited the achievement of desired outcomes. Increased transportation resulted in larger numbers of women seeking medical help in Peru. Training local women as health attendants may help, because of the resulting high likelihood that they will go back to their communities to provide services (as in Yemen).

- Context-specific support is important. In Colombia, where a high percentage of births occur under institutional supervision, Bank support for improving the quality of care provided by institutions at both the prenatal stage and during birth would be important. In countries where utilization of health facilities is low, there needs to be significant support for demand-driven incentives to convince poor households that using services is important.

- The Bank-supported termination of user fees in Ghana has been found to be effective in increasing the utilization of facilities. However, an impact evaluation suggested that these subsidies should be well targeted and expanded only when there is assurance of funding for such activities. Realistic planning and budgeting is critical.

- Costs are not always the only reason that health services are used too little. Lack of awareness of the need for women to use services can also be a problem in some countries. In such cases, there is some evidence that a door-to-door awareness-raising program may be necessary, in combination with the provision of facilities, trained female personnel, and supplies.

Source: IEG.

In Zambia, service was mainly provided through the social fund, and women benefited much more from the water components in nonwater projects (schools, health) because those brought water close to the community and eased women's labor burden. A highly efficacious project in Ghana supported provision of water to poor communities, although its contribution to country-level outcomes is not evident.[17]

The Bank has been very proactive in involving women in the management of water resources for domestic consumption—and with good results. In Ghana, Bank support demonstrated the central role women can play in the provision of services at both household and community levels. In the Philippines, field assessments found that the inclusion of women in water committees enhanced trust in the management of those committees' activities. The Tajikistan Rural Infrastructure Project was less successful in providing water to communities, and the ICR (World Bank 2008l) concluded that it was necessary to involve women in water user committees.

Although women also benefited from gender-blind projects in Yemen because water connections were made directly to households, stakeholders reiterated the importance of consulting with poor women (not just with better-off women, whose needs and priorities are different) to ensure that a sufficient quantity of water would be available at appropriate times. Furthermore, among poorer communities, the main consideration for women in deciding whether to connect to the water was the availability of household income.

In the Philippines, an assessment undertaken as part of the evaluation of bank support for decentralization (IEG 2008a) indicated that as much as 77 percent of the women in a poor village did not opt for the connection because of the tariffs and the lack of any cross-subsidization either by the local government or by the community.

Equal Access to Economic Assets and Opportunities

In this domain, IEG analyzed the results in three main areas: enhanced access to financial and economic services, increased access to economic opportunities and assets, and improved capacity and skills. In all 12 countries, women's economic empowerment was a focus, and the evaluation examined whether Bank support contributed to increased access to economic assets and opportunities. Overall, the evaluation finds that there is need to strengthen outcome-based support in this domain, where Bank support is more focused on inputs and outputs.

Support for economic empowerment of women was successful in areas where the Bank focused on gender-related outcomes.

Enhanced access to financial and economic services

Access to microfinance. The Bank has increasingly provided support for microfinance programs that target women. That support appeared to have been among its more successful efforts in this domain in Bangladesh, Benin, Ghana, Peru, and Yemen.

IEG field assessments of Bank support in Ghana and Yemen and self-assessments in Bangladesh suggested that microfinance helped empower women in many ways. Results demonstrated that microfinance programs—by requiring attendance at regular meetings, through occasional training sessions, and by making women more "visible" in the economic sphere—enhanced women's mobility and aid empowerment. Such activities also helped to establish women's or gender-balanced groups that work together on productive activities and increased individual incomes of group members.

By 2006, the Bank had provided financial and technical support to 10 microfinance intermediaries (MFIs) operating in 26 branches in nine governorates in Yemen. These intermediaries had 25,588 active borrowers and 24,617 savers and provided more than 81,000 loans totaling YER 2,430 million ($11.9 million). The IEG field assessment validated the findings of an independent evaluation undertaken at project closing: women receiving these loans felt a greater sense of empowerment within their households and within the larger community. Most important, Bank support laid the foundation for a microfinance industry, with the capacity of microfinance intermediaries strengthened and microfinance tools developed to provide financial services to poor but creditworthy groups.

In Benin, although there was evidence of success with the social fund project, which included a microfinance component, the ICR for the private sector credit (World Bank 2008d), which aimed to strengthen institutions, was completely silent on the gender dimension. In Ghana, although the microfinance component did provide women with loans, institutional strengthening appeared not to be as sustainable as in Yemen.

Access to economic services. Bank support for construction of rural roads, other economic infrastructure, and market projects has significant potential to increase the marketing of agricultural products and farmers' revenues. The evaluation found that these interventions more effectively addressed gender issues when both male and female participation was encouraged in project design and implementation (box 6.5). Of the seven relevant transport projects in the 12 countries, five were gender aware and generated positive results for both men and women. In terms of providing inputs for women in the agricultural sector, two projects addressed this issue in Ghana, leading to substantial results.

Increased equality in access to economic opportunities and assets

Increased labor force participation. Increased labor force participation helps empower women in many ways, including increasing their access to wages and income. However, Bank support in this area has generated only small or temporary results.

In Bangladesh, Colombia, Yemen, and Zambia, public works projects resulted in women receiving wages by participating in temporary construction work.[18] In Yemen, women also obtained a small percentage of the few permanent jobs created in the health, education, and water sectors.

Major efforts to influence labor markets did not particularly benefit women. In Colombia, three DPOs for programmatic labor and social reform ($600 million) provided significant support to the government, but the results have been mixed. Female participation in the labor markets fell during the evaluation period, and the gender gap in unemployment worsened, rising from 6 percent in 1998–2000 to 7 percent in 2005, moving away from the 3 percent target. An IEG review suggested that because of high minimum wages and other protective measures, women were likely to be employed in lower numbers in the formal markets. Colombians, however, obtained the right to an unemployment subsidy program. The ICR (World Bank 2007c) noted that the program was beneficial for men, who are the majority of informal sector workers, but women's welfare was affected

---

BOX 6.5

CONSULTATION WITH WOMEN IN TRANSPORT PROJECTS HELPED SUPPORT THEIR ECONOMIC EMPOWERMENT

A field assessment of Peru's rural roads project demonstrated how involving women in the design of projects is critical if the infrastructure is to meet the needs of both men and women. Through participatory assessments, the project effectively engaged women as decision makers on the scope and scale of the project and on community-based road-maintenance microenterprise grants for women. This resulted in the construction of footpaths, which women prefer because they are the easiest and safest way to take their animals to pasture and to collect firewood and water. Access to roads and paths increased women's mobility—77 percent of women said that they travel more often and farther as a result of the project. Sixty-seven percent said that travel was safer after the project. The project also increased the efficiency of women's time management, and 43 percent of women reported that the project had allowed them to obtain new sources of income.

Sources: Review of Bank support and IEG field assessment in Peru.

more because they valued access to health care for their families more than men do. However, this program benefited only 1.5 percent of the unemployed in Colombia.

In Turkey, the Bank supported a package of labor market reforms intended to raise workforce participation rates for women and youth through its Competitiveness and Employment DPO. The ICR did not discuss gender issues, and women's labor market participation decreased during the evaluation period.

Enhanced productive skills. The Bank supported training activities in the 12 countries. ICRs focused for the most part on outputs, and in its evaluation IEG relied on such information, except in a few countries where some further assessments were undertaken. Overall, these efforts appeared to have generated some results, particularly in countries where such access was limited for women (box 6.6).

In Bangladesh, Ghana, and Zambia, although women acquired new skills, unlike their male counterparts, a lack of resources and support to establish productive livelihoods prevented them from converting the training opportunity into further benefits. For example, in Bangladesh, training in aquaculture techniques benefited men more because they had better user rights to ponds than women did. In Zambia, interviews with trainees indicated that although women were more willing to take up technical training, unlike their male counterparts they were less likely to set up business enterprises. In Colombia, 62 percent of the 110,000 people trained under a program supported by the Bank were women, but there was no evidence that these women were able to find employment in the informal or private sectors.

Support for reorganizing technical and vocational education to respond to the needs of the rural productive sectors in countries such as Colombia has generated weak results. This issue is of concern, given the increasing dropout rate at the secondary level. In Yemen, the Higher Education Project could not meet its gender goals, the Vocational Training Projects' gender component was dropped, and the vocational training policy supported by the Bank was gender blind.[19]

Increased access to land. A handful of the closed projects attempted and succeeded in helping improve women's access to economic assets. Most of these improved access to land.

In Peru and the Philippines, where land transfers are mostly governed by statutory laws (rather than customary laws), small interventions have created sometimes permanent changes for women. In Peru, the Urban Property Rights Project helped increase the proportion of female property titleholders among illegal occupants in urban areas. Women report that this has resulted in their being involved in decision making concerning use of property and their views being taken more seriously at community meetings.[20] As titleholders, women had more flexibility to work outside the community, because they no longer had to stay close to home to guard their land from usurpation. However, since the project's close, the process of titling had been transferred to decentralized municipalities. This has generated problems because the municipalities preferred to follow their own administrative mechanisms.

In the Philippines, the ICR for the Bank-supported Land Administration and Management Project (World Bank 2005d) noted the issuance of a Department Administrative Order, which removed a longstanding gender bias in land titling, facilitating the registration of land in women's names. However, this important result was primarily due to the efforts of the Australian government's Overseas Aid Program, a cofinancier.[21] In Ghana and Tajikistan, Bank support (still active) is expected to address gender and land issues, but prevailing customary laws may hinder equal results.

Increased Voice of Women in Development

In all 12 countries, the key issue in this domain was one of enhancing women's voice in development planning and

---

implementation. In several countries (Bangladesh, Benin, Ghana, Peru, the Philippines, Tajikistan, Yemen, and Zambia), Bank support encouraged the presence of women on community-level decision-making committees that were either entirely women (in Yemen) or both men and women (in Ghana). Another less common measure in a few countries, such as Bangladesh, Ghana, and Yemen, was to enhance literacy for both men and women.

Bank support for improving women's participation succeeded, but more careful design is needed to improve voice in decision making.

Given the poor information on outcomes in ICRs, IEG undertook limited field assessments in Ghana, Peru, the Philippines, Tajikistan, and Zambia[22] to understand the results of such participation on women's empowerment and voice. Other Bank self-assessments and IEG work on community water user associations in the Philippines[23] also provided some observations.

The rapid and limited IEG field assessments indicated that women—whether in Zambia or in the Philippines—wanted to participate in development activities, and Bank-supported projects have helped ensure that they can. Although groups were created for specific purposes—such as microfinance, literacy, or infrastructure rehabilitation—they were able to engage in collective public action outside the immediate context (box 6.7).

The group structure provided women with a voice and a support network to enhance their status and sometimes helped solve conflicts within the group. Peer dynamics encouraged participants to save and served as a control mechanism if participants were not fully contributing. However, the field assessments are inconclusive about whether participation in income-generating activities led to control by women over the resources they earned, although women stated that the male members of the household consulted them more often once they contributed to household income.

Beneficiaries of Bank-supported projects indicated that equal opportunity to be elected or appointed to community committees did not necessarily translate into equal participation. Instead of influencing prevailing gender relations, project committees often reflected the unequal distribution of community power between men and women. In some regions of the Philippines and Peru, for example, women participated more actively in meetings and in decision-making processes and assumed leadership roles in the community.

In Bangladesh, elite capture posed risks even for poor men. For example, in a Bank-supported fisheries project, local elites had substantial influence in 40 percent of the community-based organizations; targeted poor fisher folk did not benefit, and in some cases, they were even negatively affected (World Bank 2007a). In Zambia, the field assessments found that men played key roles and women played subordinate roles. In Tajikistan, only female heads of household assumed leadership positions, with married women typically being assigned membership in the larger committees. In Yemen, the ICR for an irrigation project (World Bank 2009h) found that the criteria for membership in water users' associations must be carefully established if women were to be given a voice.

Where the Bank had adapted its approach to reflect cultural priorities, the results appeared to be better (box 6.8) for both men and women. In Yemen, microfinance was provided to women, even if the funds went to meet the needs of male family members first or went for household needs. With this start,

---

BOX 6.7

SUSTAIN SUPPORT FOR WOMEN'S PARTICIPATION IN CDD, BUT PROVIDE SIMULTANEOUS SUPPORT FOR STRENGTHENING THEIR PARTICIPATION IN LOCAL GOVERNMENTS

Bank support for women's participation in CDD activities was relevant and efficacious in all countries where field assessments were undertaken. For example, although project implementers in Peru complained that quotas for women's participation were not welcomed, they nevertheless conceded that such a requirement enhanced focus on mechanisms to make it work.

However, although gender issues were largely integrated into Bank-supported CDD activities, integration was not typical in its support for local governments. The Bank, therefore, lost significant opportunities to support gender-aware institutions and processes at the local government levels, particularly given that the majority of the Bank's clients had decentralized or were decentralizing basic services to local governments.

Bank support could have helped build the capacity of local governments to plan and manage their own development in a gender-aware manner, as it did in the Philippines Mindanao project. Or Bank support could have helped integrate gender into targets set for achievement at the local levels, as it did in a few projects in Colombia and Peru.

Sources: IEG field assessments in Ghana, Peru, Yemen, and Zambia; IEG (2008a).

both men and women appeared to become more comfortable with women borrowing money for their own purposes.

Similarly, during implementation of a natural resource management project in Peru, an unsuccessful business initiative program for indigenous women shifted from a focus on gender equality to one on gender complementarity, recognizing the gender-differentiated roles and capacities and consistent with the Bank's indigenous peoples policy requirement on provision of culturally appropriate gender support.[24] The project ICR concluded that there were no significant changes, given women's "high level of illiteracy, low self-esteem, and the patriarchal culture that still predominates in the countryside and even at the project design level, which fails to see peasant women as capable of leading the process for change" (World Bank 2004f). This may be symptomatic of ambitious project objectives.

Women's inputs varied, depending on the type of organization in which they participated. In infrastructure-related activities, their inputs were disproportionately higher yet less rewarded in monetary terms than men's. For example, Zambian men typically performed the paid skilled labor, whereas women performed the unskilled unpaid labor in all but one of the cases reviewed. Field assessments confirmed that the burden of labor was higher on women. Women, lacking access to transport technologies, carried sand, stones, firewood, and water by head-loading (and simultaneously carried babies on their backs), whereas men were able to use oxcarts, wheelbarrows, or bicycles, in addition to their regular domestic chores. For example, women who provided most of the labor to build the community school in a poor Lusaka community reported that they worked from seven in the morning to seven at night, and then did domestic chores after that.

Thus, the evaluation finds that women's participation in community committees improved their participation as beneficiaries and provided a way for them to participate outside their households. However, to sustainably influence gender relations and empower women, long-term support is needed, as well as carefully designed mechanisms that will address gender imbalances in participation, rather than strengthen existing stereotypes.

Institutional strengthening

Despite the strengthened country-level strategic mainstreaming approach, support for formulating gender-aware policies, for eliminating gender biases in laws and regulations, for strengthening institutional capacity to implement development activities to support gender equality or women's empowerment, or for generating gender-related or -disaggregated data was not common. They were found only in 4 of the 10 sample countries where such support was relevant. In the Philippines and Colombia, policies and institutions supporting gender equality are fairly advanced, and Bank support was not considered highly relevant in this area.

> A focus on institutional strengthening, critical for a strategic mainstreaming approach, was not common.

In Ghana and Zambia, the Bank and other supporters supported revised gender-aware policies, although the support was not sustained in Zambia. In Ghana, a directorate for women in agricultural development was established, and gender considerations were integrated into agricultural policies and in the delivery of extension services.

In Nigeria and Tajikistan, Bank support aimed to generate gender-aware poverty data through support for statistical agencies. ICRs for both countries rated the component as satisfactory but were silent on the gender issue. A visit to the Central Statistical Unit in Tajikistan confirmed that the Bank had provided it with gender-aware training and that gender-disaggregated data are now available.

Long-term and sustained support is required to influence institutional and policy change. In Yemen, as in Zambia,

---

BOX 6.8

INFLUENCING BOTH MALE AND FEMALE ATTITUDES IS NECESSARY TO INFLUENCE GENDER EQUALITY

There was greater resistance in some areas to women's participation until men actually saw the benefits of such participation. For example, a young couple in Gizaa, Ghana, related their story about joining the literacy program.

The wife was elated about finally being able to read and write, but her young husband did not think it would be beneficial. Unable to oppose her decision because the program was supported by the community, the husband frustrated the woman's efforts by making unreasonable demands on her time each night she tried to prepare to attend literacy classes. He only acknowledged the benefit when the group formed an income-generating activity and he saw his wife bringing in income. At that point, he not only encouraged her but also joined the group. Another woman stated that her husband had encouraged her to join when he noticed his neighbor's wife could now understand the figures on her baby's weighing card.

Source: IEG Ghana field assessment.

support for institutional strengthening of the country's gender institution started well but was dropped midway.[25] In Benin, the Bank was more ambitious, with the CAS including a gender-related trigger: the attainment of base case triggers plus effective implementation of the Family Code and other legislation protecting women's rights. This was not achieved, and the support was not sustained in the subsequent CAS.

IEG also examined 109 relevant pieces of ESW in the 12 countries to understand how the Bank supported the generation of knowledge on gender issues and their development implications. Overall, the results were mixed (table 6.4). Fewer than half of the 109 pieces of ESW integrated gender in a high or substantial manner—that is, included analysis of gender issues, backed by quantitative or qualitative data, and identified relevant actions to address issues identified.

ESW was highly gender aware in Benin, Peru, and Yemen, and substantially so in Bangladesh, Colombia, and Turkey. However, consideration of gender issues was not always consistent. For example, the report "Colombia Rural Finance—Access Issues, Challenges and Opportunities" (World Bank 2003a) did not discuss gender issues, despite significant domestic policies and laws that seek to promote and address gender issues in the area; in contrast, "Land Policy in Transition" (World Bank 2004a), a piece undertaken the same year, integrated gender issues well. Similarly, the Zambia "Smallholder Agricultural Commercialization Strategy" (World Bank 2007k) did not discuss gender issues in a sector where a majority of Zambians operated and where women provided the bulk of labor. At the same time, "Poverty and Vulnerability Assessment"

TABLE 6.4	Integration of Gender in Relevant ESW in 12 Focus Countries	
Country	No. of ESW reviewed	% of ESW with H/S gender integration
Bangladesh	14	57
Benin	3	100
Colombia	8	50
Ghana	8	13
Lebanon	3	0
Nigeria	11	27
Peru	7	86
Philippines	19	26
Tajikistan	7	29
Turkey	13	54
Yemen, Republic of	6	83
Zambia	10	40

Source: IEG.

Note: ESW = economic and sector work.

(World Bank 2007j) was notable for its data-backed gender analysis.

Gender in DPOs

In assessing results of Bank support, IEG examined 29 closed DPOs in 8 of the 12 focus countries. Gender-aware DPOs helped deliver results in education and social protection in Bangladesh, Benin, Ghana, Peru, and Turkey. Outside these areas, it was less common to find evidence of any sustained results. In Yemen, for example, a DPO supported studies on gender and land, but there was little evidence of gender-aware outcomes. In Benin, there was some discussion of gender-aware interventions in the water sector, but, once again, ICRs did not discuss the issue.

In Colombia, as discussed earlier in this chapter, three DPOs focused on labor and social protection. Although they resulted in women receiving training, the operations did not contribute to gender equality in the labor market. The third DPO in fiscal 2007 concluded that "in the long run, the vision is to reform legislation to reduce disincentives to employment, accompanied by a series of social protection schemes to protect the unemployed and to improve the employability of hard-to-employ groups (youth, women, unskilled, rural)" (World Bank 2006a).

There was also a tendency for operational documents to discuss gender issues in health and education, even when the key objectives may have been focused on other sectors. In Zambia, DPOs aiming to strengthen the credibility and institutional capacity of the public sector and enhance pro-poor growth opportunities included little discussion of gender issues except for some focus on education and HIV/AIDs. In Bangladesh, the ICR for the fourth DPO concluded that although gender aspects were not directly addressed by the operations, its IDA complement, Education Sector Development Support Credit, did contribute to achieving significant progress in ensuring gender parity in secondary enrollment.

IEG also examined ICRs available for 42 of the 53 DPOs with gender-related measures discussed in chapter 4. Information on achievement of gender issues was sparse, and the evaluation found the following:

- Fifty-four percent of the measures were effectively met, and another 22 percent were partially met. Argentina met all the measures (all related to programs on reproductive health and social protection for poor women).

- One of the most successful measures outside the human development sector was in Rwanda, which required establishment of a ministry (the Ministry of Gender and Family Promotion), issuance and implementation of a gender action plan, increased access to education for girls, and initiation of gender budgeting in five ministries. The ICR noted that all actions were completed. A more ambitious measure was also observed in Rwanda: "gender disparities and discriminations of all forms to be abolished in all forthcoming legislation" (World Bank 2008j, p. 11). The ICR noted that the government had displayed commitment, particularly in land-related law.

- Twenty-four percent of the conditions (50 percent of these were outside the human development sectors) were not addressed in ICRs, and it is assumed that they were not met. In some cases, information was provided on gender (for example on education), but not related to the specified measure.

Overall, IEG's review suggested that the practice of including gender-related measures in DPOs related to human development had generated results that complemented Bank support in reducing gender inequalities or disparity. In other sectors, particularly those highlighted by the GAP, gender issues need to be more explicitly considered as part of the social and poverty impact analysis. Additionally, as part of the strengthening of the monitoring system, CASCRs and ICRs should report on the gender-differentiated impact of DPO activities.

What Worked Well?

The Bank has demonstrated that the country-level approach, if implemented well, can contribute to progress in gender equality or women's empowerment (box 6.9). The Bank has expanded its support for gender integration in a wider variety of sectors outside of health and education. There has been an increase of gender integration in transport projects, land management and administration projects, and legal and judicial reform over the previous evaluation period. Support for microfinance in several countries has helped demonstrate that providing women with economic resources goes a long way in helping to empower them.

The Bank has demonstrated that it is possible to support gender equality outcomes in client countries.

BOX 6.9

WHAT WORKED WELL?

In Ghana and Bangladesh, where results were more favorable, the following elements of the four-step strategic approach were present:

- Timely diagnosis of gender issues

  - Timely diagnosis was done not only through freestanding CGAs, but also through several pieces of ESW that contributed to increased knowledge on gender issues.

- Effective mainstreaming of gender into CASs and country programs

  - Gender was mainstreamed within the results framework of the CASs, with a clear set of monitoring indicators to assess results in client countries.

  - Recognizing the wide-ranging gender issues in the country, both CASs required gender mainstreaming in all Bank activities, and subsequent projects followed through.

  - Relevant DPOs integrated gender issues.

- Focus on strengthened client country institutions

  - CASs included steps for institutional strengthening (such as strengthening institutional accountability and capacity for gender equality, including gender-related analysis of public expenditures in Bangladesh and support for drafting and issuing gender-aware policies in Ghana).

- Collaboration with other partners in providing support for gender equality

  - Both CASs proposed working with other development and civil society partners and discussing gender issues as part of the policy dialogue with the client.

- Sustained support for gender through different CAS periods

  - CASs proposed to intensify analytical and advisory activities and proposed more focused assessments to improve the strategic approach of gender.

  - Subsequent CASs sustained focus on gender issues.

- Focus on results was higher in these two countries.

Source: IEG.

Monitoring of gender or women's dimensions of health and education outcomes has improved, buttressed by the need to assess achievement of MDGs. There was also some evidence that the integration of gender-related or -disaggregated indicators increased the chance that gender issues would be monitored. In addition, 62 percent of the projects with high or substantial indicators delivered positive outcomes, although this was so in fewer than 30 percent of those without such indicators. Monitoring indicators also help leave behind an institutional memory on what needed to be assessed.

That said, monitoring needs to be significantly strengthened in the other two domains (increased access to economic assets and opportunities and enhanced voice of men and women in development planning and implementation), where outcomes are not as easily assessed. The 2007 GAP rightly identified the need to develop suitable and affordable indicators as one of its four key activities. The recent OPCS requirement that IDA-supported investment projects report on project beneficiaries in a gender-disaggregated manner will also improve monitoring in this area.

Monitoring and evaluation continues to be weak outside the health and education sectors.

In countries where domestic development policies and institutions were strong, the evaluation found that, despite the lack of sustained gender integration in Bank support, several activities benefited both men and women. These projects were mainly in the Philippines, where gender-blind projects benefited both men and women because of the equitable domestic processes and systems in these countries.

In countries with strong institutions and rules for gender equality, results were better.

A few of these projects were in Colombia, where, because of higher levels of gender equality, both men and women were able to access opportunities. The previous IEG evaluation (IEG 2005) found a similar situation in Vietnam and Poland. This underscores the importance of "strategic mainstreaming" and of strengthening institutional arrangements and policies in client countries.

What did not work as well?

The absence of a results framework in the 2001 Gender Strategy weakened country-level outcomes. Interventions were focused on outputs rather than on outcomes, and the lack of a considered framework resulted in inconsistent attention to gender issues, particularly outside the human development sectors.

The absence of a results framework led to interventions not focused on outcomes.

Entry points to address gender issues continued to be mostly at the sector or project levels and were not always cohesive or strategic at the country level (box 6.10). For example, the Social Fund Project in Benin included a small and successful component to provide microfinance for women. At the same time, the Cotton Sector Project (a sector where large numbers of women worked), with significant potential to affect change, did not address gender inequalities and could actually have resulted in strengthening unequal gender relations.

Similarly, in Tajikistan a social fund project included a small component for microcredit (which was eventually dropped), but at the same time larger agricultural projects were almost gender blind. In Zambia, the scattered gender advances gained through the social fund risked not being consolidated as the social fund was discontinued, and agriculture-related projects consistently failed to address gender, a key productivity and growth issue. At the same time, new project entry points opened in Transport and Public Service Reform.

Entry points for gender integration remained mainly at a project or sectoral level.

The Bank may have missed significant opportunities to support gender equalities or enhance women's empowerment. Only 47 percent of the relevant closed projects integrated gender issues well (that is, had some analysis, some consultation, and an action and included at least one gender-related indicator). Sixty-three percent of these projects delivered good results, but less than a quarter did so when gender issues were not integrated. Thus, Bank work could have been significantly more effective in its support for gender equality and women's empowerment, if project design had ensured that activities would benefit both men and women.

By failing to integrate gender into more than half the relevant closed projects, Bank support did not realize the full potential of its investments.

Thus, the evaluation finds that it is good practice to ensure an initial analysis of whether project-level activities will benefit both men and women. Although not a practice in the Bank, it may be worth noting that ADB includes a covenant in loan agreements for projects with high gender rele-

HOW COULD THE COUNTRY-LEVEL APPROACH BE STRENGTHENED?

In 10 of the 12 focus countries (Benin, Colombia, Nigeria, Lebanon, Peru, the Philippines, Tajikistan, Turkey, Yemen, and Zambia), the country-level approach was less evident:

- Timely diagnosis was undertaken in 8 of the 10 countries (in Lebanon, a CGA was undertaken in 2009; in Peru, it was not undertaken).

- All immediately subsequent CASs (except in Peru and Lebanon) substantially integrated gender issues; except for the fiscal 2002 CAS in the Philippines (World Bank 2002d), they fell short of a considered strategic gender response. That is—

  - Subsequent CASs did not address strategic gender issues, such as enhancing gender-aware policies, eliminating biases in the legal framework, and strengthening institutions to support gender equality; in Benin and Yemen, the CASs included attention to such issues, but there was little follow-through.

  - Few CASs monitored results beyond the health and education sectors, with the Nigeria CASs including no gender-related indicators.

  - Support for gender in country programs was usually a blend of reducing gender disparity in education, improving women's reproductive health, encouraging women's participation in CDD, and providing some income generation or similar activity for women. Though no doubt important, these measures were at the same time part of country programs where the bulk of support was in other economic or infrastructure sectors, with significant potential to impact gender.

- Attention to gender responses was not sustained. Subsequent CASs in Benin, Colombia, Nigeria, Peru, the Philippines, Tajikistan, Turkey, and Zambia did not maintain the focus on gender issues identified in the first CAS.

  - In Turkey, although health and education sectors were identified as priority in the 2004 CAS, the 2008 CAS suggested that women's employment would "likely" be a focus area.

  - In the Philippines, the 2002 CAS integrated gender concerns well, but this was completely lost by the time of the 2005 CAS, when there was only a focus on maternal health with no explanation for the position.

  - The 2003 Yemen CAS proposed to strengthen a consultative process by which stakeholders would design and take ownership of a gender action program. However, Yemeni stakeholders suggested that such dialogue was initiated but not sustained.

Source: IEG.

vance (where its internal rules require a gender action plan) that the government will implement the gender-related action. It may be helpful for the Bank to consider such a step or at least to include a single gender-related indicator in the agreement with governments on the key performance indicators for a project.

Findings and Recommendations

Findings

Relevance of the Bank's Gender Policy

The goals and objectives of the Bank's gender policy as reflected in OP 4.20 were and remain relevant to the Bank's mandate of supporting poverty reduction and equitable economic growth. Country teams were expected to complete CGAs in all countries where the Bank was active. Those CGAs were then expected to inform policy dialogue and CASs, which in turn would indicate whether, how, and why the Bank intended to address gender constraints. In sectors and thematic areas where a CAS had identified the need for action, Bank-supported projects and other activities were to be gender responsive. Finally, Regional vice presidencies were to report annually to their managing directors on the implementation of OP/BP 4.20. This process was envisaged as client led and tailored to country specifications, with the Bank in a supportive, if proactive, role as the facilitator of gender mainstreaming, in line with the country commitments and objectives for gender equality.

Nevertheless, two factors in particular have detracted from the relevance of the policy. One is the absence of a clear results framework underpinning the Bank's gender policy. Such a framework would help ensure rigorous analytical foundations for policy measures to support a client country's gender and development agenda. Most crucially, it would also ensure a structure for accountability within the Bank.

A second factor is the shift from a generalized integration of gender at a project level to a more selective country-level one. IEG takes the view that although gender mainstreaming needs to be selective, given limited resources, it needs to (i) address both top-down strategic institutional and policy reform and (ii) ensure that Bank-supported operations are gender responsive, so as to encourage the participation of both men and women in project activities and access to benefits.

The country-level approach should help engage the client in diagnosing and identifying strategic policy and institutional constraints to poverty reduction, as well as helping provide the framework for the Bank's gender support to a country.

Client demand is critical in this context, and Bank objectives need to be kept realistic in line with such demand, some role for advocacy notwithstanding.

Equally, at the project level, to enhance development effectiveness, Bank staff should ensure that Bank support is gender responsive and encourages the participation of both men and women in project activities and benefits. Furthermore, in many countries the country-level strategic approach cannot be implemented for various reasons, including barriers to doing CGAs, competing priorities, and lack of demand from governments. In such cases, it would be helpful to reinstate a stated minimum obligation for Bank staff to ensure through project design that both men and women benefit equitably from its support and to mitigate any disadvantageous changes that project activities may have on either. This would be consistent with the principles of OMS 2.20 and with the approach of the 2007 GAP.

Finally, the Bank is increasing support for gender through DPOs, even though OP 8.60 on DPOs does not explicitly refer to OP/BP 4.20. Many DPOs also now focus on areas where there can be no doubt about the relevance of gender-related policies and institutional arrangements for poverty reduction, notably sectors such as agriculture, health, education, water, and rural development. At the policy level, the first useful step would be to link OP 8.60 more explicitly with OP 4.20 to clarify the requirement that gender considerations be integrated into DPOs in sectors identified in CASs. A second step would be to monitor how the gender dimensions of Poverty and Social Impact Analysis are being integrated into DPOs and to acquire a better understanding of the implications of not integrating gender into such DPOs.

Implementation of the Bank's Gender Policy

Measurable progress in gender integration was made between the early 1990s and the early 2000s across all major areas of Bank operations. A large majority of CASs prepared between fiscal 2002 and 2008 discussed gender issues, but fewer than half of those shifted to an approach that focused on strategic outcomes to support gender equality. Meanwhile, the Bank's agenda at the project level has widened, with gender better addressed in important thematic areas such as access to justice and land management than during the period covered in the previous IEG evaluation (fiscal 1990–99). Additionally, more DPOs, particularly in the health and education sectors, now address gender issues.

There is, however, a concern regarding whether these gains are being sustained. The evaluation finds that there has been a clear decline since 2003 in gender integration both at the country and sector/project levels. Strategic mainstreaming at the country level is coming to a standstill, with a rapid decline in undertaking or updating CGAs and decreased meaningful attention in CASs.

Further, except in a minority of cases, the links between the CAS and integration at the project level are difficult to make. At the project level, although gender issues may be well institutionalized in the health and agriculture sectors, a decline has been evident even in the education sector over the past few years. And though the 2007 GAP may temporarily facilitate mainstreaming gender into projects in the preselected GAP sectors, it is unclear how this will be sustained when the GAP funding ends.

Nor does improvement in the Bank's performance mean that the 2001 Gender Strategy and the subsequent OP/BP were adequately institutionalized. Critical institutional elements identified by the 2001 Strategy for making the shift to a strategic approach were not realized. Incremental budgetary resources were not committed except in three of the eight years covered by this evaluation. Regions did not undertake CGAs as scheduled (despite the considerable flexibility built into the policy regarding methods). The monitoring system envisaged in the 2001 Strategy was not established, and accountabilities, although specified in the strategy, were not enforced.[1] The RGCs (occupying a pivotal position in the strategy) appear to spend less time on gender issues now, and the majority of country directors and sector managers have yet to assume the gender responsibilities as envisaged by the strategy.

The evaluation finds that the level of gender integration across the board reached its highest level around 2003–04 and the lowest in 2008 (although there has been some improvement in some infrastructure sectors, possibly as a result of the GAP).[2] The foundation of the gender policy is the comprehensive diagnosis of gender issues in the country; this identifies strategic interventions where gender disparities are recognized as inhibiting growth, poverty reduction, human well-being, and development effectiveness.

When gender diagnosis has not been undertaken, the country director (even where he or she wishes to integrate gender into the CAS) has little basis for a making a decision about the importance of gender issues for the country's program or on what the appropriate Bank response should be. Moreover, the ability to sustain attention to gender over time and the institutional memory required to do so are diminished when there is no documented foundation or traceable process for gender mainstreaming in country work. To maintain its country-level approach, the Bank needs to put this building block for gender-informed country strategies and programs firmly in place and monitor it as part of policy implementation.

Finally, there is a risk that the country-level approach will not be implemented, given the finding that CGAs—the principal means for its implementation as envisaged in the 2001 Strategy—are no longer being undertaken or updated and that fewer CASs are meaningfully addressing gender issues in the manner required. The links between CASs and gender integration in operations are also not evident. At the same time, at the project level, the requirement to examine gender issues at appraisal has been circumscribed, and the GAP is expected to end in 2010. It is unclear how results will be sustained and accountabilities established for gender integration into relevant operations once the funding stops.[3]

Results of Bank support

The contribution of Bank support to the desired strategic outcomes at the country level was notable in the majority of the 12 focus countries. About 42 percent of relevant projects delivered substantial results. In 4 of the 12 focus countries, Bank support contributed to substantial improvement in at least two of the three domains of gender equality. In other countries, either because of lower levels of results or lack of integration in several important sectors, the contribution of Bank support to gender equality or women's empowerment was more modest. Bank support was more successful in countries, where there was relatively greater demand for addressing gender concerns, such as Bangladesh and Ghana.

These results need to be understood in consideration with the length of time that is typically needed for improvement in gender inequalities. It takes longer than the eight years covered by this evaluation to achieve measurable gains in gender equality. In countries where markets have yet to fully evolve, where poverty is persistent, where women still spend long hours collecting water and fuel for domestic consumption, and where political movements for gender equality are still nascent, development interventions of short duration cannot by themselves generate the required outcomes. It is a slow process—and one that needs to be relentlessly pursued.

At the same time, the recent improvements in gender-related outcomes resulted from higher levels of gender mainstreaming in the early 2000s. In the past few years, however, gender mainstreaming has declined in Bank operations.[4] Unless this decline is reversed and mainstreaming restored to at least previous levels and sus-

Photo courtesy of Arne Hoel/World Bank.

tained, the Bank runs a high risk that future results will not be as positive as those obtained during this evaluation period.

Part of the reason for the lower efficacy of Bank support is the lack of sustained attention. The evolution of attention to education in Zambia illustrates a wider theme in the varying role of Bank investments and the changing attention to gender in several countries: an ambitiously conceived start is followed by imperfect implementation; then a new approach is introduced in which the modest gains of the previous stage are forgotten.

Furthermore, the evaluation found that, for the most part, the project, or the sector, was the most common entry point to address issues related to gender inequalities, particularly in the economic sectors. It was more uncommon to find top-down and "strategic" activities that supported governments' efforts to formulate gender-aware

policies, eliminate biases in legal and regulatory frameworks, strengthen institutions that support gender equality or women's empowerment, and encourage collection of gender-disaggregated data. A blend of both types of support is necessary to address gender inequalities in most countries with low CPIA 7 ratings.

Finally, a lack of consistent data to monitor progress in achieving gender-related objectives persists, reducing accountabilities for supporting gender equality, both in the Bank and in client countries. Even in an area such as maternal mortality, the lack of data is so pervasive that assessment becomes a challenging task.

Recommendations

The 2007 GAP, although highly relevant, needs to be anchored more clearly in the Bank's gender policy. The GAP was considered necessary because of the weak institutionalization of OP/BP 4.20. It was clear that the country-level "strategic mainstreaming" approach was not reliably leading to gender integration in sectors that are critical for gender. Thus, the GAP provided a necessary counter-measure to a hole that came from weak implementation of the country-level gender policy and a highly limited project-level entry point. It is essential, however, to ensure adequate policy underpinnings for the GAP, as well as a coherent strategy and approach, if the Bank is to achieve its gender-related goals and thereby catalyze poverty reduction.

Further, given the reality that virtually no development agency has successfully implemented a gender mainstreaming strategy (Norad 2005), a more selective approach may be worth considering. The evaluation finds that Bank support, even when it does not integrate gender considerations, generates better results in countries with stronger gender-aware institutions and policies. Thus, it may be practical to identify countries with higher levels of gender inequalities (as captured by the CPIA 7 criteria) and to address strategic issues at the country level while also integrating gender within and across relevant sectors at the project level. In countries with lower levels of gender inequalities, it may be more realistic and practical to allow gender integration as circumstances warrant—a selective integration strategy may be fully appropriate in such cases. A tracking and monitoring system should nevertheless be set up and operated to monitor integration across all countries.

Finally, Bank management commitment—especially at the country director and more senior levels—is critical to implementing the Bank's gender policy. Such commitment needs to be reflected in clear steps to institutionalize the gender policy consistently with the framework envisaged in the 2001 Gender Strategy. At the same time, IEG believes that, where appropriate, Bank staff must consider gender issues at appraisal and ensure as a minimum the obligations once enshrined in OMS 2.20—that both men and women should participate in project benefits, and that project design must mitigate to the extent possible any disadvantageous impact the project activities may have on men or women.

To ensure a better understanding of the gender policy and to ensure its effective implementation, the evaluation calls attention to several measures:

- Foster greater clarity and better implementation of the Bank's gender policy, notably by—

    - Establishing a results framework to facilitate consistent adoption of an outcome approach to gender integration in the Bank's work.

    - Establishing and implementing a realistic action plan for completing or updating country-level diagnostics, giving primacy to countries with higher levels of gender inequalities.

- Extend implementation of the 2007 GAP while formalizing and strengthening its policy basis. An alternative would be to reinstate and strengthen provisions along the lines of OMS 2.20 to restore a sector- and/or project-level entry point for gender.

    - Establish clear management accountability for the development and implementation of a system to monitor the extent to which Bank work adequately addresses gender-related concerns, including effective reporting mechanisms. The pivotal role of country directors needs to feature centrally in the accountability framework.

    - Strengthen the incentives for effective gender-related actions in client countries by continuing to provide incentive funding through the GAP to strengthen the collection, analysis, and dissemination of gender-disaggregated, gender-relevant data and statistics.

APPENDIX A

Evaluation Methodology

This appendix presents the detailed methodology for the different evaluation components.

I. Selection of Evaluation Countries

Selection of evaluation countries

Countries that have a population of more than a million people, that received more than two investment projects within the evaluation period, that had Gender-related Development Index (GDI) and Human Development Index (HDI) ratings in 2005, and that prepared a CAS or an equivalent document between fiscal 2002 and fiscal 2008 were selected. Attachment 1 to this appendix provides a list of the 93 countries; table A.5 lists the names of those countries that were excluded.

Selection of 12 countries for results examination

Of the 93 countries, 12 were selected via stratified weighted random sampling for assessing the results of Bank support (table A.1). This procedure was based on the GDI/HDI score and gender rating of the Independent Evaluation Group (IEG) as gleaned from the relevant Country Assistance Strategy (CAS) or Interim Strategy Note. GDI/HDI was chosen as a means of determining the level of gender performance because it was considered an appropriate national index for measuring gender dimensions of development outcomes. Although there are other national level indexes,[1] this one was thought to be best suited for this evaluation because of its focus on gender outcomes, especially in human development and income distribution.[2]

The GDI and HDI scores follow a 0–1 rating scale, where 0 corresponds to very low gender or human development and 1 to a very high gender or human development. HDI measures human development, whereas GDI is HDI adjusted for gender inequality, so that a country's HDI score is penalized if gender inequality is substantial. A ratio of GDI:HDI is a measure of the gender inequality or gender gap in a society. A GDI:HDI score close to 1 signifies a small gender gap, and a score close to 0 signifies a large gender gap. No prior indication existed as to what should be considered the cut-off point between high and low GDI:HDI scores separating countries with relatively weak gender performance from countries with relatively strong gender performance. Therefore, the evaluation used the simple GDI:HDI mean of 0.98 as the cut-off between countries with high versus low gender performance.[3]

The CAS gender rating was a simple "yes" or "no" given by IEG, indicating whether the CAS in question stated that the Bank would be providing specific gender-aware support to the country (rating "yes") or not (rating "no").

Based on the GDI:HDI score in 2005 and the IEG CAS gender rating, the 93 countries were divided into four mutually exclusive groups as follows:

- **Group 1 – Low, Yes:** GDI score of 0.98 or below and a CAS gender rating of "yes"

- **Group 2 – Low, No:** GDI score of 0.98 or below and a CAS gender rating of "no"

- **Group 3 – High, Yes:** GDI score of above 0.98 and a CAS gender rating of "yes"

- **Group 4 – High, No:** GDI score of above 0.98 and a CAS gender rating of "no."

The evaluation then selected countries from groups 1–3. It was concluded that improving gender performance was not a priority in those countries in Group 4, and hence the Bank's input would not need to be studied in depth there. IEG selected 12 countries made from groups 1 and 3 by means of stratification. This was based on the share of countries that fell into each group. For instance, if 25 percent of the countries had fallen into Group 1 and 75 percent into Group 3, IEG would have drawn 3 countries from Group 1 and 9 from Group 3, making the desired total of 12. Shares were rounded off to the nearest whole number.

TABLE A.1	Countries Selected
	Bangladesh
	Benin
	Colombia
	Ghana
	Lebanon
	Nigeria
	Peru
	Philippines
	Tajikistan
	Turkey
	Yemen, Rep. of
	Zambia

II. Assessment of Country Gender Assessments

County Gender Assessments (CGAs) were scored (1–4) across four indicators noted in figure 4.1 of the main report. A final score (1–16) was derived by adding the individual indicator scores. The list of CGAs assessed is provided in table A.2. CGAs that fell between 10 and 16 were considered "high" and "substantial" quality, and those below 10 were considered to be of "modest" or "low" quality (table A.2).

III. Rapid Assessment of 74 Poverty Assessments

A rapid assessment of 74 Poverty Assessments, prepared between fiscal 2001 and 2008 in the 93 evaluation countries, was undertaken. The sole objective was to gain an understanding of whether Poverty Assessments could have constituted as CGAs in countries where there were no CGAs. Each Poverty Assessment was assessed using the following criteria:

- Scope and quality of diagnosis (clear analysis backed by data) of gender issues

- Discussion of monitoring indicators to assess gender issues in the sector

- Gender aware recommendations.

IV. Assessment of CASs

For the 93 countries, IEG reviewed 140 country strategy documents[4] (plus two for Afghanistan) prepared between fiscal 2002 and 2008. The criteria are provided in figure 4.3 of the main report.[5]

V. Methodology for Sector/Project-Level Analysis

All investment projects approved between fiscal 2002 and 2008 in the 93 countries were selected from a Bank data-

base. Economic Recovery Loans, supplementaries, and additional financing documents were removed, and Project Appraisal Documents (PADs) were not available for six projects. This left 1,183 projects for which PADs were available (tables A.3 and A.4).

Given the more selective gender strategy of the Bank, the evaluation first examined whether gender was relevant based on a review of project objectives and the components. Based on this review, the evaluation excluded 293 projects for which gender was considered of low relevance. These were projects that were likely to benefit both men and women and did not involve involuntary resettlement or affect indigenous peoples.

The criteria for assessment are mentioned in figure 4.6 of the report. Each criterion was rated on a scale of 1–4 and projects receiving a composite rating of 15–16 were rated "high"; projects with 9–14 were rated "substantial"; projects with 8 or 7 were rated "modest," and projects with 4–6 were rated "low." Thus, a project received an overall substantial rating even if it had modest analysis and no consultation, as long as it had at least a single measure to address the identified issue and included at least one relevant monitoring indicator.

VI. Methodology for Results Assessment in Peru

The Peru study began with a review of the PAD for all 14 Bank-financed projects that closed between 2002 and 2008. This review identified three projects with defined gender strategies and five projects likely to have different impacts on men and women but with no defined gender strategy. The objectives of the other six projects were considered too broad to make worthwhile case studies.[6] From the eight possible projects, two were selected that had clearly spelled-out gender objectives and defined strategies for achieving these objectives (the Sierra Natural Resource Management and Poverty Reduction Project and the Second Rural Roads Project), and one project was selected that had targets for the participation of women but no defined strategy for achieving these targets (the Urban Property Rights Project). Each case study then described the project, its approaches to gender, how gender issues were addressed during implementation, and the gender-related impacts. These impacts concerned women's access to economic opportunities, access to services (such as transport, water, education, and health), and participation and voice.

IEG assessed the Bank's contribution to achieving gender objectives, as well as the question of what difference the existence of gender objectives and a gender strategy actually makes to gender and development and to the empowerment of women.

TABLE A.2 CGAs Assessed

Country	Type of report	Region	Fiscal year
Albania	Labor Assessment/Poverty Assessment	Europe and Central Asia	2003
Algeria	CGA	Middle East and North Africa	2002
Bangladesh	CGA	South Asia	2007
Benin	Draft CGA	Sub-Saharan Africa	2002
Bosnia	Gender Review	Europe and Central Asia	2003
Brazil	Gender Review	Latin America and the Caribbean	2002
Bulgaria	Draft CGA	Europe and Central Asia	2003
Burkina Faso	CGA	Sub-Saharan Africa	2003
Cambodia	CGA	East Asia and Pacific	2004
Chile	CGA	Latin America and the Caribbean	2007[a]
China	Gender Review	East Asia and Pacific	2006
Colombia	Gender Review	Latin America and the Caribbean	2003
Costa Rica	Regional	Latin America and the Caribbean	2002
Dominican Republic	Regional Draft	Latin America and the Caribbean	2002
Ecuador	Gender Review	Latin America and the Caribbean	2004
Egypt	CGA	Middle East and North Africa	2003
El Salvador	Regional	Latin America and the Caribbean	2002
Ethiopia	Draft CGA	Sub-Saharan Africa	2005
Ghana	Draft CGA	Sub-Saharan Africa	2002
Guatemala	Regional	Latin America and the Caribbean	2003
Guinea	CGA	Sub-Saharan Africa	2003
Haiti	Regional Draft	Latin America and the Caribbean	2002
Honduras	Regional	Latin America and the Caribbean	2002
Indonesia	CGA	East Asia and Pacific	2006[a]
Jamaica	Regional Draft	Latin America and the Caribbean	2002
Jordan	CGA	Middle East and North Africa	2005
Kenya	CGA	Sub-Saharan Africa	2003
Lao PDR	Country CGA	East Asia and Pacific	2005
Malawi	CGA	Sub-Saharan Africa	2003
Mali	Draft CGA	Sub-Saharan Africa	2006
Mauritania	CGA	Sub-Saharan Africa	2007
Mongolia	CGA	South Asia	2005
Mozambique	CGA	Sub-Saharan Africa	2006
Nepal	CGA	South Asia	2006
Nicaragua	Regional	Latin America and the Caribbean	2002
Nigeria	CGA	Sub-Saharan Africa	2004
Pakistan	CGA	South Asia	2005
Panama	Regional	Latin America and the Caribbean	2002
Paraguay	Draft Gender Review	Latin America and the Caribbean	2003
Poland	CGA	Europe and Central Asia	2004
Russia	Gender Profile	Europe and Central Asia	2004
Senegal	Draft CGA	Sub-Saharan Africa	2006
Tajikistan	Draft CGA	Europe and Central Asia	2005
Tanzania	CGA	Sub-Saharan Africa	2004
Turkey	CGA	Europe and Central Asia	2004
Uganda	CGA	Sub-Saharan Africa	2005
Ukraine	Gender Review	Europe and Central Asia	2002
Vietnam	CGA	East Asia and Pacific	2006[a]
Yemen, Rep. of	Gender Note	Middle East and North Africa	2002
Zambia	CGA	Sub-Saharan Africa	2004

Source: IEG.

Note: CGA = Country Gender Assessment.

a. Indicates existence of a prior CGA also reviewed.

TABLE A.3	Sector-Wise Allocation of 1,183 Projects
Sector	US$ commitments
Agriculture and Rural Development	13,018
Economic Policy	278
Education	9,006
Energy and Mining	9,818
Environment	961
Financial and Private Sector Development	5,412
Financial Management	11
Global Information/Communications Technology	178
Health, Nutrition, and Population	6,932
Procurement	24
Public Sector Governance	3,989
Social Development	1,528
Social Protection	4,001
Transport	19,324
Urban Development	6,472
Water	6,904
Total	87,856

Source: World Bank.

Sample design and data collection instruments

Each case study covered the following groups: project beneficiaries (interviewed individually and in groups); similar communities not affected by the projects; project implementing agencies; consultants involved in different components of the project (for example, gender training or the management of the economic development programs); other international agencies familiar with the projects; women's organizations; and the Ministry of Women and Social Development.

As some of the projects were designed more than a decade ago and all had been closed for several years, locating officials who had been involved during the different project stages presented a major challenge, as did ensuring reliable recall after so many years.[7] Triangulation was therefore used to obtain and compare information from different sources (for example, data from interviews with different officials was compared with details given in project documents). A time line was developed for each project, on which information was placed from different respondents in the correct chronological order.[8]

Data collection had to be completed for all three projects in three widely dispersed regions in just two and a half weeks. Consequently, the sample sizes were relatively small. Across the three projects, the following numbers of interviews were conducted in total:

- 12 focus groups with project beneficiaries (a total of 75–100 respondents)

- 36 individual interviews with project beneficiaries

- 3 focus groups with nonbeneficiaries (a total of 15–20 respondents)

- 7 individual interviews with nonbeneficiaries

- 23 interviews with representatives of implementing agencies

- 13 interviews with directors of implementing agencies and their respective ministries

- 8 interviews with international agencies, women's organizations, consultants, and nongovernmental organizations.

The two main data collection instruments were focus groups (with beneficiaries and similar communities that did not have access to project services and benefits) and in-depth individual interviews with implementing agencies and other nonbeneficiary groups.

Given the time and data constraints of the evaluation and the fact that it was conducted up to five years after the completion of the projects, it was not possible to use quasi-experimental evaluation designs, which might have been preferable. In these, changes in the conditions of project populations would have been compared with changes in matched comparison groups. Consequently, the assessments of the contribution of the projects to the observed changes in beneficiary populations were obtained by drawing on the impact evaluations that had been commissioned by the Bank toward the end of the projects or after their completion, and comparing these estimates with the opinions of the stakeholders and beneficiaries interviewed during this eval-

TABLE A.4	Commitments Evaluated				
	Number of investment projects	%	Amount of commitment (US$ million)	%
Approved investment loans for 93 countries, fiscal 2002–08	1,417		97,199	
(Additional Financing and Supplementaries)	(166)		(5,199)	
(Emergency Loans)	(68)		(4,144)	
Number of projects	1,183	83.5	87,856	90.4

Source: World Bank.

uation. No similar studies were available for use in assessing the contribution of the Bank to the observed changes.

Consequently, this assessment was based on the interviews conducted with implementing agencies and other stakeholders, combined with information available in the relevant PADs, Implementation Completion and Results Reports, and other project documents.

VII. Methodology for Results Assessment in Zambia

The Zambia study began with a review of a total of 49 Bank operations, of which two were Institutional Development Fund grants; 36 of the operations had closed, comprising 21 investment projects, 13 policy operations, and 2 Institutional Development Fund grants. The PADs were reviewed for 13 active operations (1 Development Policy Operation and 12 investment projects) for the extent to which gender was addressed in the preparatory documents. Of the sample of Bank projects, three closed projects were selected for more intensive examination because of their explicit concern with gender. These three projects were the Zambian Social Investment Fund; the Technical Educational, Vocational and Entrepreneurship Training; and the Drought Recovery Project.

Programmatic documents reviewed include three CASs (World Bank 1999b, 2004g, 2008n); a Country Assistance Evaluation (IEG 2002), and a Country Gender Assessment (World Bank 2004h), as well as two Poverty Reduction Strategy Papers (World Bank 2000b, 2007i), which are in effect the multiyear National Development Plans.

Sample design and data collection instruments

The methodology was openly qualitative, resources being insufficient to support a quantitative survey. It is in essence a meta-evaluation, supported by a small field ground-validating exercise. Brief field investigations were conducted in three localities, two rural and one urban, to supplement information obtained from informants and documentary analysis. Interviews were held with key local project implementers and with beneficiaries.

An attempt was also made to identify and interview beneficiaries of the drought relief program. Individuals or groups

TABLE A.5	Excluded Countries
	Czech Republic
	Equatorial Guinea
	Estonia
	Fiji
	Gabon
	Hungary
	Korea (Republic of)
	Malaysia
	Montenegro
	Namibia
	Serbia
	Seychelles
	Slovenia
	South Africa
	Sudan
	Swaziland
	Syrian Arab Republic
	Thailand
	Togo
	Turkmenistan
	Zimbabwe

Source: IEG.

of beneficiaries gave semistructured interviews; a more freeform approach was used for key informants, starting with the narrative of project execution and leading to issues of gender-specific economic and social outcomes, particularly relating to women's economic empowerment and decision making.

The broader cohort of operations was subjected to a more generic analysis of key documents: PADs (SARs) and program documents, Implementation Completion and Results Reports, and, where available, Project Performance Assessment Reports.

For the country context, a comparative content analysis of gender was done for the CASs and portfolio reviews. These findings were then related to the evolving context over the last 10 years and to the gender approaches of government planners, of some of the key cooperating partners, and of a few Bank and project staff and civil society organizations.

Country	Region	Gender-related development index	Country	Region	Gender-related development index
Angola	AFR	0.439	Albania	ECA	0.797
Benin	AFR	0.422	Armenia	ECA	0.772
Burkina Faso	AFR	0.364	Azerbaijan	ECA	0.743
Burundi	AFR	0.409	Belarus	ECA	0.803
Cameroon	AFR	0.524	Bulgaria	ECA	0.823
Central African Rep.	AFR	0.368	Bosnia and Herzegovina	ECA	...
Chad	AFR	0.37	Croatia	ECA	0.848
Congo	AFR	0.54	Georgia	ECA	...
Congo, Dem. Rep. of	AFR	0.398	Kazakhstan	ECA	0.792
Côte d'Ivoire	AFR	0.413	Kyrgyz Rep.	ECA	0.692
Eritrea	AFR	0.469	Latvia	ECA	0.853
Ethiopia	AFR	0.393	Lithuania	ECA	0.861
Gambia	AFR	0.496	Macedonia	ECA	0.795
Ghana	AFR	0.549	Moldova	ECA	0.704
Guinea	AFR	0.446	Poland	ECA	0.867
Kenya	AFR	0.521	Romania	ECA	0.812
Lesotho	AFR	0.541	Russian Federation	ECA	0.801
Madagascar	AFR	0.53	Slovak Rep.	ECA	0.86
Malawi	AFR	0.432	Tajikistan	ECA	0.669
Mali	AFR	0.371	Turkey	ECA	0.763
Mauritania	AFR	0.543	Ukraine	ECA	0.785
Mauritius	AFR	0.796	Uzbekistan	ECA	0.699
Mozambique	AFR	0.373	Argentina	LCR	0.865
Niger	AFR	0.355	Bolivia	LCR	0.691
Nigeria	AFR	0.456	Brazil	LCR	0.798
Rwanda	AFR	0.45	Chile	LCR	0.859
Senegal	AFR	0.492	Colombia	LCR	0.789
Sierra Leone	AFR	0.32	Costa Rica	LCR	0.842
Tanzania	AFR	0.464	Dominican Rep.	LCR	0.773
Uganda	AFR	0.501	Ecuador	LCR	0.716
Zambia	AFR	0.425	El Salvador	LCR	0.726
Cambodia	EAP	0.594	Guatemala	LCR	0.675
China	EAP	0.776	Haiti	LCR	0.462
Indonesia	EAP	0.721	Honduras	LCR	0.694
Lao People's DR	EAP	0.593	Jamaica	LCR	0.732
Mongolia	EAP	0.695	Mexico	LCR	0.82
Viet Nam	EAP	0.732	Nicaragua	LCR	0.696
Papua New Guinea	EAP	0.529	Panama	LCR	0.81
Philippines	EAP	0.768	Lebanon	MNA	0.759
Paraguay	LCR	0.744	Morocco	MNA	0.621
Peru	LCR	0.769	Tunisia	MNA	0.75
Uruguay	LCR	0.849	Yemen, Rep. of	MNA	0.472
Venezuela, R. B. de	LCR	0.787	Bangladesh	SAR	0.539
Algeria	MNA	0.72	India	SAR	0.6
Egypt, Arab. Rep. of	MNA	0.634	Nepal	SAR	0.52
Jordan	MNA	0.76	Pakistan	SAR	0.525
			Sri Lanka	SAR	0.735

Source: IEG.

Note: ... = no index for the country for this year. AFR = Sub-Saharan Africa; EAP = East Asia and Pacific; ECA = Europe and Central Asia; LCR = Latin America and Caribbean; MNA = Middle East and North Africa; SAR = South Asia.

Summary Findings of Literature Review on Gender, Poverty Reduction, and Economic Growth

There are many channels or pathways through which gender equality, poverty reduction, and economic growth are linked (for reviews of these transmission mechanisms, see Klasen 2002; Morrison, Raju, and Sinha 2007). For purposes of this appendix, four critical and interconnected pathways are considered, through which gender differences relevant for growth and poverty reduction are manifested: (i) human capital; (ii) employment and entrepreneurship; (iii) access to productive assets and resources; and (iv) legal status, rights, and voice.

Gender-based differences in each of these areas have a profound effect on economic opportunities for men and women, the productivity of men's and women's labor, the performance and potential of their businesses, and the incentives facing men and women as economic agents. These in turn affect the nature, pace, and impact of economic growth and poverty reduction. This appendix briefly reviews the evidence in each of these areas.

Human Capital: Building Economic Capability

Many studies find that gender-based inequalities in education reduce economic growth, because such inequalities decrease the overall human capital available within the country. Notwithstanding the methodological limitations alluded to earlier, Morrison, Raju, and Sinha (2007) report striking findings from work undertaken by Klasen (2002). Klasen estimates the effect of the gender gap in years of total schooling in the adult population on per capita income growth, using cross-country and panel regressions for the 1960–92 period for 109 industrial and developing countries. He finds that the direct and indirect effects of gender inequality in educational attainment account for 0.95 percentage points of the 2.5 percentage point gap in growth rates between South Asia and East Asia; 0.56 percentage points of the 3.3 percentage point gap between Sub-Saharan Africa and East Asia; and 0.85 percentage points of the 1.9 percentage point gap between the Middle East and North Africa and East Asia.

Many studies demonstrate the positive externalities of educating women and the important intergenerational effects of female education. Educated women contribute to the welfare of the next generation by reducing infant mortality, lowering fertility, and improving the nutritional status of children (World Bank 2005h, 2001a; Lagerlöf 2003; Klasen 1999; Smith and Haddad 1999).

Country studies confirm significant effects on health and educational outcomes. In India, children of literate mothers spend two hours more per day studying than children of illiterate mothers (Behrman and others 1999). In Guatemala and Nigeria, educated mothers are more likely to adopt health-seeking behaviors such as immunization (Pebley, Goldman, and Rodriguez 1996; Gage, Sommerfelt, and Piani 1997). In Brazil, income received by mothers has four times the impact on stunting indicators of children than the same amount received by fathers (Thomas 1990). Within the household, more educated women have a stronger bargaining position, which in turn contributes to better intrahousehold resource allocation. The long-term impact on adolescent girls is striking (box B.1).

Employment and Entrepreneurship: Building Economic Opportunity

Women's participation in the labor force has progressed over the years, and women are now estimated to comprise around 40 percent of the global labor force. Yet women still predominate in the informal sector (ILO 2002), and, despite improvements in education, women still earn less than men. Estimates of wage differences show marked Regional variations: in the Middle East and North Africa, women earn 93 percent of men's wages; in Sub-Saharan

LONG-TERM EFFECTS OF FEMALE EDUCATION

The education of girls provides one strong test of a government's commitment to equality of opportunity. Many obstacles stop girls from completing their schooling: family financial pressure, lack of safety, even things as basic as inadequate toilet facilities. But if these obstacles can be overcome, the payoff is very high. Educated women have fewer, healthier children, and they have them at older ages. Their children are then more successful in school, largely because they benefit from their mother's education. Educating girls and integrating them into the labor force is thus one way to break an intergenerational cycle of poverty.

Source: Commission on Growth and Development (2008).

Africa, 87 percent; in Latin America and the Caribbean, 78 percent; in Europe, 76 percent; and in high-income Asian countries, 74 percent (Tzannatos 2008; Buvinic and others 2008). There is also some evidence (although less robust at this stage) that, as is the case for education disparities, gender inequality in employment similarly reduces economic growth (for example, Klasen 1999; Klasen and Lamanna 2003).

Higher female labor force participation can be seen to have a positive impact on income growth. Recent microsimulations for eight countries in Latin America addressed dimensions of gender inequality in relation to four specific labor market issues: entry into the labor market; occupational status of men and women; wage discrimination between men and women; and differences in characteristic endowments of men and women. These simulations confirmed that removing gender inequality in labor market participation would lead to a significant reduction in poverty, growth in income, and decline in inequality. This is especially relevant in the countries concerned, as there is a marked gender gap in labor force participation; the average female participation rate is about 56 percent, whereas the male rate is greater than 80 percent (Costa, Silva, and Vaz 2009).

In the Middle East and North Africa, higher female labor force participation rates in the 1990s are estimated to have increased per capita gross domestic product growth rates by 0.7 percent (Klasen and Lamanna 2003). Analysis in India (Esteve-Volart 2004; Besley, Burgess, and Esteve-Volart 2005) indicates that a 10 percent increase in the female-to-male ratio of managers would increase real output per capita by 2 percent, and a 10 percent increase in the female-to-male ratio of total workers would increase real output per capita by 8 percent. The study by Besley, Burgess, and Esteve-Volart concludes that gender inequality in the access to labor markets acts as a brake on development. Moreover, the efficiency costs of such inequality are large.

It is important to bear in mind, however, that these relationships are not always one sided or universally positive. Country circumstances and institutions matter. For example, views on the impact of gender pay gaps on economic performance are mixed, with some studies suggesting that high gender inequality in wages, coupled with low gender gaps in education and employment, were a contributing factor to the growth experience of middle-income exporting countries. A study by Galor and Weil (1996) suggests that large gender pay gaps will reduce economic growth. Such pay gaps reduce female employment, increase fertility, and lower economic growth.

In contrast, Blecker and Seguino (2002) highlight a different mechanism, leading to contrasting results. They suggest that high gender pay gaps and associated low female wages increase the competitiveness of export-oriented industrializing economies and thus boost the growth performance of these countries.

Again, as with education, women's greater labor force participation has important intrahousehold and intergenerational effects. For example, the development of the garment industry in Bangladesh has increased women's access to a lucrative labor market and expanded their ability to influence household choices. A comparative study of the Philippines, Indonesia (Sumatra), and Ghana shows that changes in labor market opportunities for women can influence increasing equality in patterns of land inheritance and investments in schooling.

An increasing share of cash income in women's hands is also shown to increase household food expenditure, controlling for average per capita expenditure, household expenditure and demographic characteristics, resulting in better nutrition and child health (Hoddinott and Haddad 1994). Thomas, Beegle, and Frankenberg (2003) have shown that greater incomes of mothers can have up to 20 times the effect on the nutritional status of children than if the same income increment goes to fathers.

The importance of women's entrepreneurship, and of women in the corporate sector, is increasingly recognized. Women own between 13 and 38 percent of enterprises worldwide. In China, it is estimated that women own one-third of all small and medium-sized businesses, with more than one in five employing more than 1,000 workers. In Latin America, among both microenterprises and small and medium-sized enterprises, between one-quarter and one-third are women-owned. In Egypt, Jordan, Saudi Arabia, and the West Bank and Gaza, the share of female-owned firms that have recently increased their workforce exceeds the share of male-owned firms, and fewer female-owned firms have decreased their workforce. Women's entrepreneurship is increasingly recognized as an important untapped source of economic growth. Women's businesses in Africa make an important contribution to growth and poverty reduction (box B.2).

There appear to be positive correlations between women's representation on corporate boards and corporate performance, suggesting that women are both good business and good for business. In 2000, women made up only 12.5 percent of corporate officers, 4.1 percent of top earners, and 6.2 percent of top managers. But those organizations with the most women in top managerial positions are far more likely to see a strong return on investment for shareholders. Fortune 500 companies with the highest percentages of women corporate officers yielded, on average 35.1 percent higher return on equity and 34 percent higher total return to shareholders than those with the lowest percentages of women corporate officers. Again, it is important to stress that these links do not imply that there is a causal relationship between women's presence on boards and in management and company performance. However, as a recent study of Fortune 500 companies concludes, they do "give us a factual snapshot that can only argue in favor of greater gender diversity" (McKinsey and Company 2007).

Access to Assets and Resources: Building Economic Security

There is empirical evidence that women have less ownership of economic resources and assets and several studies suggest that enhanced access to such assets and resources lead to increased productivity of women. Increased equality in access to economic assets is shown to raise the productivity of female producers (Blackden and Bhanu 1999; World Bank 2002e, 2001a; Bamberger and others 2002). This in turn helps improve household welfare through better bargaining power (World Bank 2006g; Doss 1996).

A global study of land policy addresses women's land rights (World Bank 2003c). The study concludes that increasing women's control over land could have a strong and immediate effect on the welfare of the next generation and on the level and pace at which physical and human capital are accumulated. Given the significant participation of women in agricultural production in Africa, gender differences in security of tenure—and access to inputs and technology—are likely to account for much of the poor performance of the sector.

For example, in Ghana, the greater precariousness of women's land rights has direct implications for productivity and yields (box B.3). In Latin America, a study showed that the gender inequality in land ownership in 12 countries is the combined results of biases: male preference in inheritance, male privilege in marriage, male bias in state programs of land distribution, and gender inequality in the land market (Deere and Leon 2001). Analysis of country-level data from Honduras and Nicaragua suggests a positive correlation between women's land rights and their overall role in the household economy: women gain greater control over agricultural income, gain higher shares of business and labor market earnings, and more frequently receive credit (Katz and Chamorro 2003).

There is growing empirical evidence that although there are forms of structural discrimination against women in relation to access to credit networks (Mayoux 2001), women borrowers have a lower risk of default because there is a lower prevalence of corruption and bribes among women's

---

BOX B.2

GENDER AND COMPETITIVENESS IN AFRICA

Women's businesses in Africa are at least as productive as those of their male counterparts. Once men and women entrepreneurs are operating their businesses, the constraints and obstacles they face affect them in largely the same way, and differences based on gender tend to disappear.

The absence of significant gender-based barriers in operating a business does not mean that there are no gender-based obstacles to entrepreneurship. It is very likely that barriers to entry into business present greater obstacles for women than for men. Consequently, measures aimed at facilitating entry into entrepreneurship through legal, regulatory, and other reforms are likely to have a more positive impact on women entrepreneurs.

The finding that there are no or few significant differences between female and male entrepreneurs once they are already operating businesses is encouraging. It suggests, for example, that Africa does indeed have considerable hidden growth potential in its women and that tapping that potential, including through removal of barriers that exist at entry and removing disparities in access to and control of resources by empowering women economically, can make a substantial difference for Africa's growth and poverty reduction

Source: Bardasi, Blackden, and Guzman (2007).

WOMEN AND LAND: PRECARIOUS RIGHTS, LOWER YIELDS

Complex, multiple, and overlapping rights to land in Akwapim, Ghana, are, according to a recent study, associated with barriers to investment in land fertility. Individuals who are not central in the networks of social and political power that permeate these villages cannot be confident of maintaining their rights over land while it is fallow. Hence, they fallow their land less than would be technically optimal, and farm productivity for these individuals is correspondingly reduced.

There is a strong gender dimension to this pattern, because women are rarely in positions of sufficient political power to be confident of their rights to land. So women fallow their plots less than their husbands and achieve much lower yields

Source: Goldstein and Udry (2008).

groups (Swamy and others 2001) and higher repayment rates among women borrowers (Khandker, Kahn, and Baqui 1995). Such findings have strengthened demands for gender-based policies to ensure that women have a greater possibility of accessing economic opportunities. Consequently, there has been a rapid expansion of microcredit schemes for women and this has now become a preferred form of gender-based intervention. There is some evidence that increased access to resources such as microcredit allows women to gain direct access to raw materials and other resources allowing them some chance for their households to rise above poverty (Khandker, Koolwal, and Sinha 2008).

Legal Rights and Voice: Building Economic Empowerment

Little appears in the governance literature that is deliberately gender disaggregated, and women seem to get lumped with the poor or those who are more generally "subordinate" (Goetz 2004). This needs to be corrected, because the significance is clear: power and authority differentials between women and men are not restricted to the private sphere of the family and kinship network but also play out in the public sphere, in the process shaping the form of governance that prevails.

The gender literature is of greater use. Much of it dwells on the question of the extent to which the public world of governance could provide an answer to women's inferior position in the domestic sphere. Very often it seems to be assumed that the local arena of governance is better suited to female participation than regional and national levels (Evertzen 2001). However, if this were true, there would be more women engaged in local governance than national level politics, something that Mukhopadhyay (2005) stresses is not the case anywhere outside Latin America. Moreover, as Beall, Mkhize, and Vawda (2004) show in the South African context, rather than being a political apprenticeship arena for women (Evertzen 2001), local government is often more

hierarchical and embedded in local social structures than national government, making it harder for women to penetrate as independent political actors, let alone raise gender issues.

Though the terms of local participation are often not stacked in women's favor, depending on the country context, various institutional innovations are possible that facilitate more equitable gender participation in governance and involve planning and monitoring functions that are more accountable to both genders' interests. Goetz (2004), for example, discusses the establishment of rules to secure institutionalized spaces for women's participation in planning, monitoring, auditing, and reviewing expenditures, ring fencing portions of budgets for women-only deliberations, and conducting gender-sensitive revenue and spending analyses.

There is empirical evidence that encouraging the participation of women in community activities can lead to empowerment of women and their increased presence in community affairs and activities. Deininger, Galab, and Olsen (2005) found in Andhra Pradesh that women's involvement in community-driven development led to improvements in women's participation that seem to transcend the realm of the family and extend to the community level. The change in the share of women who always know of or participate in village assemblies, who are aware of other types of community institutions, and who are able to freely interact with government officials and villagers of another caste or religion is significantly higher in intervention than in control villages.

The 2006 World Development Report (World Bank 2006g) also confirms that countries with more secure property rights have higher average incomes and that better institutions and secure property rights are associated with greater political equality. However, as pointed out by Morrison, Raju, and Sinha (2007), although these gender-based obstacles have been well documented, little work has been done to address the impact of these obstacles on productivity and output.

Econometric Analysis

This appendix presents an econometric analysis undertaken to explore (i) the link between CGA and the integration of gender issues in subsequent CASs, and (ii) the extent of gender integration in Bank's investment lending operations over time and across Regions and sectors.

The analysis finds that the CASs preceded by CGAs are more likely to be better gender integrated, and there is decline in the level of gender integration in projects during fiscal 2007 and fiscal 2008.

Gender Integration in CAS

Data and regression specification

The data cover 140 CASs approved between fiscal 2002 and 2008. The dependent variable is the level of gender integration in the CASs as assessed by the evaluation team. For the econometric analysis, the four-point rating scale used to rate the CASs is converted to a two-point scale by combining high and substantial ratings into one category and modest and low ratings into another.

The reduced-form specification is motivated by the 2001 Gender Strategy, which viewed CGA as the principal means through which gender-responsive policies and actions are integrated into country dialogue and the country assistance program. So the main explanatory variable of interest is the presence of CGA prior to the CAS.

One of the most plausible determinants of level of gender integration in CAS is the gender situation in the country. This has been controlled for by incorporating the Country Policy and Institutional Assessment (CPIA) ratings for gender and/or country-level gender outcome variables such as female adult literacy rate and female labor force participation rate. The income level of the country can also be a possible determinant. Accordingly, country income level dummies have been included in the specifications. The data analysis shows regional variations as well as a reduction in the level of gender integration in CASs in the post-fiscal 2005 period. Consequently, regional dummies as well as dummies for CASs approved after fiscal 2005 have been incorporated in the regression specifications. Moreover, correlations among explanatory variables also determined choice of explanatory variables as well as specifications to avoid multicollinearity problems.

Estimation methodology

The problem of estimating the effect of a CGA on the level of gender integration in the subsequent CAS is the possibility of a self-selection bias. The countries that had undertaken a CGA might have pressing gender concerns that would have been addressed in the CAS even in the absence of a CGA. In other words, the decision to undertake a CGA might not be random, in which case, treating CGA as a random variable will overestimate the effect of CGA on the level of gender integration in the subsequent CAS.

A probit model was used to examine the factors that might influence the decision of a country to undertake a CGA. However, of country gender CPIA ratings, income level, and gender outcome variables such as female literacy rate, access to potable water, and female labor force participation rate, none could predict the probability of undertaking a CGA. So the decision to undertake a CGA is either random (in which case a probit would be justified) or driven entirely by unobserved variables (in which case a probit would overestimate the effect). For example, the degree of gender awareness of country teams might influence the decisions to undertake a CGA as well as integrating gender into CAS. Subject to the presence of such unobserved factors, the results (reported in table C.1) should be treated with caution.

Results

- Countries with CGAs are more likely to have better gender-integrated CASs.

- Countries with lower levels of female literacy are also more likely to have higher levels of gender integration in CASs.

- CASs undertaken during fiscal 2007 and fiscal 2008 are more likely to have a lower level of gender integration than CASs undertaken prior to fiscal 2006. However, the result is no longer significant once the presence of CGAs is controlled for. In other words, the fewer CGAs undertaken in the post-fiscal 2005 period could explain the lower level of gender integration in the CASs during this period. Similarly, Regional differences in gender integration in CASs—a lower level of integration in the Europe and Central Asia Region compared to other Regions—could be explained by higher female adult literacy rates.

- Lower-income countries and countries with low gender CPIA rating are more likely to have better gender-integrated CASs. However, this is not significant across specifications, possibly because their effects are captured by other variables.

Gender Integration in Projects

The purpose of this analysis is to examine the extent of gender integration in the Bank's investment projects over time and across Regions and sectors. In particular, the analysis addresses the following questions: (i) Is there any Regional and sectoral differences in project-level gender integration? (ii) Is there a decline in the levels of gender integration during the post-fiscal 2005 period?

Data and specification

The analysis has been conducted at the project level covering 890 investment loans approved between fiscal 2002 and fiscal 2008, which have been identified by the evaluation team as relevant for gender integration. The dependent variable is the level of gender integration in the projects as assessed by the evaluation team.

Like the CAS gender ratings, the four-point rating scale has been converted into a two-point scale. The explanatory variables of interest are the fiscal year dummies, the Regional dummies, and the sector board dummies. In addition, size of the loan, country CPIA gender ratings, dummies for income level of the countries, and country-level gender outcome variables such as adult female literacy rate and female labor force participation rate have been included as control variables. The specifications have been estimated using a probit model. The results are presented in table C.2.

Results

- There is a decline in the level of gender integration in projects during fiscal 2007 and 2008. Gender integration in projects approved in fiscal 2008 is more likely to be lower than projects approved in previous years.

- Projects in Europe and Central Asia Region and the Sub-Saharan Africa Region are more likely to have lower levels of gender integration.

- Compared with education sector board, projects in Health, Nutrition, and Population; Social Development;

TABLE C.1	Gender Integration in CAS—Probit Regressions					
	(1)	(2)	(3)	(4)	(5)	(6)
CGA dummy			0.59**	0.56**	0.57**	0.83***
CPIA rating	−0.48***	−0.24	−0.24	0.01		
Upper middle income		−0.15	−0.11	0.02	0.06	−0.10
Lower income		0.54**	0.49*	0.67*	0.34	0.01
Female literacy					−0.02**	−0.02***
Female labor participation					0.00	−0.01
Fiscal 2006	−0.48	−0.46	−0.24	−0.33	−0.28	
Fiscal 2007	−0.67**	−0.82**	−0.60	−0.60	−0.52	
Fiscal 2008	−0.81**	−0.85**	−0.58	−0.51	−0.57	
Sub-Saharan Africa				0.65	−0.05	
East Asia and Pacific				0.98**	0.54	
Latin America and the Caribbean				0.72*	0.50	
Middle East and North Africa				1.80***	1.18*	
South Asia				1.27*	0.67	
Constant	1.90***	0.81	0.53	−1.17	0.75	1.44**
No. of observations	140	140	140	140	131	131
LR Chi²	17.4	22.2	27.4	39.5	39.8	31.3
Prob>Chi²	0.00	0.00	0.00	0.00	0.00	0.00

Source: IEG.

Note: Marginal effects are available on request. *significant at 10% level; ** significant at 5% level; *** significant at 1% level.

TABLE C.2 Gender Integration in Projects—Probit Regressions

	(1)	(2)	(3)	(4)	(5)
CPIA rating	−0.20***	−0.25***	−0.22**	−0.19**	−0.10
Lower income	0.24**	0.28***	0.28**	0.29**	0.22
Upper middle income	−0.22	−0.27*	−0.20	−0.24*	−0.24
Female literacy					−0.01***
Female labor participation					0.00
Fiscal year					
2002	−0.18				
2004	−0.17				
2005	−0.10				
2006	−0.11	0.01	−0.02		
2007	−0.35**	−0.22	−0.20	−0.19	
2008	−0.42***	−0.26**	−0.37***	−0.37***	−0.36***
Loan Size		0.00	0.00		
ARD		0.40***	0.46***	0.45***	0.41***
FPD		−1.28**	−1.28***	−1.30**	−1.30***
GICT		0.69	0.64		
Sector					
Transport		−0.44**	−0.50***	−0.50**	−0.54***
Urban		−0.49**	−0.54***	−0.55**	−0.63***
Public Sector Governance		−0.37*	−0.38**	−0.40*	−0.27
Health, Nutrition, and Population		0.63***	0.66***	0.64**	0.70***
Social Protection		0.37*	0.55**	0.53**	0.59***
Water		−0.28	−0.34*	−0.36*	−0.39*
Environment		0.07	0.01		
Energy		−0.52**	−0.53**	−0.52**	−0.56**
Sustainable Development		0.99***	0.96***	0.95***	0.96***
Region					
Sub-Saharan Africa			0.62***	−0.25**	−0.59***
Latin America and the Caribbean			0.83***		
East Asia and Pacific			0.95***		
South Asia			0.82***		
Middle East and North Africa			0.56**	−0.29	−0.40*
Europe and Central Asia				−0.87***	−0.75***
Constant	0.99***	0.95***	0.25	1.03***	1.38***
No. of observations	890	890	890	890	841
LR Chi²	47.6	170.0	211.3	209.1	214.2
Prob > Chi²	0.00	0.00	0.00	0.00	0.00

Source: IEG.

*significant at 10% level; ** significant at 5% level; *** significant at 1% level.

Social Protection; and Agriculture and Rural Development are more likely to have higher levels of gender integration, whereas projects in Financial and Private Sector, Transport, Urban Development, Water, and Energy and Mining are more likely to have lower levels of gender integration.

- The level of gender integration in projects is more likely to be higher in lower-income countries. Similarly, countries with relatively lower CPIA gender ratings are more likely to have better gender-integrated projects. However, none of them is significant when female literacy rate and female labor force participation rate at the country level are controlled for. Countries with high adult female literacy rates are more likely to have lower level of gender integration in projects.

Inclusion and Women's Empowerment in Afghanistan

This special study of Afghanistan's ongoing gender mainstreaming was undertaken at the request of some members of the Committee on Development Effectiveness. Over the evaluation period (fiscal 2002–08), the World Bank has committed more than $1.4 billion for 33 development and emergency reconstruction projects and 2 budget support operations in Afghanistan. In Afghanistan, funds were channeled through a multidonor Trust Fund, making it different from any other project country.[1]

This evaluation assesses the result of closed projects that are relevant for the Bank's stated objectives in Afghanistan. Fourteen projects have closed, including education rehabilitation, emergency public works, reconstruction of infrastructure, emergency transport rehabilitation, and the first phase of a public administration project. Three budget support operations are also complete.

The new Afghan Constitution states that all citizens, men and women, have equal rights under the law. The country's National Development Framework 2002 stresses the need to pay special attention to women and girls by enhancing their capabilities and participation at all stages of reconstruction planning and development. It suggested that this will be accomplished partly through increased capacity building by the Ministry of Women's Affairs. Consistent with these broader government policies, the Bank's 2001 Transitional National Strategy for Afghanistan prioritizes greater diagnostics and analytic work, including a gender assessment completed in partnership with the United Nations Development Programme. The Transitional National Strategy primarily focuses on health and education reform—calling for projects to address nonformal education opportunities for poor and illiterate women, increased health facilities and access, increased employment opportunities, and increased capacities for women's nongovernmental organizations (see table D.1).

This assessment uses the same methodology and criteria as that used for the overall evaluation and is based entirely on a desk review. Although a lack of data (in comparison with other evaluation countries) made assessment of results difficult, the study did triangulate the findings using other available independent assessments (Norad 2005). Still, to disaggregate the results of Bank support is very difficult through this desk review.

Overall, the assessment finds that the strategy in Afghanistan was highly relevant and the country documents and projects integrated gender in a manner consistent with client priorities.[2] A gender assessment was identified as a necessary diagnostic, and although it was set to be delivered in 2003, it was not completed until 2006. The evaluation finds slow but clear improvement in all three domains (table D.1) in Afghanistan.

Lessons for Consideration

1. *Full integration of women at all project levels takes time but is vital.* Women are integrated across levels in the National Solidarity Project and have roles in community mobilization and awareness, Community Development Council (CDC) elections, and Council membership and participation. However, this was implemented over time, in an incremental manner, using culturally relevant strategies. For instance, although the initial voting policy did not require female participation, later versions called for women to vote, influencing gender and power dynamics within communities. In addition, these practices often "spilled over" to other local communities, spreading the interest of women to participate.

2. *Involving women in Afghanistan may be resource intensive but nevertheless needs to be encouraged.* Despite the necessity of retaining female staff to ensure women's effective participation in the National Solidarity Project, the higher costs associated with recruiting

TABLE D.1 Country-Level Objectives and Summary Results for Bank Support for Afghanistan

Objectives stated in 2002 and 2003 INS	Results
Enhanced human capital	
Education • Increase gross enrollment at the primary, secondary, and tertiary levels, with a focus on creating more equal opportunity for girls and women. • Improve literacy among young women • Provide technical and vocational training to vulnerable groups to enable their participation in the modern economy (Primary gross enrolment rate has been estimated most recently at 30 percent for girls)	*Improvement* • **Skills Development in Afghanistan (October 2008):** Although the gender gap has narrowed in the past few years, it is still large. Nearly twice as many boys are enrolled at the primary level. At the secondary level, this gap widens to about three times as many boys, as illustrated by the gender-parity ratio, which is the ratio of numbers of girls to numbers of boys at each level. • **National Emergency Employment Program for Rural Access (2008) ICR:** Enrolled students in 17 primary schools, 22 secondary schools, and 5 high schools connected by the sample roads increased by 36 percent during the post project period. Proportion of girls availing education facilities increased from 29 to 36 percent. **PRSP 2008:** School enrollments have more than quadrupled to over six million children, one-third of whom are girls. Female literacy 18 percent.
Health • Increase the number of female health workers • Reduce maternal mortality and fertility through expanding service delivery and increasing equity (starting point: estimated mortality rate of 16 (per 1,000 live births.) Almost half of all deaths among women of reproductive age are a result of pregnancy and childbirth—¾ of which were preventable. Trained health care provider attended fewer than 8 percent of deliveries countrywide (2002).	*Improvement* • **INS 2003:** Maternal mortality, at 1,700. • **Strengthening Health Activities for the Poor Project Paper (2009):** Maternal mortality is the second highest in the world; with a ratio of 1,600 maternal deaths per 100,000 live births, women's survival remains a top priority for the health sector. Data from a 2006 household survey of women in rural areas suggest that utilization of health services is improving but still far too low to put the country on track for reaching MDGs 4 and 5. • **National Emergency Employment Program for Rural Access (2008) ICR:** Rehabilitated sample rural roads provided better connectivity to 23 hospitals, and all villages located within a maximum distance of 7.5 km from these hospitals availed the improved access to health services. Outpatients availing the hospital facilities increased by 30 percent, women seeking prenatal care has gone up by 90 percent, and women seeking delivery care and services doubled during the postproject period. Ratio of women availing delivery services to prenatal services from these hospitals has gone up from 41 to 51 percent in the benefited villages. Increased access to female health care workers. The percentage of primary health care facilities with at least one female doctor, nurse or midwife has increased from 26 percent in 2004 to 81 percent in 2007.
Equal access to economic assets and opportunities	
Economic empowerment • Number of person-days of employment provided through public works programs (including number for women)	*Improvement* • **CGA (2006):** The Bank has approached gender and economic empowerment through greater involvement of women within agricultural and livestock sector—Afghanistan's leading production framework—as well as increased access to microcredit and lending programs. Although increases in employment for women were not at the level expected between the 2001 and 2003 strategies, by 2006 the strategy introduced a focus on strengthening women's roles as producers in the rural economy, particularly horticulture and livestock, job creation in industrial sectors and better infrastructure for women's employment (for example, transport, facilities and so forth) The CGA calls for programming in the form of access to training, credit facilities, and expanding marketing opportunities and greater support to businesswomen through access to credit, raw materials, training and markets. • **The Empowerment Program for Rural Access Project** (fiscal 2003–08) utilized innovative solutions such as the production of building materials from home or other socially acceptable locations to facilitate a cooperate and coordinative environment including women to build a respond to issues of gender, ethnicity, local poverty conditions, community dynamics and the institutional context.

(Table continues on the following page.)

Objectives Stated in 2002 and 2003 INS	Results
	• **National Emergency Employment Program for Rural Access (2008) ICR:** Options for women to participate in the workforce were promoted, using innovative solutions such as the production of building materials from home or other socially acceptable locations.
	• **Expanding Microfinance Outreach and Improving Sustainability Project (2007 Technical Annex):** Microfinance program reportedly reached 119,000 people, 85 percent of whom are women. A 2008 evaluation of the ongoing microcredit program in finds that "participation in microfinance has certainly brought a number of benefits to female clients including: better economic posturing than their peers who did not join the program and improved financial status including increased savings at a rate much higher than men." The project has had gender-relevant goals since its outset and will most likely see continued gains for women through its forward leaning approach. There are also three operationally sustainable management and finance plans. Additionally, all 15 plans cover 89 percent of their operational costs from income earned on their outstanding loan portfolios.
	• **INS 2006:** 8.8 million days of employment—of this 1–2 percent paid to women; National Emergency Employment Program, and microfinance programs reaching 119,000, people of whom 85 percent are women; the relatively short-term gains of this pillar have been realized.
	• **CGA (2006):** Currently, close to one-third of all teachers are female; women's labor force participation rates in Afghanistan are comparable to the rest of the Region at 35.8 percent.
Improved Voice of Women in Development Planning and Implementation	
Enhance women's voice through participation in community-driven development (fiscal 2003) • Gender assessment to be carried out through a participatory process • Encouraging women in community-driven development	*Improvement* • **INS 2006:** Gender assessment completed 2006 • **The National Security Program (NSP) additional financing paper (2009):** Revealed progress in "enabling a critical mass of women to become members of the decision-making bodies… provide them with valuable practical skills and experience." To date the program has seen the creation of 22,618 Community Development Councils. Three-and-a-half percent of all CDC representatives are women and 47 percent of women confirm their participation in decision making. Moreover, 21 percent of women are active in development activities outside the NSP. The participation of women in village life represents an important transformation in a society where women are largely absent from public fora. Eighty-nine percent of men and 77 percent of women rated CDCs as being the main decision-making bodies that address critical development needs. CDC representatives receive training in office bearer duties, book keeping, and accounting.
Public administration • Correct the gender imbalance and promote the role of women in civil service • Develop systems and processes for women in senior economic management • Support gender analysis and balance across government (21 percent of all government employees were women pre-2001)	*No evident improvement* • **Strengthening Institutions DPO (2009):** "Building on the 2005 gender assessment (National Reconstruction and Poverty Reduction—The Role of Women in Afghanistan's Future), the International Development Association will continue the dialogue on women in the civil service. Although civil service reforms such as the introduction of meritocracy are an opportunity to enhance the role of women in the government, realizing this opportunity requires targeted programs."

Source: IEG.

Note: CDC = Community Development Council; ICR = Implementation Completion and Results Report; INS = interim national strategy.

women (for example, *maharam* salaries and higher travel costs) may result in the reduction of female staff. Greater recruitment of women in selected localities provides a valuable model for communities and increases the potential for women's effective engagement in the CDCs. However, specific policies may be needed to ensure increased recruitment of female staff.

3. *Promoting women's empowerment without triggering a political and social backlash will necessitate dissemination of regional best practices, both in country in a culturally compatible manner, as well as within the Bank team.* However, early recognition of these challenges can allow for appropriate project design and response. Approaches would need to be flexible, sensitive to cultural norms, and reviewed as both male and female stakeholders become comfortable. The Emergency Education Quality Improvement Program, for example, facilitated gender-separate community meetings for each affected area to inform the local population about their rights under the project. The National Emergency Empowerment Program for Rural Access Project used innovative solutions such as the production of building materials from women's homes or other socially acceptable locations to facilitate women's participation. Forward-looking actions, such as capacity building and training for women, involved in local nongovernmental organizations but not the CDCs directly, and were implemented to inoculating new leadership.

Endnotes

Management Response

1. As a thematic issue, gender falls under several Bank policies, which should be read together for a comprehensive picture of the Bank's policy framework for gender. The gender policy (OP/BP 4.20), in conjunction with other policies (notably OP/BPs 8.60; 4.10, 4.12, 2.30, and 4.30), is also highly relevant to address gender equality and women's empowerment in operations.

2. These Agriculture and Rurual Development targets are, by the end of 2010, to raise above 50 percent: the share of rural projects in the Sub-Saharan Africa Region with gender-responsive design (at 43 percent in 2005); the share of rural projects in all Regions with gender-informed monitoring and evaluation (17 percent in 2005); and the share of land policy and administration projects in all Regions guided by gender analysis in design and in the support of regulatory reform (37 percent in 2005).

3. The share of loans in "economic sectors" (Agriculture and Rural Development, Economic Policy, Energy and Mining, Financial Management, Financial and Private Sector, Public Sector Governance, Transport, Urban Development, and Water) rose from 62.7 percent in 2006 to 64.6 percent in 2008.

Chapter 1

1. Three World Conferences of the International Women's Year were organized in Mexico (1975), Copenhagen (1980), and Nairobi (1985).

2. Noting that women are sometimes "a particularly important group of project participants and beneficiaries," the OMS called for several analyses during project appraisal. Specifically, it called for (i) examination of whether the project design adequately took account of local circumstances that impeded or encouraged the participation of women, (ii) assessment of the contribution that women could make to achieving the project's objectives and the changes the project would introduce that might be disadvantageous to women, and (iii) consideration of whether the implications for women were included in the provisions for monitoring the impact of the project.

3. Management notes that the World Bank OPs stated, "A system of OMSs and [Operational Policy Notes] was initiated in the 1970s; after 1987, they were consolidated into [Operational Directives]. All these statements included elements of policy, procedure, and guidance" (World Bank 1997).

4. Such strategic measures included supporting governments to do three things: (i) design gender-sensitive policies and programs to ensure that overall development efforts are directed to attain impacts that are equitably beneficial for both men and women; (ii) review and modify legal and regulatory frameworks to improve women's access to assets and services, and take institutional measures to ensure that legal changes are implemented in actual practice, with due regard to cultural sensitivity; and (iii) strengthen the database for, and train country officials in, gender analysis, particularly in countries with inadequate gender-disaggregated data.

5. IEG notes that the statements in chapter 4 of the 2001 Strategy (along with the minutes of the Bank Board's discussion of the Strategy paper and subsequent management actions) can be interpreted as reflecting an intent to update and strengthen the language of OMS 2.20 on Gender Issues in the appraisal of investment lending as part of the process of converting OMSs to OP/BP statements. In fact, the subsequent absorption of the gender provisions of OMS 2.20 into OP 4.20 can be viewed as having narrowed the Bank's gender policy applicable to investment projects, in a manner not explicitly foreshadowed in 2001. For the purposes of the evaluation, however, IEG accepts management's view that the strategy reflected an intent to shift to a country-level approach.

6. Management notes that the 2003 OP/BP 4.20 is consistent with the 2001 Strategy. The OP/BP's requirement for comprehensive analysis at the country level and selective integration into projects came directly from the strategy. Following the strategy, the Board's advice to management was to "revise the OP to reflect the Gender Strategy" and when this revision was completed and sent out for review, comments received from IEG in 2003 confirmed the alignment of the approach adopted in OP/BP 4.20 with the Gender Strategy.

7. IEG considers that the GAP takes a sector- or project-level approach to integrating gender considerations into operations. First, the reason the GAP was developed was the fact that gender was not being integrated into operations in the economic sectors. Second, Action 1 of the GAP aims to intensify gender mainstreaming into Bank and International Finance Corporation operations (projects and programs) and in key regional ESW in selected predetermined sectors. Third, the key performance indicator for assessing the implementation of this action is "increased percentage of operations (projects and programs) in agriculture, transport, energy, water, mining, and private sector development with

highly satisfactory gender mainstreaming." Fourth, subsequent monitoring reports prepared by management have monitored and reported the percentage of integration in Bank operations (projects and programs). Finally, the core set of guiding principles stated in the 2007 GAP paper does not require any linkage with the CAS or the CGA. In fact, it explicitly notes that the GAP funding is "based on incentives, rather than mandates and obligations."

8. Management disagrees with this view of the GAP. The GAP was conceived fully within the framework of the 2001 Gender Strategy and OP/BP 4.20, with the explicit purpose to improve implementation by addressing the poor record since 2001 in a subset of lagging sectors. It is correct, as the evaluation notes, that GAP funding is not restricted to Bank staff working on gender-related activities narrowly identified in CGAs. This would defeat the objective of mainstreaming gender in Bank activities. The GAP has funded a wide range of activities that were clearly deemed to be priority activities by Country Management Units (CMU). Clearance by those units is a requirement for GAP funding. Management notes that the GAP takes a sector-based (not project-based) approach; the evaluation seems to imply that sector approaches are incompatible with country-driven approaches, ignoring the fact that the Bank's matrix structure integrates sectors and countries. The GAP does not weaken country-led approaches or CASs; on the contrary, it is an instrument to improve the ability of the Bank's country-led approach, based on the CASs, and delivered through tools that include ESW and operations, focusing on the sectors where gender mainstreaming was weakest; $4.2 million in GAP funds has supported 56 pieces of analytical work, many directly linked to key country policy dialogue.

Chapter 2

1. Management notes that there is no requirement for a formal CGA document to be prepared for each country. The country director does oversee the preparation of CASs, where a gender assessment—relying on Bank or third party analysis—is expected to be presented. OP/BP 4.20 states that this assessment can also be carried out by the country government or an organization other than the Bank. Management notes that, despite the recognition of a broad definition of CGA, the evaluation considers only a small subset of ESW that could function as CGAs. Excluded from the analysis are Poverty Assessments, Poverty and Social Impact Assessments, Country Economic Memoranda, Public Expenditure Reviews, Development Policy Reviews, Investment Climate Assessments, and employment studies, to name just a few. The GAP, for example, has supported the integration of gender analysis in combined poverty-social-gender assessments (Mozambique and Lesotho), Investment Climate Assessments (Ethiopia and Nigeria), rural Investment Climate Assessments (Ethiopia), a Country Economic Memorandum (Senegal), and employment studies (Macedonia, Kosovo, Turkey, and Moldova). A CGA does not need to be labeled as such to provide an actionable gender diagnostic.

2. The country-level approach has been a part of the Bank's gender policy since the issuance of the 1994 OP 4.20.

3. "The overarching goal of the strategy is to reduce poverty by promoting inclusive development. From a gender perspective, this means ensuring that both women and men have a voice in the development of their community and country, that both are able to benefit from the new opportunities that development brings, that both have access to the resources needed to be productive members of society, and that both share in a higher level of wellbeing"(World Bank 2002b, p. 1).

Chapter 3

1. "Growth regressions have limitations, however, and those that use gender-disaggregated data are no exception. One serious limitation is the ad hoc nature of extensions to the augmented Solow model, which underlies growth regressions. Variables have been added to capture economic openness, government spending, political instability, ethnic diversity, and a host of other potential determinants of growth—frequently with little or no justification in economic theory. A second weakness is a simultaneity problem that results in biased results: gender equality affects growth, but growth presumably also affects gender equality, because the economic pressure in rapidly growing markets makes gender discrimination much more costly. Finding appropriate identification factors to address this bias is extremely difficult, which leads to a search for other evidence" (World Bank 2007e, p. 108).

2. In anticipation, a crude tracking system to assess gender integration in investment projects initiated in 1987 was abandoned.

3. Management notes that there is no requirement for a formal CGA document to be prepared for each country. The country director does oversee the preparation of CASs, where a gender assessment—relying on Bank or third party analysis—is expected to be presented. OP/BP 4.20 states that this assessment can also be carried out by the country government or an organization other than the Bank. Management notes that, despite the recognition of a broad definition of CGA, the evaluation considers only a small subset of ESW that could function as CGAs. Excluded from

the analysis are Poverty Assessments, Poverty and Social Impact Assessments, Country Economic Memoranda, Public Expenditure Reviews, Development Policy Reviews, Investment Climate Assessments, and employment studies, to name just a few. The GAP, for example, has supported the integration of gender analysis in combined poverty-social-gender assessments (Mozambique and Lesotho), Investment Climate Assessments (Ethiopia and Nigeria), rural Investment Climate Assessments (Ethiopia), a Country Economic Memorandum (Senegal), and employment studies (Macedonia, Kosovo, Turkey, and Moldova). A CGA does not need to be labeled as such to provide an actionable gender diagnostic.

4.   For such a results framework, see the Bank's Transport Business Strategy for 2008–12; *Making Sustainable Commitments: An Environment Strategy for the World Bank* (World Bank 2001b); and "Empowering People by Transforming Institutions: Social Development in World Bank Operations" (World Bank 2005b). Other development agencies such as the Canadian International Development Agency and International Fund for Agricultural Development have also established such frameworks to indicate the types of desired outcomes that their support must aim for, and to allow for measurement of whether the goal is being achieved.

5.   Management notes that this project, approved in June 1999, was prepared under OMS 2.20, not under OP/PB 4.20.

Chapter 4

1.   Management notes that there is no requirement for a formal CGA document to be prepared for each country. The country director does oversee the preparation of CASs, where a gender assessment—relying on Bank or third party analysis—is expected to be presented. OP/BP 4.20 states that this assessment can also be carried out by the country government or an organization other than the Bank. Management notes that, despite the recognition of a broad definition of CGA, the evaluation considers only a small subset of ESW that could function as CGAs. Excluded from the analysis are Poverty Assessments, Poverty and Social Impact Assessments, Country Economic Memoranda, Public Expenditure Reviews, Development Policy Reviews, Investment Climate Assessments, and employment studies, to name just a few. The GAP, for example, has supported the integration of gender analysis in combined poverty-social-gender assessments (Mozambique and Lesotho), Investment Climate Assessments (Ethiopia and Nigeria), rural Investment Climate Assessments (Ethiopia), a Country Economic Memorandum (Senegal), and employment studies (Macedonia, Kosovo, Turkey, and Moldova). A CGA does not need to be labeled as such to provide an actionable gender diagnostic.

2.   Management notes that there is no requirement for a formal CGA document to be prepared for each country. The country director does oversee the preparation of CASs, where a gender assessment—relying on Bank or third party analysis—is expected to be presented. OP/BP 4.20 states that this assessment can also be carried out by the country government or an organization other than the Bank. Management notes that, despite the recognition of a broad definition of CGA, the evaluation considers only a small subset of ESW that could function as CGAs. Excluded from the analysis are Poverty Assessments, Poverty and Social Impact Assessments, Country Economic Memoranda, Public Expenditure Reviews, Development Policy Reviews, Investment Climate Assessments, and employment studies, to name just a few. The GAP, for example, has supported the integration of gender analysis in combined poverty-social-gender assessments (Mozambique and Lesotho), Investment Climate Assessments (Ethiopia and Nigeria), rural Investment Climate Assessments (Ethiopia), a Country Economic Memorandum (Senegal), and employment studies (Macedonia, Kosovo, Turkey, and Moldova). A CGA does not need to be labeled as such to provide an actionable gender diagnostic.

3.   The 2001 Gender Strategy placed the responsibility on OPCS and the Gender Group to monitor progress on whether the intended number of CGAs was delivered (including through vehicles such as Poverty Assessments and Country Economic Memoranda). GAD monitoring reports until fiscal 2004–05 counted the number of CGAs that were undertaken. The Bank's gender Web page included a list of the number of CGAs conducted, and all these were considered as CGAs for purposes of the evaluation.

4.   See the 2001 Gender Strategy: "The country gender analysis may, for example, be a stand-alone document or a section of a country poverty or economic analysis. The CGA may contain original, analytical work or may simply refer to such work produced by the Bank or by other agencies (government, international, academic)" (World Bank 2002b, p. xiii).

5.   The Latin America and the Caribbean Regional report was prepared in partnership with national ministries and led to identification of strategic issues in each country. Unlike the Latin America and the Caribbean report, a single gender report in Europe and Central Asia covered 29 countries (22 of the 93 countries). However, the evaluation did not count the Europe and Central Asia's report's individual CGAs because the analysis was not country specific; the report was not prepared in collaboration with the country partners to ensure ownership; and it failed to identify any country-level strategic entry points, resulting only in broad Regional recommendations. Additionally, the report itself noted that separate CGAs would need to be undertaken in each country.

6. Management notes that there is no requirement for a formal CGA document to be prepared for each country. The country director does oversee the preparation of CASs, where a gender assessment—relying on Bank or third party analysis—is expected to be presented. OP/BP 4.20 states that this assessment can also be carried out by the country government or an organization other than the Bank. Management notes that, despite the recognition of a broad definition of CGA, the evaluation considers only a small subset of ESW that could function as CGAs. Excluded from the analysis are Poverty Assessments, Poverty and Social Impact Assessments, Country Economic Memoranda, Public Expenditure Reviews, Development Policy Reviews, Investment Climate Assessments, and employment studies, to name just a few. The GAP, for example, has supported the integration of gender analysis in combined poverty-social-gender assessments (Mozambique and Lesotho), Investment Climate Assessments (Ethiopia and Nigeria), rural Investment Climate Assessments (Ethiopia), a Country Economic Memorandum (Senegal), and employment studies (Macedonia, Kosovo, Turkey, and Moldova). A CGA does not need to be labeled as such to provide an actionable gender diagnostic.

7. Management notes that there is no requirement for a formal CGA document to be prepared for each country. The country director does oversee the preparation of CASs, where a gender assessment—relying on Bank or third party analysis—is expected to be presented. OP/BP 4.20 states that this assessment can also be carried out by the country government or an organization other than the Bank. Management notes that, despite the recognition of a broad definition of CGA, the evaluation considers only a small subset of ESW that could function as CGAs. Excluded from the analysis are Poverty Assessments, Poverty and Social Impact Assessments, Country Economic Memoranda, Public Expenditure Reviews, Development Policy Reviews, Investment Climate Assessments, and employment studies, to name just a few. The GAP, for example, has supported the integration of gender analysis in combined poverty-social-gender assessments (Mozambique and Lesotho), Investment Climate Assessments (Ethiopia and Nigeria), rural Investment Climate Assessments (Ethiopia), a Country Economic Memorandum (Senegal), and employment studies (Macedonia, Kosovo, Turkey, and Moldova). A CGA does not need to be labeled as such to provide an actionable gender diagnostic.

8. See 2001 Gender Strategy: "For purposes of monitoring and quality assurance, it is important that the CAS discusses the CGA and identify the rationale for particular gender-responsive actions (or their absence)" (World Bank 2002b).

9. CASs in Georgia, Poland, and Romania explained that there were no critical gender issues in the country; this approach was considered adequate.

10. Management notes that this better integration of gender into CASs does not make it more likely that gender integration in projects is better. Bank financial and knowledge programs to countries reflect need, country demand, and what the government is doing with support from other development partners and its own resources. This means that the Bank cannot and should not be seeking to lead and finance actions in all sectors. It does need to report on the status of gender issues as part of its gender assessment in CASs. So it could well be the CGA leads to more gender-related discussion in CASs but not necessarily more gender-related actions.

11. This difference may have resulted from stricter evaluation criteria. For high or substantial gender integration, the evaluation required at least one relevant indicator.

12. The development literature shows a differential impact of climate change based on gender—women and girls are more vulnerable in societies with lower levels of gender equality. They account for the largest number of deaths in natural calamities, are likely to be taken out of school to support mothers with increased workloads, and have lower levels of access to resources as these become scarce (Terry 2008; Neumayer and Plümper 2007; Aguilar and others 2007; Aguilar 2004; Nelson and others 2002).

13. As part of the evaluation, IEG undertook a survey on the relevance of the Bank's Gender Strategy and on integrating gender into operational work. Out of 713 country directors, sector managers, and task team leaders surveyed, 248 (35 percent) responded. Given the low response rate, the evaluation used the results only for triangulation purposes.

14. Management disagrees with this conclusion. The Gender Group's analysis of lending operations shows an increase in gender integration during 2006–08.

Management also disagrees with the assertion that using a composite indicator with four criteria is better than using a disaggregated one, especially to inform future Bank responses. This is particularly the case when one of the criteria used in the indicator is debatable (around consultation).

IEG Response: The criteria for assessing project design was adjusted from a rating system provided by the Gender Group dated May 13, 2003, which notes that the participation of both male and female beneficiaries is essential for the success of the project at all different stages of a project cycle. Moreover, IEG disagrees that using just one criteria (discussion of gender issues with quantitative data and extensive background information) is sufficient by itself to assess project design without any measures or monitoring indicators. Finally, the four criteria noted in the approach paper dated November 24, 2008, were shared and discussed with the Gender Group and sent to the Committee on Development Effectiveness.

15. Management notes that changing portfolio composition could also be a main reason for the decline in gender integration found by the evaluation, even if sector by sector, results were improving. An analysis of the sectoral composition of loans approved between fiscal 2002 and 2008 shows that the fiscal 2003 peak integration of gender corresponds to a peak in the share of education and health projects. The subsequent downward trend of gender integration also corresponds to the downward trend of the share of education and health projects in the overall portfolio. (The Inter-American Development Bank has observed a pattern of the degree of gender mainstreaming varying with the composition of the loan portfolio: years with higher gender mainstreaming are years with a higher proportion of social sector projects in the portfolio.)

IEG Response: The evaluation found that even after excluding health and education sector projects from the analysis the percent of gender integration declined by around 20 percent between 2003 and 2008.

16. The sample of DPOs reviewed for the previous evaluation was significantly smaller (19 program documents); discussion of gender issues and measures were found only in two (about 11 percent).

17. Management disagrees with this finding of the evaluation. As noted before, the Gender Group's analysis, based on a larger sample, indicates an improvement in gender integration between fiscal 2006 and 2008.

IEG Response: IEG disagrees that there is a difference in the findings. When measured by one of IEG's four criteria (Gender Analysis) similar to that used by management, the evaluation also finds an improvement between fiscal 2006 and 2008.

18. Management notes that the World Bank OPs stated, "A system of OMSs and [Operational Policy Notes] was initiated in the 1970s; after 1987, they were consolidated into [Operational Directives]. All these statements included elements of policy, procedure, and guidance" (World Bank 1997).

19. Management notes that there is no requirement for a formal CGA document to be prepared for each country. The country director does oversee the preparation of CASs, where a gender assessment—relying on Bank or third party analysis—is expected to be presented. OP/BP 4.20 states that this assessment can also be carried out by the country government or an organization other than the Bank. Management notes that, despite the recognition of a broad definition of CGA, the evaluation considers only a small subset of ESW that could function as CGAs. Excluded from the analysis are Poverty Assessments, Poverty and Social Impact Assessments, Country Economic Memoranda, Public Expenditure Reviews, Development Policy Reviews, Investment Climate Assessments, and employment studies, to name just a few. The GAP, for example, has supported the integration of gender analysis in combined poverty-social-gender assessments

(Mozambique and Lesotho), Investment Climate Assessments (Ethiopia and Nigeria), rural Investment Climate Assessments (Ethiopia), a Country Economic Memorandum (Senegal), and employment studies (Macedonia, Kosovo, Turkey, and Moldova). A CGA does not need to be labeled as such to provide an actionable gender diagnostic.

Management also notes that this conclusion contradicts the findings reported in chapter 4 that "about 25 percent of the CASs proposed gender mainstreaming into operations. However, an examination indicated that the difference between gender integration in operations in countries where CASs indicated that gender would be mainstreamed into operations and those that did not was only about 4 percentage points." Thus, getting gender into the CASs may be necessary—but it is not sufficient to successfully promote gender equality actions in Bank operations; complementary actions and approaches are needed.

20. Management notes that the GAP does not weaken country-led approaches or the CAS; on the contrary, it is an instrument to improve the ability of the Bank's country-led approach, using the tools of ESW as well as operations, to focus on the sectors where gender mainstreaming was weakest. Moreover, the GAP requires that Country Management Units approve proposals submitted for funding, providing for consistency with CASs.

21. A gender and transport initiative in several countries was ongoing from fiscal 2002 onward, which resulted in the availability of resources for staff to undertake gender work. This initiative spurred higher levels of gender integration into transport projects, but it seems to have waned since the initiative terminated.

Chapter 5

1. The findings in this chapter are based on a desk review of Bank documents, interviews with RGCs, interviews with other staff members of the PREM Gender Group, and discussions with staff of other development partner organizations (ADB, IADB, CIDA, the UK Department for International Development, Norad, Swiss Agency for Development and Cooperation, Swedish International Development Cooperation Agency, and United Nations Development Programme) and independent nongovernmental organizations in Washington, DC. The evaluation team additionally discussed Bank support and activities with stakeholders in Colombia, the Philippines, and Yemen to ensure a client perspective. It also met with donor representatives in Ghana, Peru, and Yemen to discuss their views on Bank collaboration at the country level. The evaluation also compared its findings with partnership assessments undertaken by the Netherlands and CIDA of gender integration into partnership activities.

2. Management disagrees with this assessment. Monitoring systems are in place, and the Gender Group reports annually on the progress in the implementation of the gender

mainstreaming strategy, although it recognizes that these systems are always a work in progress. It has monitored and rated gender integration into lending, diagnostic ESW, and CASs starting in fiscal 2002. From fiscal 2000 to 2007, the Quality Assurance Group Quality at Entry and Quality of Supervision Assessments tracked and rated gender integration in lending; this work was taken over by Gender and Development for fiscal 2008 and 2009 and is in process. Since fiscal 2002, Gender and Development has reviewed and rated Bank diagnostic ESW (Poverty Assessments, Public Expenditure Reviews, Country Economic Memorandums, and Development Policy reviews) and all CAS products discussed by the Board each fiscal year, using criteria developed in consultation with Bank staff involved in producing ESW and CASs. The treatment of gender in CASs was included in a fiscal 2009 CAS retrospective discussed by the Board in September 2009.

3. ADB and the IADB have functioning systems for screening and categorizing projects according to their gender relevance.

4. Management notes that the GAP does not provide financial incentives in the form of rewards for staff who integrate gender in their activities. These financial incentives consist of providing resources for the Bank's analytical and operational activities to integrate gender considerations.

5. ADB, for example, notes that its action plan has budgeted for four gender specialists at its headquarters in Manila. In addition, there are 10 national staff and consultants in their countries (see *Biennial Thematic Report on Gender and Development, 2006–2007*, paragraph 40; ADB 2009). For the three Regions common to institutions (East Asia and Pacific, South Asia, and Central Asia [sub-Region]), the equivalent number of Bank staff working on gender would be slightly higher. The evaluation of gender mainstreaming in the United Nations Development Programme (2006) suggests that there are fewer staff focused on gender in the organization. In early 2005, it had five specialists in its central unit (the Bank had 16). In addition, it had a gender adviser in each of its regions (full time as opposed to part time) and focal points in several countries.

6. Titles were identified that contained any of the search words "gender," "women or woman," "maternal," "female or male," or "girl or boy."

7. During 2001–02, for example, a GENFUND grant co-funded the pioneering work of operationalizing gender into 47 projects financed by the World Bank in Central America and Ecuador.

8. GAP has mobilized significant resources from both the Bank's own funds and donor contributions and is helping mainstream gender into these selected areas. To date it has received $29 million, exceeding the original four-year budget of $24 million, and additional amounts have been pledged by Australia, Canada, Denmark, Finland, Germa-

ny, Iceland, Italy, Norway, Spain, Sweden, and the United Kingdom.

9. Management disagrees with this assessment. The GAP has contributed to implementing a country-level approach through the integration of gender analysis in combined poverty-social-gender assessments (Mozambique and Lesotho), Investment Climate Assessments (Ethiopia, Nigeria), rural Investment Climate Assessments (Ethiopia), a Country Economic Memorandum (Senegal), and employment studies (Macedonia, Kosovo, Turkey, and Moldova). In addition, the GAP funding has supported strategic country programs in Afghanistan, Ghana, Kenya, Lao PDR, Liberia, and Sudan.

10. In Europe and Central Asia, a total of $50,000 was provided for gender integration to which the RGC and country focal points charged their time.

11. This rough calculation assumes that funds for gender at a country or project level remained the same before and after the policy.

12. The harmonized guidelines were made possible through the ODA-GAD Network, which continues to meet regularly and serve as a venue for coordination/partnership among the different development agencies in the Philippines.

13. No institutional focal point engages in donor forums on gender at the country level, so gender is "rarely" raised in high-level dialogues, and Bank staff seem "disengaged" from some critical areas in this regard.

14. OPCS was expected to review all CASs, taking into account—among other variables—the quality of the gender diagnostic and the consistency between diagnosis and the proposed program, as well as incorporating overall assessment into the CAS retrospective. OPCS was also expected to collaborate with the Gender and Development Board to monitor progress in delivering the intended number of CGAs (including through vehicles such as Poverty Assessments or Country Economic Memoranda) and the gender aspects of lending operations. (World Bank 2002b, table 2.1)

15. Management disagrees with this assessment. Monitoring systems are in place, and the Gender Group reports annually on the progress in the implementation of the gender mainstreaming strategy, although it recognizes that these systems are always a work in progress. It has monitored and rated gender integration into lending, diagnostic ESW, and CASs starting in fiscal 2002. From fiscal 2000 to 2007, the Quality Assurance Group Quality at Entry and Quality of Supervision Assessments tracked and rated gender integration in lending; this work was taken over by Gender and Development for fiscal 2008 and 2009 and is in process. Since fiscal 2002, Gender and Development has reviewed and rated Bank diagnostic ESW (Poverty Assessments, Public Expenditure Reviews, Country Economic Memorandums, and Development Policy reviews) and all CAS products discussed by the Board each fiscal year, using

criteria developed in consultation with Bank staff involved in producing ESW and CASs. The treatment of gender in CASs was included in a fiscal 2009 CAS retrospective discussed by the Board in September 2009.

16. Gender Monitoring Reports were produced in fiscal 2006 and fiscal 2007 but were never formalized or presented to the Bank's Board.

17. For example, the 2008 monitoring report did not assess whether CGAs were undertaken. Instead, it focused on whether gender was integrated in other ESW and CASs.

Chapter 6

1. In Bangladesh, the evaluation relied on a 2001 CAS and a progress report from 2003. In Lebanon, the evaluation relied on objectives stated at the project level.

2. In Peru, for example, assessments of the projects' contribution to the observed changes in beneficiary populations were obtained by drawing on the impact evaluations commissioned by the Bank toward the end of the projects or after their completion and comparing these estimates with the opinions of the stakeholders and beneficiaries interviewed during this evaluation.

3. In Lebanon, a participatory CGA was undertaken in fiscal 2009. Bank lending, however, did not generate any evident results. The ICR for the Agriculture Infrastructure Development Project rates achievement of gender outcomes as modest. The Vocational and Technical Education Project aimed to support productive employment of women, but the ICR provides no information on results.

4. The Global Gender Gap Index, an initiative of the World Economic Forum, aims to capture the magnitude of the gap between women and men in four critical areas: economic participation and opportunity, political empowerment, educational attainment and health, and survival. Unlike other indices that assess gender dimensions, the Global Gender Gap indices were available for most countries for the last three years of the evaluation.

5. Some external commentators have criticized safety nets, stating that they reinforce traditional gender roles and help reproduce existing patterns of gender inequality in the household and the larger society (Brym and others 2005). In Bangladesh, however, a survey issued by the Bank in 2007 indicated that girls who obtain education cite having "voice" as the most important achievement (World Bank 2008g). The study also notes tentative findings that the presence of more educated children seems to restrain violence inflicted on mothers and wives and that there is an intergenerational change in gender norms, exemplified by younger women's more liberal views on gender equality. Their attitudes toward equal education of spouses, to son preference, divorce, and domestic violence all signify that younger women are more liberal than their mothers and grandmothers.

6. The Joint Staff Assessment (World Bank 2008e) stated, "The net enrollment rates have increased at an even faster pace, reaching 69 percent in the academic year 2005–06, up from 59 percent in 2004–05. While the gender parity index rose to 0.95 in 2005–06, up from 0.93 in 2004–05, it was still below the 1.0 target in the Growth and Poverty Reduction Strategy (GPRS) II." Data in 40 deprived regions were not provided in the ICR.

7. In Zambia, a two-stage Adaptable Program Loan was designed with a sectorwide approach (15 partners) just before the evaluation period. The United States Agency for International Development, Danish International Development Agency, and United Nations Children's Fund took the lead, with the Bank making no serious attempt to mainstream gender considerations even in training, planning, or M&E. In later years, the Bank's own investments went specifically to constructing two secondary schools, incurring high costs and a delay in closing. During the evaluation period, the Bank dropped the second Adaptable Program Loan and left the sector to other agencies.

8. Gender parity is not the same as gender equality. Other issues related to gender equality include gender stereotyping in textbooks, unbalanced expectations by parents and school staff, lack of appropriate vocational training, weak links to labor markets, and inadequate availability of information on labor market opportunities.

9. "Poverty and gender issues have not received particular attention in the implementation process. No related information exists and when available could not be verified" (World Bank 2007g, p. 13). See also IEG (2008c).

10. "Another factor to consider in this area is the sexist content that is still seen in school textbooks and that predispose women to take on traditional roles such as choosing professions that are not only considered feminine but also have a lower social value and thus lower salaries" (JICA 2005).

11. See World Bank (2007a, p. 18). See also: http://www.irinnews.org/Report.aspx? ReportId=82444.

12. In Bangladesh, the Bank-supported Secondary Education Quality and Access Enhancement Project built on the achievements of an earlier project that supported a government program targeting not only girls but also poor boys. This issue was also to be addressed in Colombia as part of the Cundimamarca Education Quality Improvement Project, but the ICR is silent on whether any measures were implemented and on the results thereof.

13. The evaluation selected this indicator because there was significant Bank support for reducing maternal mortality, because data were unavailable in ICRs to assess whether gender-related constraints to health services were addressed and because maternal mortality does pertain to the well-being of women. Data even in this area turned out to be patchy, and the evaluation had to rely on CASs, project documents, and available databases.

14. See the Project Performance Assessment Report of the Health and Population Project (1999) (IEG 2005) and ICR Review of National Nutrition Project (P050751), which notes that the projects only partially achieved their objectives. Further, the Bangladesh Poverty Assessment (World Bank 2008c) indicates that although women from better-off families saw an increase in trained attendance at birth (from 30 to 39 percent) and a reduction in home births (from 81 to 68 percent), poor women experienced very little change in their use of these services during this period. See also the "Whispers to Voices" report (World Bank 2008m). In Peru, the 2002 CAS's stated target for reducing maternal mortality to 160 per 100,000 has been met through a set of DPO measures and project support, particularly in those regions with the highest degree of disparity. However, the Project Appraisal Document for the second phase of the Health Reform Project (World Bank 2009e) states that Peru's maternal mortality rate was almost double the Latin American average and that the official rate may have understated the extent of the problem, as the World Health Organization, the United Nations' Children's Fund, and the Economic Commission for Latin America and the Caribbean suggested that the rate was closer to 240 per 100,000. The contribution of Bank support to the reduction of maternal mortality may have been notable, but it was impossible to assess this accurately.

15. In Colombia, the latest CAS states that there was no intervention to address maternal health during the evaluation period. DPOs—although gender blind—helped strengthen those safety nets that predominately reached women (62 percent). However, outcomes in this area are unlikely to be significant. In the Philippines, the support for health programs provided through the Second Social and Expenditure Management Project did not focus on those factors related to maternal mortality, and an ongoing project includes a component addressing maternal mortality issues.

16. Malaria causes about 20 percent of maternal mortalities in Zambia. In terms of HIV/AIDS support, the focus is typically on pregnant women.

17. According to a survey carried out by the government, 57 percent of households had access to safe water in 2004, compared to 56 percent in 1994. That reflects a slight improvement (see World Bank 2008e).

18. In Colombia, the 1999 National Household Survey showed that only 2 percent of the total labor force of women was involved in construction work. The Community Works Project (fiscal 2000), therefore, included specific measures to target women. The actual numbers (75,000 women) exceeded the original target of 50,000, and these were mainly women out of the labor force.

19. "The objective to achieve gender equity in [higher education] enrollment through the establishment of an equitable funding mechanism was not examined as the developed formula was not piloted. Some of the key activities were totally dropped (for example, development of Financial Management Information System, student aid) and thus this component was the least successful" (World Bank 2009g, p. 26).

20. Households in a field assessment undertaken by the Bank estimated the title increased the value of their property by 20 to 30 percent.

21. See World Bank (2008h, p. 18). The PAD did not integrate any gender considerations, which was mainly part of the Australian government's Overseas Aid Program appraisal documents.

22. In 2009, two local consultants, guided by an international consultant, conducted three weeks of fieldwork in Mazabuka, Petauke, and Lusaka districts to obtain beneficiary and stakeholder views on the extent to which three Bank-financed projects implemented in the districts had contributed to women's economic and decision-making power at local levels.

23. The evaluation relied on a field assessment undertaken for IEG's evaluation of Bank support for decentralization in three regions in the Philippines (IEG 2008a).

24. Fifty-four percent of the participants in business initiatives were women, and 40 percent of the workers were women. Sixty-seven percent of wives in the target population participated in Conservation Committee meetings, and 52 percent of these held elected seats on the committees.

25. Interview with the Deputy Head, Women's Development Agency, Sana.

Chapter 7

1. Management disagrees with this assessment. Monitoring systems are in place, and the Gender Group reports annually on the progress in the implementation of the gender mainstreaming strategy, although it recognizes that these systems are always a work in progress. It has monitored and rated gender integration into lending, diagnostic ESW, and CASs starting in fiscal 2002. From fiscal 2000 to 2007, the Quality Assurance Group Quality at Entry and Quality of Supervision Assessments tracked and rated gender integration in lending; this work was taken over by Gender and Development for fiscal 2008 and 2009 and is in process. Since fiscal 2002, Gender and Development has reviewed and rated Bank diagnostic ESW (Poverty Assessments, Public Expenditure Reviews, Country Economic Memorandums, and Development Policy reviews) and all CAS products discussed by the Board each fiscal year, using criteria developed in consultation with Bank staff involved in producing ESW and CASs. The treatment of gender in CASs was included in a fiscal 2009 CAS retrospective discussed by the Board in September 2009.

2. Management disagrees with this finding and points to analysis by Bank staff that shows an increasing trend between 2006 and 2008 when using a larger sample that includes DPLs (World Bank 2009d).

3.   Management notes that there is no requirement for a formal CGA document to be prepared for each country. The country director does oversee the preparation of CASs, where a gender assessment—relying on Bank or third party analysis—is expected to be presented. OP/BP 4.20 states that this assessment can also be carried out by the country government or an organization other than the Bank. Management notes that, despite the recognition of a broad definition of CGA, the evaluation considers only a small subset of ESW that could function as CGAs. Excluded from the analysis are Poverty Assessments, Poverty and Social Impact Assessments, Country Economic Memoranda, Public Expenditure Reviews, Development Policy Reviews, Investment Climate Assessments, and employment studies, to name just a few. The GAP, for example, has supported the integration of gender analysis in combined poverty-social-gender assessments (Mozambique and Lesotho), Investment Climate Assessments (Ethiopia and Nigeria), rural Investment Climate Assessments (Ethiopia), a Country Economic Memorandum (Senegal), and employment studies (Macedonia, Kosovo, Turkey, and Moldova). A CGA does not need to be labeled as such to provide an actionable gender diagnostic.

4.   Management disagrees with this finding and points to analysis by Bank staff that shows an increasing trend between 2006 and 2008 when using a larger sample that includes DPLs (World Bank 2009d).

Appendix A

1.   Other overall national gender indexes are the World Economic Forum's Global Gender Gap Index, the Human Development Report's Gender Empowerment Measure, and the World Bank's Country Policy and Institutional Assessment gender score.

2.   The idea was to ascertain the "gender discount," that is, the difference between HDI nonadjusted for gender and the gender adjusted HDI. If the straight GDI had been used as a measure of gender performance, it would have been too heavy on the human development parts and would not have single out gender sufficiently.

3.   At first sight, 0.98 would seem like an amount so close to the HDI that it appears that gender inequality has been pretty much ignored. However, it should be stressed that in relation to the HDI, the gender discount tended to be small, meaning that there was a large difference, for example, between countries that had a GDI/HDI of 0.95 compared with

0.98. Essentially, it is the relative number that matters, not the absolute number.

4.   For example, Joint Country Assistance Strategies, Interim Country Assistance Strategies, Transitional Support Strategies, and Country Partnership Strategies.

5.   Indicators for health and education in the results framework were insufficient by themselves to be rated satisfactory for the monitoring and evaluation criterion, unless the CAS noted that these were the key sectors constraining gender equality.

6.   The projects not considered appropriate candidates for the present evaluation included Programmatic Sector Reform Loans, two Decentralization and Competitiveness Loans, a Programmatic Reform for Growth, a Fiscal Management and Competitiveness Loan, and a Judicial Reform Loan.

7.   It proved possible to identify and interview many of the key officials who had been involved in the planning and implementation of each of the three projects. Many of the officials were still with the same agency, but in different positions, and others were now working as independent consultants.

8.   Defining the time line proved to be both important and a challenge, because many projects were implemented in phases in different regions. (In the case of the Urban Property Rights Project, there was a lapse of three to four years between the launch of the first project in Lima and the launch of some of the other projects in the country's interior.) Also, many respondents had been assigned to different regions at different times, so it was difficult for them to recall where and when different activities (such as gender training) had taken place.

Appendix D

1.   The Afghanistan Reconstruction Trust Fund (ARTF) is a multidonor trust fund set up to facilitate donor coordination and externally supported development interventions in Afghanistan.

2.   Number of children in school, disaggregated by gender and number of person-days of employment; provided through public works programs (including number for women) for the first Transitional National Strategy; and clearer indicators in the 2003 Transitional National Strategy: 10 percent net enrollment increase (yearly) in primary education and an increase in the enrollment of girls from 40 percent net to 50 percent. Number of people reached by quality microcredit programs, especially women.

Bibliography

Abu-Ghaida, Dina, and Stephan Klasen. 2004. "The Costs of Missing the Millennium Development Goal on Gender Equity." *World Development* 32: 1075–107.

ADB (Asian Development Bank). 2009. *Biennial Thematic Report on Gender and Development 2006–2007*. Manila: ADB.

———. 2006. *Implementation Review of the Policy on Gender and Development*. Manila: ADB.

Adato, M., T. Roopnaraine, N. Smith, E. Altinok, N. Çelebioğlu, and S. Cemal. 2007. *An Evaluation of the Conditional Cash Transfer Program in Turkey: Second Qualitative and Anthropological Study*. Washington, DC: International Food Policy Research Institute.

Agarwal, B. 1991. *A Field of Her Own*. Oxford: Oxford University Press.

Aguilar, L. 2004. *Gender and Climate Change*. San José, Costa Rica: International Union for Conservation of Nature.

Aguilar, L., A. Araujo, and A. Quesada-Aguilar. 2007. *Climate Change and Disaster Mitigation*. Gland: The World Conservation Union.

Ahmed, Akhter U., Agnes R. Quisumbing, and John F. Hoddinott. 2007. "Relative Efficacy of Food and Cash Transfers in Improving Food Security and Livelihoods of the Ultra-Poor in Bangladesh," International Food Policy Research Institute, in collaboration with Dhaka University, American University, and Data Analysis and Technical Assistance Limited, http://documents.wfp.org/stellent/groups/public/documents/liaison_offices/wfp144615.pdf.

Alyanak, Leyla. 1998. "Tight Economic Situation Unleashes a Flood of 'Reverse' Migration in Asia." *World of Work* 25: 10–2.

Alzate, Mónica M. 2008. "The Sexual and Reproductive Rights of Internally Displaced Women: The Embodiment of Colombia's Crisis." *Disasters* 32(1): 131–48.

Andrić-Ružićić, D. 1999. *(Ne) Živjeti s Nasiljem ((Not) Living with Violence)*. Zenica: Medica Zenica-Infoteka.

Antoine, P. 1995. « Population et Urbanisation en Afrique. » *Chronique du CEPED* 17: 1–4.

Anwar, A. T., M. Iqbal, Japhet Killewo, Mahbub-E-Elahi, K. Chowdhry, and Sushil Kanta Dastgupta. 2004. "Bangladesh: Inequalities in Utilization of Maternal Health Care Services – Evidence from Matlab." HNP Discussion Paper, Reaching the Poor Program Paper No. 2, World Bank, Washington, DC.

Bamberger, Michael, Mark Blackden, Lucia Fort, and Violeta Manoukian. 2002. *Gender: A Sourcebook for Poverty Reduction Strategies* (ed. Jeni Klugman), chapter 10 pp. 333–74. Washington DC: World Bank.

Ban, Ki-moon. 2009. "Remarks to Special Event on Philanthropy and the Global Public Health Agenda." New York, February 23. http://www.un.org/apps/news/infocus/sgspeeches/search_full.asp?statID=437.

Bardasi, Elena, Mark Blackden, and Juan Carlos Guzman. 2007. *Gender, Entrepreneurship, and Competitiveness in Africa*. Africa Competitiveness Report 2007. Geneva: World Economic Forum.

Başlevent, Cem, and Özlem Onaran. 2003. "Are Married Women in Turkey More Likely to Become Added or Discouraged Workers?" *Labour* 17 (3): 439–58.

Beall, J., S. Mkhize, and S. Vawda. 2004. "Navigating Tradition, Traditional Authorities, and Governance in Thekwini Metropolitan Municipality, South Africa." *Development Planning Review* 24 (4): 457–76.

Behrman, Jere R., Andrew D. Foster, Mark R. Rosenzweig, and Prem Vashishtha. 1999. "Women's Schooling, Home Teaching, and Economic Growth." *Journal of Political Economy* 107 (4): 682–714.

Besley, Timothy, Robin Burgess, and Berta Esteve-Volart. 2005. "Operationalizing Pro-Poor Growth India Case Study." World Bank Policy Research Working Paper Series, Washington, DC.

Blackden, C. Mark, and Chitra Bhanu. 1999. "Gender, Growth, and Poverty Reduction in Sub-Saharan Africa." World Bank Technical Paper No. 428, Washington, DC.

Blecker, Robert, and Stephanie Seguino. 2002. "Macroeconomic Effect of Reducing Gender Wage Inequality in an Export-Oriented, Semi-Industrialized Economy." *Review of Development Economics* 6 (1): 103–19.

Borland, Elizabeth, and Barbara Sutton. 2007. "Quotidian Disruption and Women's Activism in Times of Crisis, Argentina 2002–2003." *Gender & Society* 21 (5): 700–22.

Bourguignon, François, Agnès Bénassy-Quéré, Stefan Dercon, Antonio Estache, Jan Willem Gunning, Ravi Kanbur, Stephan Klasen, Simon Maxwell, Jean-Philippe Platteau, and Amedeo Spadaro. 2008. *Millennium Development Goals at Midpoint: Where Do We Stand and Where Do We Need to Go?* Brussels: European Commission.

Braithwaite, M. 2003. *Thematic Evaluation of the Integration of Gender in EC Development Co-operation with Third Countries*. Volume 1. Brussels: European Commission.

Brown, Katrina, and Sandrine Lapuyade. 2001. "A Livelihood from the Forest: Gendered Visions of Social, Economic and Environmental Change in Southern Cameroon." *Journal of International Development* 13 (8): 1131–49.

Brym, R., S. Chung, S. Dulmage, C. Farahat, M. Greenberg, M. Ho, K. Housein, D. Kulik, M. Lau, O. Maginley, A. Nercessian, E. Reyes Le Blanc, A. Sacher, N. Sachewsky, A. Sadovsky, S. Singh, S. Sivananthan, N. Toller, S. Vossoughi, K. Weger, and T. Wu . 2005. "In Faint Praise of the World Bank's Gender Development Policy." *Canadian Journal of Sociology.* http://www.cjsonline.ca/articles/brymetal05.html.

Buvinic, Mayra, Andrew R. Morisson, A. Waafas Ofosu-Amaah, and Mirja Sjöblom. 2008. *Equality for Women: Where Do We Stand on Millennium Development Goal 3?* Washington, DC: World Bank.

Čačeva, V., and Lj Čoneva. 2000. *Semejno Nasilstvo (Domestic Violence).* Skopje: ESE.

Cameron, Lisa. 2002. "Women and the Labour Market During and After the Crisis." In *Women in Indonesia: Gender, Equity and Development*, eds. Kathryn May Robinson and Sharon Bessell. Singapore: Institute of Southeast Asian Studies, 144–57.

Carvajal-Escobar, Y., M. Quintero-Angel, and M. Garcia-Vargas. 2008. "Women's Role in Adapting to Climate Change and Variability." *Advances in Geosciences* 14: 277–80. Copernicus Publications on behalf of the European Geosciences Union.

CIDA (Canadian International Development Agency). 2005. "CIDA's Framework for Assessing Gender Equality Results:. Report No. 0-662-40865-9. http://www.acdi-cida.gc.ca/INET/IMAGES.NSF/vLUImages/GenderEquality3/$file/GE-framework.pdf.

CIEL (Center for International Environmental Law) and Gender Action. 2007. *Gender Justice: A Citizen's Guide to Gender Accountability at International Financial Institutions.* http://www.ciel.org/Publications/GenderJustice_Jun07.pdf or http://www.genderaction.org/images/Gender%20Justice_Final%20LowRes.pdf

Catalyst. 2007. *The Bottom Line: Corporate Performance and Women's Representation on Boards.* http://www.catalyst.org/publication/200/the-bottom-line-corporate-performance-and-womens-representation-on-boards.

Cerrutti, Marcela. 2000. "Economic Reform, Structural Adjustment and Female Labor Force Participation in Buenos Aires, Argentina." *World Development* 28 (5): 879–91.

Chant, S., and C. McIlwaine. 1995. "Gender and Export Manufacturing in the Philippines: Continuity or Change in Female Employment? The Case of the Mactan Export Processing Zone." *Gender, Place and Culture – A Journal of Feminist Geography* 2 (2): 147–76.

Commission on Growth and Development. 2008. *The Growth Report: Strategies for Sustained Growth and Inclusive Development.* Washington, DC: World Bank.

Ćopić, Sanja. 2004. "Wife Abuse in the Countries of the Former Yugoslavia." *Feminist Review* 76 (1): 46–64.

Cord, Louise, Marijn Verhoeven, Camilla Blomquist, and Bob Rijkers. 2009. *The Global Economic Crisis: Assessing Vulnerability with a Poverty Lens.* Washington, DC: World Bank.

Correia, Maria. 2002. "Gender Dimensions of Vulnerability to Exogenous Shocks: The Case of Ecuador." In *Crisis and Dollarization in Ecuador: Stability, Growth, and Social Equity*, eds. Paul Beckerman and Andres Solimano. Washington, DC: World Bank, 177–215.

Costa, Joana, Elydia Silva, and Fabio Vaz. 2009. "The Role of Gender Inequalities in Explaining Income Growth, Poverty, and Inequality: Evidences from Latin American Countries." Working Paper No. 52, International Policy Center for Inclusive Growth, Brasilia, Brazil.

Deere, Carmen Diana, and Magdalena Leon. 2001. *Empowering Women: Land and Property Rights in Latin America.* Pittsburgh, PA: University of Pittsburgh Press.

Deere, C. D., H. Safa, and P. Antrobus. 1997. "Impact of Economic Crises on Poor Women and Their Households." In *The Women, Gender and Development Reader*, ed. Nalini Visvanathan. London: Zed Books.

Deininger, Klaus, Shaik Galab, and Tore Olsen. 2005. "Empowering Poor Rural Women in India: Empirical Evidence from Andhra Pradesh." Presentation at the Annual Meeting of the American Agricultural Economics Association, Providence, RI, July 24–27.

DFID (Department for International Development). 2007. *Gender Inequality and Growth: Evidence and Action.* London: DFID.

Dixon-Mueller, Ruth, and Adrienne Germain. 2007. "Fertility Regulation and Reproductive Health in the Millennium Development Goals: The Search for a Perfect Indicator." *American Journal of Public Health* 97 (1): 45–51.

Dollar, David, and Roberta Gatti. 1999. "Gender Inequality, Income, and Growth: Are Good Times Good for Women?" World Bank Policy Research Report Working Paper No. 1, Washington, DC.

Doss, Cheryl R. 1996. "Women's Bargaining Power in Household Economic Decisions: Evidence from Ghana." Staff Paper 13517, University of Minnesota, Department of Applied Economics.

Douglas, Carol Anne, Moira McCauley, Melissa Ostrow, and Melissa Wimbrow. 2003. "Russia: Women Face Increased Violence." *Off Our Backs* 33 (5/6): 6–7.

Drexhage, J. 2006. *Climate Change Situation. Analysis – Final Report.* Gland: The World Conservation Union.

ECOSOC (Economic and Social Council). 1997. *Report of the Economic and Social Council for 1997.* Washington, DC: World Bank.

Elson, Diane. 2007. "Macroeconomic Policy, Employment, Unemployment, and Gender Equality." In *Towards Full and Decent Employment,* eds. José Antonia Ocampo and K.S. Jomo. London: Zed Books.

Elson, Diane, and Nilufer Cagatay. 2000. "The Social Content of Macroeconomic Policies." *World Development* 28 (7): 1347–64.

Esteve-Volart, Berta. 2004. "Gender Discrimination and Growth: Theory and Evidence from India." STICERD Development Discussion Paper No. 42, London School of Economics, London.

Evertzen, Annette. 2001. *Gender and Local Governance.* The Hague: SNV—Netherlands Development Organisation.

Fallon, Peter R., and Robert E. B. Lucas. 2002. "The Impact of Financial Crises on Labor Markets, Household Incomes, and Poverty: A Review of Evidence." *World Bank Research Observer* 17 (1): 21–45.

Fiszbein, Ariel, Paula Giovagnoli, and Norman Thurston. 2003. *Household Behavior in the Presence of Economic Crisis: Evidence from Argentina, 2002.* Washington, DC: World Bank.

Floro, Maria and Gary Dymski. 2000. "Financial Crisis, Gender, and Power: An Analytical Framework." *World Development* 28 (7): 1269–83.

Friedman, Jed, and Duncan Thomas. 2009. "Psychological Health Before, During, and After an Economic Crisis: Results from Indonesia, 1993-2000." *World Bank Economic Review* 23 (1): 57–76.

Fukada-Parr, Sakiko. 2008. "The Human Impact of the Financial Crisis on Poor and Disempowered People and Countries." United Nations General Assembly's Interactive Panel on the Global Financial Crisis, New York, October. http://www.un.org/ga/president/63/interactive/gfc/sakiko_p.pdf.

Gage, Anastasia J., A. Elisabeth Sommerfelt, and Andrea L. Piani. 1997. "Household Structure and Childhood Immunization in Niger and Nigeria." *Demography* 34 (2): 295–309.

Galasso, Emanuela, and Martin Ravallion. 2004. "Social Protection in a Crisis: Argentina's Plan Jefes y Jefas." *World Bank Economic Review* 18 (3): 367–99.

Galor, Oded, and David Weil. 1996. "The Gender Gap, Fertility, and Growth." *American Economic Review* 86: 374–87.

Gavrilova, Natalia S., Victoria G. Semyonova, Galina N. Evdokushkina, and Leonid A. Gavrilov. 2000. "The Response of Violent Mortality to Economic Crisis in Russia." *Population Research and Policy Review* 19 (5): 397–419.

Gelles, Richard J. 1997. *Intimate Violence in Families.* London: Sage Publications.

Germain, Adrienne, and Rachel Kyte. 1995. *The Cairo Consensus: The Right Agenda for the Right Time.* New York: International Women's Health Coalition.

Gill, Stephen. 2002. "Constitutionalizing Inequality and the Clash of Globalizations." *International Studies Review* 4 (2): 47–65.

Gilligan, D., H. Jacoby, and J. Quizon. 2000. "The Effects of the Indonesian Economic Crisis on Agricultural Households: Evidence from the National Farmers Household Panel Survey (PATANAS)." Unpublished working paper, Center for Agro-Socioeconomic Research and the World Bank, Bogor.

Goetz, Anne Marie. 2004. "Striving for Gender Equality in an Unequal World." In *Striving for Gender Equality in an Unequal World,* ed. United National Development Program. New York: UNDP.

Goldstein, Markus, and Christopher Udry. 2008. "The Profits of Power: Land Rights and Agricultural Investment in Ghana." *Journal of Political Economy* 116 (6): 981–1022.

Gurmu, Eshetu, and Ruth Mace. 2008. "Fertility Decline Driven by Poverty: The Case of Addis Ababa, Ethiopia." *Journal of Biosocial Science* 40 (3): 339–58.

Haboush, J. K. 1991. "The Confucianization of Korean Society." In *The East Asian Region Confucian Heritage and its Modern Adaptation,* ed. Gilbert Rozman. Princeton: Princeton University Press, 84–110.

Hamilton, Sarah. 2002. "Neoliberalism, Gender, and Property Rights in Rural Mexico." *Latin American Research Review* 37 (1): 119–43.

Hirsch, Joachim. 1995. *Der Nationale Wettbewerbsstaat Staat, Demokratie und Politik im Globalen Kapitalismus.* Berlin: ID-Archiv.

Hoddinott, J., and L. Haddad. 1994. "Does Female Income Share Influence Household Expenditures? Evidence from the Côte d'Ivoire." Working Paper Series 94.17, Centre for the Study of African Economies, University of Oxford, Oxford, UK.

Howes, Candace, and Ajit Singh. 1995. "Long-Term Trends in the World Economy: The Gender Dimension." *World Development* 23 (11): 1895–911.

Hudson, Valerie M., Mary Caprioli, Bonnie Balif-Spanvill, Rose McDermott, and Chad F. Emmett. 2009. "The Heart of the Matter: The Security of Women and the Security of States." *International Security* 33 (3): 7–45.

IADB (Inter-American Development Bank). 2003. Gender Mainstreaming Action Plan. March 2003–June 2005. SDS/GED. Washington, DC: IDB.

IEG (Independent Evaluation Group). 2008a. *Decentralization in Client Countries: An Evaluation of World Bank Support, 1990-2007.* IEG Study Series. Washington, DC: World Bank.

———. 2008b. "Evaluation of Bank Support for Gender." Approach Paper, World Bank, Washington, DC.

———. 2008c. "Nigeria: Second Primary Education Project and Universal Basic Education Program." Project Performance Assessment Report No. 44360, World Bank, Washington, DC.

———. 2008d. "Tajikistan Farm Privatization Support Project (PPAR)." Report No. 44359, World Bank, Washington, DC.

———. 2006. "Bangladesh—Fourth Population and Health and Health and Population Program Projects." Project Performance Assessment Report No. 36564, World Bank, Washington, DC.

———. 2005. *Evaluating a Decade of World Bank Gender Policy, 1990–1999.* IEG Study Series. Washington, DC: World Bank.

———. 2002. "Zambia—Country Assistance Evaluation." Report No. 25075, World Bank, Washington, DC.

———. 2001a. "The Gender Dimension of Bank Assistance: An Evaluation of Results." Report No. 23119, World Bank, Washington, DC.

———. 2001b. *Integrating Gender in World Bank Assistance.* IEG Study Series. Washington, DC: World Bank.

———. 1997a. "Evaluating Health Projects: Lessons from the Literature." World Bank Discussion Paper No. 356, World Bank, Washington, DC.

———. 1997b. "Mainstreaming Gender in World Bank Lending: An Update." Report No. 17169, World Bank, Washington, DC.

———. 1994. "Gender Issues in World Bank Lending." IEG Report No. 79, World Bank, Washington, DC.

IFAD (International Fund for Agricultural Development). 1999. *The Asian Crisis and the Rural Poor: How IFAD Will Respond?* Rome: IFAD.

ILO (International Labour Organization). 2005. "Thematic Evaluation Report: Gender Issues in Technical Cooperation." ILO Governing Body, Committee on Technical Cooperation Paper, ILO, Geneva.

———. 2002. *Men and Women in the Informal Economy: A Statistical Picture.* Geneva: ILO.

———. 2000. "Towards Gender Equality in the World of Work in Asia and the Pacific." Technical Report for Discussion at the Asian Regional Consultation on Follow-up to the Fourth World Conference on Women, Manila, 6–8 October 1999. Bangkok: ILO.

———. 1999. *The Impact of the Asian Crisis on Women.* Geneva: ILO.

IPCC (Intergovernmental Panel on Climate Change). 2001. *Summary for Policymakers. Climate Change 2001: Impacts, Adaptation, and Vulnerability.* Geneva: IPCC.

Jahangeer, Shirin A., Wafaas Ofosu Amaah, and Faaria Islam. 2006. "Integrating Gender into the World Bank's Bangladesh Country Program: A Review of the Portfolio." Background Paper for the Bangladesh Gender Assessment, World Bank, Dhaka Office.

JICA Colserver Network Ltda. 2005. *Columbia: Country Gender Profile.* http://www.jica.go.jp/activities/issues/gender/pdf/05col.pdf.

Jokisch, Brad, and Jason Pribilsky. 2002. "The Panic to Leave: Economic Crisis and the 'New Emigration' from Ecuador." *International Migration* 40 (4): 75–102.

Katz, Elizabeth, and Juan Sebastian Chamorro. 2003. "Gender, Land Rights, and the Household Economy in Rural Nicaragua and Honduras." Paper presented at the annual conference of the Latin American and Caribbean Economics Association, Puebla, Mexico, October 9–11.

Kelly, P.M., and W.N. Adger. 2000. "Theory and Practice in Assessing Vulnerability to Climate Change and Facilitating Adaptation." *Climatic Change* 47: 325–52.

Khandker, Shahidur R. 1998. *Fighting Poverty with Microcredit: Experience in Bangladesh.* Oxford: Oxford University Press.

Khandker, Shahidur R., Gayatri Koolwal, and Nistha Sinha. 2008. "Benefits of Improving Young Women's Labor Market Opportunities: Evidence from Group-Based Credit Programs in Bangladesh." Background paper for Adolescent Girls Initiative, World Bank, Washington, DC.

Khandker, Shahidur R., Zahed H. Kahn, Khalily M.A. Baqui. 1995. "Sustainability of a Government Targeted Credit Program." World Bank Discussion Paper No. 316, Washington, DC.

Kim, Haejin, and Paula B. Voos. 2007. "The Korean Economic Crisis and Working Women." *Journal of Contemporary Asia* 37 (2): 190–208.

Klasen, Stephan. 2002. "Low Schooling for Girls, Slower Growth for All? Cross-Country Evidence on the Effect of Gender Inequality in Education on Economic Development." *The World Bank Economic Review* 16 (3): 345–73.

———. 1999. "Does Gender Inequality Reduce Growth and Development? Evidence from Cross-Country Regressions." World Bank Policy Research Report Working Paper No. 7, Washington, DC.

Klasen, Stephan, and Francesca Lemanna. 2003. "The Impact of Gender Inequality in Education and Employment on Economic Growth in the Middle East and North Africa." Mimeo, University of Munich.

Kristof, Nicholas D., and Sheryl WeDunn. 2009. "The Women's Crusade." *New York Times Magazine* (August 17).

Kulakowska, Elisabeth. 2000. "For East Europe's Women, a Rude Awakening." *UNESCO Courier* 53 (2): 37–39.

Lagerlöf, Nils-Peter. 2003. "Gender Equality and Long-Run Growth." *Journal of Economic Growth* 8: 403–26.

Lee, Kye Woo, and Kisuk Cho. 2005. "Female Labour Force Participation during Economic Crises in Argentina and the Republic of Korea." *International Labour Review* 144 (4): 423–49.

Lee, Rebecca Anne. 2005. "When Work Empowers: Women in Mexico City's Labour Force." PhD Dissertation, McGill University, Montreal.

Levine, David, and Minnie Ames. 2003. "Gender Bias and the Indonesian Financial Crisis: Were Girls Hit Hardest?" Working paper C03-130, Center for International and Development Economics Research, Institute for Business and Economic Research, University of California, Berkeley.

Lim, Joseph Y. 2000. "The Effects of the East Asian Crisis on the Employment of Women and Men: The Philippine Case." *World Development* 28 (7): 1285–1306.

Mayoux, Linda. 2001. "Women's Empowerment and Poverty Reduction: Implications for Impact Assessment. " http://www.enterprise-impact.org.uk/approaches/tsp/povelimempowerwomen.shtml.

McKinsey and Company. 2006. "Women Matter: Gender Diversity: A Corporate Performance Driver." http://www.europeanpwn.net/files/mckinsey_2007_gender_matters.pdf.

Mehra, Rekha, and Geeta Rao Gupta. 2006. *Gender Mainstreaming: Making It Happen.* Washington, DC: International Center for Research on Women and World Bank.

Metoyer, Cynthia Chavez. 2001. "Hurricane Mitch, Alemán, and Other Disasters for Women in Nicaragua." *International Studies Perspectives* 2 (4): 401–15.

Morrison, Andrew, Dhushyanth Raju, and Nistha Sinha. 2007. "Gender Inequality, Poverty, and Economic Growth." World Bank Policy Research Working Paper No. 4349, Washington, DC.

Moser, Caroline O., and A. Moser. 2005. "Gender Mainstreaming since Beijing: A Review of Success and Limitations in International Institutions." *Gender and Development* 13 (2).

———. 1997. *Household Responses to Poverty and Vulnerability. Volume I: Confronting Crisis in Cisne Dos, Guayaquil, Ecuador.* Nairobi: Urban Management Programme.

———. 1993. *Gender Planning and Development: Theory, Practice and Training.* New York: Routledge.

Mukhopadhyay, Maitrayee. 2005. "Decentralisation and Gender Equity in South Asia." http://nppdin/node/8.

Munné, Myriam I. 2005. "Alcohol and the Economic Crisis in Argentina: Recent Findings." *Addiction* 100 (12): 1790–99.

Nathan, Dev, and Govind Kelkar. 1999. "Agrarian Involution, Domestic Economy and Women: Rural Dimensions of the Asian Crisis." *Economic and Political Weekly* 34 (19): 1135–41.

Nelson, V., K. Meadows, T. Cannon, J. Morton, and A. Martin. 2002. "Uncertain Predictions, Invisible Impacts, and the Need to Mainstream Gender in Climate Change Adaptations." *Gender and Development* 10 (2): 51–9.

Neumayer, Eric, and Thomas Plümper. 2007. "The Gendered Nature of Natural Disasters: The Impact of Catastrophic Events on the Gender Gap in Life Expectancy, 1981–2002." *Annals of the American Association of Geographers.* http://ssrn.com/abstract=874965.

Niederle, Muriel, and H. Alexandra Yestrumskas. 2008. "Gender Differences in Seeking Challenges: The Role of Institutions." NBER Working Paper 13922, National Bureau of Economic Research, Inc.

Nijeholt, G. L., V. Vargas, and S. Wieringa (eds). 1998. *Women's Movements in Public Policy in Europe, Latin American and the Caribbean.* New York: Garland.

Nikolić-Ristanović, Vesna. 2002. *Social Change, Gender and Violence: Post-communist and War Affected Societies.* London: Kluwer Academic Publishers.

Nordås, Hildegunn Kyvik. 2003. Trade Liberalization a Window of Opportunity for Women." WTO Staff Working Paper ERSD-2003–03.

Norad (Norwegian Agency for Development Cooperation). 2006. "Lessons from Evaluations of Women and Gender Equality in Development Cooperation." Synthesis Report 2006/1 Oslo: Norad, ISBN: 978-82-7548-182-3. http://www.oecd.org/dataoecd/19/37/37880765.pdf.

———. 2005. "Evaluation of the Strategy for Women and Gender Equality in Development Cooperation (1997–2005)." Norad Evaluation Report 5/2005, Oslo.

Notzon, F. C., Yu M. Komarov, S. P. Ermakov, Ch. T. Sempos, J. S. Marks, and E. V. Sempos. 1998. "Causes of Declining Life Expectancy in Russia." *Journal of the American Medical Association* 279 (10): 793–800.

OECD/DAC WP-EV. 2003. "Review on Gender and Evaluation." OECD/DAC Working Party on Aid Evaluation, Paris.

Oxford Policy Management, Social Development Direct, and Working Together Ltd. 2008. "Making Aid More Effective through Gender, Rights and Inclusion: Evidence from Implementing the Paris Declaration." http://www.opml.co.uk or www.oecd.org/dac.

Özler, Süle. 1999. "Globalisation, Employment, and Gender—Background Paper Prepared for the UNDP Human Development Report." New York, UNDP.

Parrado, Emilio A., and Rene M. Zenteno. 2001. "Economic Restructuring, Financial Crises, and Women's Work in Mexico." *Social Problems* 48 (4): 456–77.

Pebley, A., N. Goldman, and G. Rodriguez. 1996. "Prenatal and Delivery Care and Childhood Immunization in Guatemala: Do Family and Community Matter?" *Demography* 33: 231–47.

Pouliotte, J., B. Smit, and L. Westerhoff. 2009. "Adaptation and Development: Livelihoods and Climate Change in Subarnabad, Bangladesh." *Climate and Development* 1: 31–46.

Pyle, Jean. 2001. "Sex, Maids, and Export Processing: Risks and Reasons for Gendered Global Production Networks." *International Journal of Politics, Culture, and Society* 15 (1): 55–76.

Quy-Toan Do, and Lakshmi Iyer. 2003. "Land Rights and

Economic Development: Evidence from Vietnam." World Bank Policy Research Working Paper 3120, Washington DC.

Rakowski, Cathy A. 2003. "Women's Coalitions as a Strategy at the Intersection of Economic and Political Change in Venezuela." *International Journal of Politics, Culture, and Society* 16 (3): 387–405.

Ravallion, Martin. 2008. "Bailing out the World's Poorest." World Bank Policy Research Working Paper WPS4763, Washington, DC.

Room, R., D. Jernigan, B. Carlini-Marlatt, O. Gureje, K. Mäkelä, M. Marshall, M. E. Medina-Mora, M. Monteiro, C. Parry, J. Partanen, L. Riley, and S. Saxena. 2002. *Alcohol in Developing Societies: A Public Health Approach.* Helsinki: Finnish Foundation for Alcohol Studies (in collaboration with the World Health Organization).

Rose, Pauline, and Ramya Subrahmanian. 2005. "Evaluation of DFID Development Assistance: Gender Equality and Women's Empowerment. Volume 1. Synthesis Report." DFID Working Paper, London.

Rukumnuaykit, Pungpond. 2004. "Economic Crises and Demographic Outcomes: Evidence from Indonesia." PhD Dissertation, Michigan State University, East Lansing.

Sachs, Jeffrey D. 2001. *Macroeconomics and Health: Investing in Health for Economic Development. Report of the Commission on Macroeconomics and Health.* Geneva: World Health Organization.

Samarina, O. 2001. "The Social Protection of Women and Family Policy in Contemporary Russia." *Problems of Economic Transition* 44 (1): 72–80.

Schechter, Susan. 1982. *Women and Male Violence: The Visions and Struggles of the Battered Women's Movement.* Boston: South End Press.

Seguino, Stephanie. 2000a. "Gender Inequality and Economic Growth: A Cross-Country Analysis." *World Development* 28: 1211–30.

———. 2000b. "Accounting for Gender in Asian Economic Growth." *Feminist Economics* 6 (3): 27–58.

Shahidur, R. Khandker, Zahed H. Khan, and M. A. Baqui Khalily. 1995. "Sustainability of a Government Targeted Credit Program." World Bank Discussion Paper 316, Washington DC.

Shin, K. 1999. "Where Did Many Unemployed Women Go? Female Unemployment in a Paternalistic Society." *Trend and Prospect* 40: 70–88.

Sigit, H., and S. Surbakti. 1999. *The Social Impact of the Financial Crisis in Indonesia.* Manila: Economics and Development Resource Center, Asian Development Bank.

Silvey, Rachel M. 2001. "Migration under Crisis: Household Safety Nets in Indonesia's Economic Collapse." *Geoforum* 32 (1): 33–45.

———. 2000. "Stigmatized Spaces: Gender and Mobility Under Crisis in South Sulawesi, Indonesia." *Gender, Place and Culture – A Journal of Feminist Geography* 7 (2): 143–61.

Silvey, Rachel M., and Rebecca Elmhirst. 2003. "Engendering Social Capital: Women Workers and Rural-Urban Networks in Indonesia's Crisis." *World Development* 31 (5): 865–79.

Singh, Ajit, and Ann Zammit. 2000. "International Capital Flows: Identifying the Gender Dimension." *World Development* 28 (7): 1249–68.

Singh, Susheela, Jacqueline E. Darroch, Michael Vlassof, and Jennifer Nadeau. 2003. *Adding It Up: The Benefits of Investing in Sexual and Reproductive Health Care.* New York: The Alan Guttmacher Institute.

Smith, Daniel Jordan. 2004. "Contradictions in Nigeria's Fertility Transition: The Burdens and Benefits of Having People." *Population and Development Review* 30 (2): 221–38.

Smith, L. C., and L. Haddad. 1999. *Explaining Child Malnutrition in Developing Countries—A Cross-Country Analysis.* Washington DC: International Food Policy Institute.

Smith, James P., Duncan Thomas, Elizabeth Frankenberg, Kathleen Beegle, and Graciela Teruel. 2002. "Wages, Employment and Economic Shocks: Evidence from Indonesia." *Journal of Population Economics* 15 (1): 161–93.

Song, Jesook. 2008. "The Making of 'Undeserving' Homeless Women: A Gendered Analysis of Homeless Policy in South Korea from 1997 to 2001." *Feminist Review* 89 (1): 87–101.

South Centre. 1999. *Financing Development. Key Issues for the South.* Geneva: South Centre.

Sparreboom, Theo. 2009. *Global Employment Trends for Women – March 2009.* Geneva: International Labour Organization.

Stosky, Janet. 2006. "Gender and Its Relevance to Macroeconomic Policy: A Survey." International Monetary Fund Working Paper WP/06/233, Washington, DC.

Swamy, Anand, Steve Knack, Young Lee, and Omar Azfar. 2001. "Gender and Corruption." *Journal of Development Economics* 64 (1): 22–55.

Tanga, Pius T., Timothy O. Mbuagbo, and Celestin Ndeh Fru. 2002. "Coping with the Economic Crisis: Women in Cameroon's Formal Sector." *Area* 34 (3): 325–28.

Tauli-Korpuz, V. 1998. "Asia-Pacific Women Grapple with Financial Crisis and Globalization." *Third World Resurgence* 94.

Terry, G. 2008. "Why Gender Matters to Climate and Equity." Presentation at the Gender and Climate Change Workshop, Kønsnet (Gender Net), Denmark, November 6.

Thomas, D. 1990. "Intra-Household Resource Allocation: An Inferential Approach." *Journal of Human Resources* 25: 635–64.

Thomas, Duncan, Kathleen Beegle, and Elizabeth Frankenberg. 2003. "Labour Market Transitions of Men and Women During an Economic Crisis: Evidence from Indonesia." In *Women in the Labour Market in Changing Economies: Demographic Issues,* eds. Brígida Garcia, Richard Anker and Antonella Pinnelli. Oxford: Oxford University Press, 37–58.

Tol, R.S.J., S. Fankhauser, R.G. Richels, and J.B. Smith. 2000. "How Much Damage Will Climate Change Do? Recent Estimates." Sustainability and Global Change Research Unit Working Paper SCG-2, Hamburg University.

Truong, Thanh-Dam. 2000. "A Feminist Perspective on the Asian Miracle and Crisis: Enlarging the Conceptual Map of Human Development." *Journal of Human Development* 1 (1): 159–64.

Tzannatos, Zafiris. 2008. "Monitoring Progress in Gender Equality in the Labor Market." In *Equality for Women: Where Do We Stand on Millennium Development Goal 3?* Ed. Mayra Buvinic. Washington, DC: World Bank.

UN (United Nations). 2000. *Millennium Declaration.* New York: United Nations.

———. 1996. *Report of the Fourth World Conference on Women, Beijing, 4-15 September 1995.* New York: United Nations.

———. 1995. *Report of the International Conference on Population and Development, Cairo, 5–13 September 1994.* New York: United Nations.

UNDP (United Nations Development Programme). 2008. "Innovative Approaches to Women's Economic Empowerment." Paper for the Partnership Event on September 25, 2008: MDG3—Gender Equality and Empowerment of Women—A Prerequisite for Achieving all MDGs by 2015, United Nations, New York.

———. 1995. *Human Development Report 1995.* Oxford: Oxford University Press for the UNDP.

———. 2006, *Evaluation of Gender Mainstreaming in UNDP.* New York: United Nations.

UNICEF (United Nations Children's Fund). 2008. *Progress for Children: A Report Card on Maternal Mortality.* New York: UNICEF. Available at: http://www.unicef.org/publications/files/Progress_for_Children-No._7_Lo-Res_082008.pdf.

———. 2006. *Millennium Development Goals: Improve Maternal Mortality.* http://www.unicef.org/mdg/maternal.html.

———. 1999. Women in Transition. Innocenti Research Centre (IRC) – MONEE Project Florence:UNICEF. http://ideas.repec.org/p/ucf/remore/remore99-1.html.

United Nations Commission on the Status of Women. 1997. Report on the Forty-First Session, New York, March 10–21.

http://www.un.org/documents/ecosoc/cn6/1997/reporten/e1997-27content.htm.

United Nations Conference on Trade and Development. 1998. *Trade and Development Report, 1998.* Geneva: United Nations. http://www.unctad.org/en/docs/tdr1998_en.pdf.

United Nations Division for the Advancement of Women. 1999. *1999 World Survey on the Role of Women in Development: Globalization, Gender and Work.* New York: United Nations.

United Nations Inter-Agency Network on Women and Gender Equality. 2009. "Issues Paper." Paper presented to the Interactive Expert Panel: Gender Perspectives of the Financial Crisis, 53rd Session of the Commission on the Status of Women. New York, March 5. http://www.un.org/womenwatch/daw/csw/csw53/papers/financial%20crisis%20FINAL%20Rev1.REFORMATTED.pdf.

United Nations Millennium Project. 2005. *Investing in Development: A Practical Plan to Achieve the Millennium Development Goals – Overview.* New York: UNDP.

UNRISD (United Nations Research Institute for Social Development). 2005. *Gender Equality: Striving for Justice in an Unequal World.* Geneva: United Nations.

Vidaković, I. 2002. "Raspostranjenost Nasilja u Porodici." In *Porodično Nasilje u Srbiji (Domestic Violence in Serbia),* ed. Vesna Nikolić-Ristanović. Belgrade: The Victimology Society of Serbia and Prometej, 13–73.

Vimard, P., A. Guillaume, and A. Quesnel. 1991. « Modification des Coûts et Bénéfices des Enfants Supportés par les Parents: Differentiation Socioeconomique et son Impact sur la Fécondité. Evolution de la Fécondité et Rôle des Enfants en Milieu Rural Ouest-Africain. » Paper presented at the Seminar on the Course of Fertility Transition in Sub-Saharan Africa, Harare.

Vishnevsky, A. G. 1998. *Population of Russia in 1998. Annual Demographic Report.* Moscow: Center of Demography and Human Ecology.

Witter, Sophie, S. Adjei, M. Armar-Klemesu, and W. Graham. 2007. "Providing Free Maternal Health Care: Ten Lessons from an Evaluation of the National Delivery Exemption Policy in Ghana." http://www.globalhealthaction.net/index.php/gha/article/view/1881/2126.

WHO (World Health Organization). 2002. *WHO's Contribution to Achievement of the Development Goals of the United Nations Millennium Declaration.* Geneva: WHO.

Wordsworth, Anna. 2008. "Moving to the Mainstream: Integrating Gender in Afghanistan's National Policy." Afghanistan Research and Evaluation Unit, Kabul.

World Bank. 2009a. "Afghanistan—Strengthening Health Activities for the Rural Poor (SHARP) Project: Environmental Assessment: Infection and Management Environmental Plan." World Bank Report No. E2082, Washington, DC.

———. 2009b. "Afghanistan—Strengthening Institutions Development Policy Grant Program." Document No. 48167, Washington, DC.

———. 2009c. "Country Assistance Strategies: Retrospective and Future Directions." World Bank Report No. 50284, Washington, DC.

———. 2009d. *Implementing the Bank's Gender Mainstreaming Strategy: FY08 Annual Monitoring Report.* Washington, DC: World Bank.

———. 2009e. "Peru—Second Phase Adaptable Program Loan of the Health Reform Project." World Bank Project Appraisal Document No. 35901, Washington, DC.

———. 2009f. "Republic of Yemen: CAS for the Period FY2010–2013." World Bank Report No. 47562, Washington, DC.

———. 2009g. "Yemen—Higher Education Learning and Innovation Project." World Bank Implementation Completion and Results Report No. ICR891, Washington, DC.

———. 2009h. "Yemen—Irrigation Improvement Project." World Bank Implementation Completion and Results Report No. ICR1125, Washington, DC.

———. 2008a. "Afghanistan—National Emergency Employment Program for Rural Access." World Bank, Implementation Completion and Results Report No. ICR625, Washington, DC.

———. 2008b. "Afghanistan—Poverty Reduction Strategy Paper and Joint IDA-IMF Staff Advisory Note." World Bank, Poverty Reduction Strategy Paper No. 43431, Washington, DC.

———. 2008c. "Bangladesh—Poverty Assessment for Bangladesh: Creating Opportunities and Bridging the East-West Divide." World Bank, Report No. 44321, Washington, DC.

———. 2008d. "Benin—Private Sector Development Project." Implementation Completion and Results Report No. ICR774, World Bank, Washington, DC.

———. 2008e. "Ghana—Poverty Reduction Strategy Paper Annual Progress Report and Joint IDA-AMF Staff Advisory Note." World Bank, Poverty Reduction Strategy Paper No. 42865, Washington, DC.

———. 2008f. "The Growth Report: Strategies for Sustained Growth and Inclusive Development." World Bank Discussion Paper, Washington DC.

———. 2008g. *Healthy Development: The World Bank Strategy for Health Nutrition and Population Results.* Washington, DC: World Bank.

———. 2008h. "Philippines—Land Administration and Management Project." World Bank Implementation Completion and Results Report 31728, Washington, DC.

———. 2008i. "Poverty Assessment for Bangladesh: Creating Opportunities and Bridging the East-West Divide."
World Bank Poverty Assessment Report No. 44521, Washington, DC.

———. 2008j. "Rwanda—First, Second, and Third Poverty Reduction Support Credit/Grant." World Bank Implementation Completion and Results Report No. ICR326, Washington, DC.

———. 2008k. *Safe, Clean, and Affordable… Transport for Development: The World Bank's Transport Business Strategy.* Washington, DC: World Bank.

———. 2008l. "Tajikistan—Rural Infrastructure Rehabilitation Project." World Bank Implementation Completion and Results Report No. ICR642, Washington, DC.

———. 2008m. "Whispers to Voices: Gender and Social Transformation in Bangladesh." World Bank Working Paper No. 43045, Washington, DC.

———. 2008n. "Zambia—Country Assistance Strategy." World Bank Report No. 43352, Washington, DC.

———. 2007a. "Bangladesh—Fourth Fisheries Project." World Bank Implementation Completion and Results Report No. ICR23, Washington, DC.

———. 2007b. "Bangladesh—National Nutrition Project." World Bank Implementation Completion and Results Report No. ICR242, Washington, DC.

———. 2007c. "Colombia –First and Second Series of Programmatic Labor Reform and Social Structural Adjustment Loans and a Third Labor Reform and Social Development Policy Loan." World Bank Implementation Completion and Results Report No. ICR522, Washington, DC.

———. 2007d. "Expanding Women's Work Choices to Enhance Chile's Economic Potential: Chile Country Gender Assessment." World Bank Report No. 36228, Washington, DC.

———. 2007e. *Global Monitoring Report 2007—Millennium Development Goals: Confronting the Challenges of Gender Equality and Fragile States.* Washington, DC: World Bank.

———. 2007f. "Nicaragua—Country Partnership Strategy." World Bank Report No. 39637, Washington, DC.

———. 2007g. "Nigeria: Universal Basic Education Project." World Bank Implementation Completion and Results Report No. ICR62, Washington, DC.

———. 2007h. "Sector Strategy Implementation Update: Third Review." Board Report No. 42128, World Bank, Washington DC.

———. 2007i. "Zambia—Poverty Reduction Strategy Paper Third Annual Progress Report." World Bank Poverty Reduction Strategy Paper No. 38307, Washington, DC.

———. 2007j. "Zambia—Poverty and Vulnerability Assessment." World Bank Report No. 32573, Washington, DC.

———. 2007k. "Zambia—Smallholder Agricultural Commercialization Strategy." World Bank Report No. 36573, Washington, DC.

———. 2006a. "Colombia—Third Labor and Social Development Policy Loan Project." World Bank Report No. 35739, Washington, DC.

———. 2006b. "Gender Equality as Smart Economics: A World Bank Group Gender Action Plan (Fiscal Years 2007–10)." World Bank Report No. 37008, Washington, DC.

———. 2006c. *Implementing the Bank's Gender Mainstreaming Strategy: Annual Monitoring Report for FY04 and FY05.* Washington, DC: World Bank.

———. 2006d. "Interim Strategy Note for Islamic Republic of Afghanistan for the Period FY07–08." World Bank Report, Washington DC.

———. 2006e. "Issue Brief: Gender." World Bank, Washington, DC.

———. 2006f. *The Other Half of Gender: Men's Issues in Development.* Washington, DC: World Bank.

———. 2006g. *World Development Report: Equity and Development.* Washington, DC: World Bank.

———. 2005a. "Afghanistan—Country Gender Assessment: National Reconstruction and Poverty Reduction—The Role of Women in Afghanistan's Future." World Bank Report No. 35606, Washington, DC.

———. 2005b. "Empowering People by Transforming Institutions: Social Development in World Bank Operations." Board Report No. 31494, World Bank, Washington, DC.

———. 2005c. "Lebanon—Agriculture Infrastructure Development Project." World Bank Implementation Completion and Results Report No. 31457, Washington, DC.

———. 2005d. "Philippines—Land Administration and Management Program." World Bank Implementation Completion and Results Report No. 31728, Washington, DC.

———. 2005e. "Project Performance Assessment Report: Bangladesh Integrated Nutrition Project (Credit 2735-BD)." World Bank Project Performance Assessment Report No. 32563, Washington, DC.

———. 2005f. "Pro-Poor Growth in the 1990s: Lessons and Insights from 14 Countries." Agence Française de Développement, Bundesministerium für Wirtschaftliche Zusammenarbeit und Entwicklung, U.K. Department for International Development, World Bank, Washington, DC.

———. 2005g. *Results Focus in Country Assistance Strategies: A Stocktaking of Results-Based Country Assistance Strategies.* Washington, DC: World Bank.

———. 2005h. "Sustainable Pathways to an Effective, Equitable and Efficient Education System for Preschool through Secondary School Education." World Bank Report No. 32450-TU, Washington DC.

———. 2004a. "Colombia—Land Policy in Transition." World Bank Report No. 27942, Washington, DC.

———. 2004b. *Gender and Development in the Middle East and North Africa: Women in the Public Sphere.* Washington, DC: World Bank.

———. 2004c. "Good Practice Note for Development Policy Lending: Using Poverty and Social Impact Analysis to Support Development Policy Operations." World Bank Report No. 31812, Washington, DC.

———. 2004d. "Implementing the Bank's Gender Mainstreaming Strategy: Second Annual Monitoring Report: FY03." World Bank Report No. 27812, Washington, DC.

———. 2004e. "Land Policy in Transition." World Bank Report No. 27942, Washington, DC.

———. 2004f. "Peru-Sierra Natural Resources Management and Poverty Alleviation Project." World Bank Implementation Completion and Results Report No. 29990, Washington, DC.

———. 2004g. "Zambia—Country Assistance Strategy." World Bank Report No. 27654, Washington, DC.

———. 2004h. "Zambia—Strategic Country Gender Assessment." World Bank Report No. 33776, Washington, DC.

———. 2003a. "Colombia—Rural Finance: Access Issues, Challenges and Opportunities." World Bank Report No. 27269, Washington, DC.

———. 2003b. "Implementation of the Gender Mainstreaming Strategy: First Annual Monitoring Report, FY02." World Bank Report No. 25575, Washington, DC.

———. 2003c. "Land Policies for Growth and Poverty Reduction." World Bank Policy Research Report, Washington, DC.

———. 2003d. "Operational Policy Statement 4.20—Gender and Development." World Bank, Washington, DC.

———. 2003e. *Social Analysis Sourcebook: Incorporating Social Dimensions into Bank-Supported Projects.* Washington DC: World Bank.

———. 2002a. "Gender in Transition." World Bank Report, Human Development Unit, Eastern Europe and Central Asia Region, Washington DC.

———. 2002b. *Integrating Gender into the World Bank's Work: A Strategy for Action.* Washington, DC: World Bank.

———. 2002c. "Pakistan—Country Assistance Strategy." World Bank Report No. 24399, Washington, DC.

———. 2002d. "Philippines Country Assistance Strategy." World Bank Report No. 24042, Washington, DC.

———. 2002e. "A Sourcebook for Poverty Reduction Strategies." PREM Network Report No. 29800, Washington, DC.

———. 2002f. "Vietnam—Country Assistance Strategy." World Bank Report No. 24621, Washington, DC.

———. 2001a. *Engendering Development through Gender Equality in Rights, Resources, and Voice.* Washington, DC, and New York: World Bank and Oxford University Press.

———. 2001b. *Making Sustainable Commitments: An Environmental Strategy for the World Bank*. Washington, DC: World Bank.

———. 2000a. *World Development Report 2000/2001—Attacking Poverty*. Washington, DC: World Bank.

———. 2000b. "Zambia—Interim Poverty Reduction Strategy Paper and Assessment." World Bank Report No. 21183, Washington, DC.

———. 1999a. "Operational Directive 4.20: Gender Dimension of Development." World Bank Policy Document, Washington, DC.

———. 1999b. "Zambia—Country Assistance Strategy." World Bank Report No. 19889, Washington, DC.

———. 1997. "World Bank Operational Policies: Lessons of Experience and Future Directions." OPCS Report No. CODE97-73, World Bank, Washington, DC.

———. 1994. "Enhancing Women's Participation in Economic Development." World Bank Policy Paper No. 13415, Washington DC.

———. 1990. *World Development Report 1990—Poverty*. Washington, DC: World Bank.

———. 1984. "Operational Manual Statement 2.20—Project Appraisal." World Bank, Washington, DC.

World Bank and DFID (UK Department for International Development). 2006. *Unequal Citizens: Gender, Caste and Ethnic Exclusion in Nepal*. Kathmandu, Nepal: DFID and World Bank.

World Bank, FAO (Food and Agriculture Organization), and IFAD (International Fund for Agricultural Development). 2009. *Gender in Agriculture Sourcebook*. Washington, DC: World Bank.

Yasmeen, Gisèle. 2001. "Stockbrokers Turned Sandwich Vendors: The Economic Crisis and Small-Scale Food Retailing in Southeast Asia." *Geoforum* 32 (1): 91–102.

Young, Brigitte. 2003. "Financial Crises and Social Reproduction: Asia, Argentina and Brazil." In (eds): *Power Production and Social Reproduction: Human In/Security in the Global Political Economy*, eds. Isabella Bakker and Stephen Gill. Houndmills: Palgrave Macmillan, 99–123.

Zhiqin, Shao. 2000. *Women and Social Security: Impact of the Financial Crisis*. Jinan: Shandong Academy of Social Sciences.